PROFESSIONAL DEVELOPMENT IN EDUCATION

New Paradigms and Practices

P. O. W. E. R.

Planning,

Owning,

Welcoming,

Educational

Reform

PROFESSIONAL DEVELOPMENT IN EDUCATION

New Paradigms and Practices

EDITED BY

Thomas R. Guskey

AND

Michael Huberman

FOREWORD BY

Matthew B. Miles

TEACHERS COLLEGE PRESS

Teachers College, Columbia University
New York and London

Published by Teachers College Press, 1234 Amsterdam Avenue, New York, NY 10027

Library of Congress Cataloging-in-Publication Data

Professional development in education : new paradigms and practices /
  edited by Thomas R. Guskey and Michael Huberman.
      p.   cm.
  Includes bibliographical references and index.
    ISBN 0-8077-3426-8 (cloth : acid-free paper). – ISBN 0-8077-3425-X (paper
: acid-free paper
    1. Teachers–In-service training. 2. Educational change. I. Guskey,
  Thomas R. II. Huberman, A. M.
  LB1731.P7274 1995
  371.1'46–dc20   94-46506

ISBN 0-8077-3425-X (paper)
ISBN 0-8077-3426-8 (cloth)
Printed on acid-free paper
Manufactured in the United States of America
02 01 00 99 98   8 7 6 5 4 3

Contents

Foreword

MATTHEW B. MILES

Let's frame the issue in extreme terms. A good deal of what passes for "professional development" in schools is a joke—one that we'd laugh at if we weren't trying to keep from crying. It's everything that a learning environment shouldn't be: radically underresourced, brief, not sustained, designed for "one size fits all," imposed rather than owned, lacking any intellectual coherence, treated as a special add-on event rather than as part of a natural process, and trapped in the constraints of the bureaucratic system we have come to call "school." In short, it's pedagogically naive, a demeaning exercise that often leaves its participants more cynical and no more knowledgeable, skilled, or committed than before. And all this is accompanied by overblown rhetoric about "the challenge of change," "self-renewal," "professional growth," "expanding knowledge base," and "lifelong learning."

Do I have your attention? If yes, perhaps we can proceed to a more temperate level of discourse. Not all professional development is like that. More and more, we can see practical evidence that it's possible to treat the learning and work of adults in schools as a serious, well-designed enterprise, one that uses the best we know about pedagogy, about organizational life in schools, and about the change process. There may be hope.

The well-conceptualized chapters of this book contribute to that hope by helping us rethink professional development in fundamental terms. The authors consider basic issues about the growth and learning of teachers as professionals over time, and how those processes can be supported and facilitated. The diversity across chapters is large. We are led through the moral and emotional dimensions of teaching, constructivist teaching and learning, the social psychology of organizational life, careers and life cycles, adult learning, teaching as a labor process, the nature of focused training, the dynamics of collaborative and collegial learning, and the meta-skills of teachers' inquiry, among others. We are a long way from Kansas, as Dorothy said to Toto.

To aid the reader in exploring each chapter, I propose some cross-cutting questions that might be used as "lenses" through which to view and critique the ideas presented.

1. What do the ideas in the chapter suggest as a "curriculum": what *conceptual understandings* are key; what *skills* (or "meta-skills") are seen as desirable outcomes; what *moral, purposive* issues are involved?
2. What do the core ideas and the implicit "curriculum" of the chapter suggest about the *design* of professional development programs? We need concrete images of how programs built on these ideas would look. What sorts of support structures would be needed? What strategies would need to be followed over time? The thoughtful chapters by Huberman and Eraut make a start in this direction, but much more is needed. What, for example, would a serious "department of human resources" look like in a school district? To put it another way: How can schools and school districts become more professional, more sophisticated, about professional development?
3. What is the connection to the lives of *students*? Many of the ideas proposed have profound implications for the way children should be learning, living, and working in school. The Borko and Putnam chapter shows us well how crucial it is for professional development programs to be *congruent* with classroom environments; active learning by children requires active learning by teachers. Empowered, liberated teachers should (but do not always) empower kids or liberate them.
4. How might the ideas have relevance for *administrators*? They are almost invisible in these accounts or dismissed as "managers," yet they are key partners in the professional development enterprise—and have professional development needs of their own.
5. How can the ideas be used to link the domains of *personal learning, organizational functioning,* and *school change* in a serious way? Some of the chapters treat school organizations merely as presenting annoying or menacing contextual constraints, rather than as a target for organization development work in their own right. Some chapters (e.g., Fullan, Smylie) carefully address issues of school reform, innovation, improvement, and restructuring, and others are silent on this topic. Yet any professional development program that isn't a joke must work with persons *and* with organizations that are *both* enmeshed in change.
6. Looking across the chapters, is there a set of *core ideas*, and core *"building blocks"* of professional development (such as time use, observation of practice, feedback structures), that can be discerned behind the diversity of approaches taken?

   In short, I suggest an active, skeptical, sifting, reflective approach to the ideas presented in these pages. Anything less would fall short of the tribute the authors deserve for helping us think more deeply about these matters. The debt we owe them can only be discharged through further reflective inquiry and action. More work along the lines of their strong contributions will help professional development in schools get genuinely serious in our time.

Matthew B. Miles
Center for Policy Research

PROFESSIONAL DEVELOPMENT IN EDUCATION

New Paradigms and Practices

INTRODUCTION

THOMAS R. GUSKEY AND MICHAEL HUBERMAN

Never before in education has there been greater recognition of the need for ongoing professional development. Inservice training and other forms of professional development are a crucial component in nearly every modern proposal for educational improvement. Regardless of how schools are formed or reformed, structured or restructured, the renewal of staff members' professional skills is considered fundamental to improvement.

To some observers this emphasis on professional development implies that practitioners in education today are doing an inadequate job. They see the demand for increased inservice education as an indication of deficiencies in the knowledge and skills of educators, especially classroom teachers. According to this view, efforts must be made to correct these inadequacies if educational institutions are to meet the demands of our increasingly complex society.

Our work with educators throughout the world, however, offers little evidence to support this point of view. The vast majority of teachers and school administrators we have encountered are dedicated professionals who work hard under demanding conditions. Our view is rather that the current emphasis on professional development comes from growing recognition of education as a dynamic, professional field. Educational researchers are constantly discovering new knowledge about teaching and learning processes. As this professional knowledge base expands, new types of expertise are required of educators at all levels. And like practitioners in other professional fields, educators must keep abreast of this emerging knowledge base and be prepared to use it to continually refine their conceptual and craft skills.

Along with growing recognition of the importance of professional development in education has come growing awareness of current shortcomings. The literature on professional development is fraught with descriptions of failings, and a broad spectrum of solutions have been proposed (Epstein, Lockard, & Dauber, 1988; Griffin, 1983; Guskey, 1986; Joyce & Showers, 1988; Lieberman & Miller, 1979; Orlich, 1989; Wood & Thompson, 1980, 1993). Still, reformers attempting to synthesize these various solutions quickly find themselves faced with seemingly incompatible dichotomies. For instance:

- Some researchers suggest that professional development efforts designed to facilitate change must be teacher-specific and focus on the day-to-day activities at the classroom level (McLaughlin, 1990; Weatherley & Lipsky, 1977; Wise, 1991). Others indicate that an emphasis on individuals is detrimental to progress and more systemic or organizational approaches are necessary (Tye & Tye, 1984; Waugh & Punch, 1987).
- Some experts stress that reforms in professional development must be initiated and carried out by individual teachers and school-based personnel (Joyce, McNair, Diaz, & McKibbin, 1976; Lambert, 1988; Lawrence, 1974; Massarella, 1980). Others emphasize that the most successful programs are those guided by a clear vision that sees beyond the walls of individual classrooms and schools, since teachers and school-based individuals generally lack the capacity to conceive and implement worthwhile improvements on their own (Barth, 1991; Clune, 1991; Mann, 1986; Wade, 1984).
- Some reviewers argue the most effective professional development programs are those that approach change in a gradual and incremental fashion, not expecting too much at one time (Doyle & Ponder, 1977; Fullan, 1985; Mann, 1978; Sparks, 1983). Others insist that the broader the scope of a professional development program, the more effort required of teachers, and the greater the overall change in teaching style attempted, the more likely the program is to elicit the enthusiasm of teachers and to be implemented well (Berman & McLaughlin, 1978; McLaughlin & Marsh, 1978).

These and other similar dichotomies in the professional development literature leave reformers feeling confused and inept. Many question how successful professional development programs can be designed and implemented when even researchers and experts in the field cannot agree on what should be done.

There are, of course, a variety of perspectives from which the professional development of educators can be viewed. Each of these perspectives has its own conceptual premises and is informed by different bodies of research. Some perspectives are derived from theoretical models that have been extended to offer implications for practice. Others are based on systematic observations of practice from which generalizations have been drawn and models constructed. As a result of these differences, each perspective leads to a somewhat different prescription for improvement.

Those familiar with the professional development literature generally are aware that these differences in perspective exist. Nevertheless, few understand the precise nature of the differences. In large part this is because no attempt has been made in the professional development field to lay bare these differences. There has been no systematic effort to clearly illustrate the conceptual grounds from which each perspective is derived or to show the connections between the prescriptions each offers for practice.

This book is an attempt to offer just such a description. Each chapter is written by an individual or group of individuals well known for their work in the area of professional or career development of educators. The authors represent researchers and practitioners drawn from different regions throughout the world. They represent Australia, Canada, England, Israel, The Netherlands, Switzerland, and the United States. To this task they bring a variety of different theoretical foundations, research traditions, and practical solutions.

To provide a common frame of reference for these varied perspectives, we asked each author or author team to address a common set of issues and questions. These included the following:

1. What philosophical or theoretical premises underlie your view of professional development or career development in education?
2. Exactly how do these premises inform your conceptualization of professional development, and what kinds of operational or prescriptive implications have you drawn in your work? In other words, does your work lead to some kind of "model" for describing or organizing the process of professional development? If so, can you map that model graphically or the parts of the model that seem most clear to you?
3. What bodies of research have informed your ideas, and how? Has there been an evolution in the way you have thought about these ideas?
4. What are the practical implications of your work? That is, what are the chief operational components of the vision you hold of professional development? What problems might practitioners anticipate in accepting, planning, and implementing it, and how might these problems be addressed?
5. In what ways do we need to expand the knowledge base in the fields of professional or career development of educators? What kinds of information or tools are lacking? How might we go about providing them, and what sort of research agenda is required?

While we expected each author or team to go beyond this set of guiding questions in describing their perspectives, we believed these unifying themes would aid readers in their efforts to synthesize the ideas presented. Specifically, we wanted to assemble a coherent set of unique points of view for understanding, investigating, and improving the practice of professional development.

What resulted is a diverse collection of carefully articulated perspectives that tap a wide array of professional development issues. Evident in each chapter are the authors' intellectual struggles and emotional engagements with the challenges and complexities of professional development in education. Also evident is a clear sense of the authors' histories, circumstances, and philosophical leanings.

As we reflected upon this collection of perspectives, we discovered they fell quite naturally into four broad categories. Although these categories are not mutually exclusive, and the perspectives of several of the authors transcend category distinctions, we found the categories useful in grouping our presentation of these highly diverse perspectives into the four parts of this book.

The first category focuses on the role of personal bases and characteristics in professional development. The authors of the two chapters in Part I tend to view professional development as a personal journey to find appreciation and meaning in one's work.

A second group of perspectives centered on social-psychological and institutional factors that promote or impinge on professional development. The authors of the three chapters in Part II present a compelling view of professional development fashioned principally by modern developments both in and outside of education that result in an ever-expanding professional knowledge base.

A third category of chapters emphasize professional development phases, models, and requisite supports. The authors of the four chapters in Part III present professional development in education broadly and holistically, and then describe what are considered career- or life-cycle perspectives.

The final group of perspectives stress the present and future of professionalism in professional development. The authors of the two chapters in Part IV challenge current paradigms regarding the complexity, orientation, and scope of professional development in education; they then propose the development of more ambitious models.

The perspectives presented in these chapters are obviously diverse. Equally diverse are the prescriptions offered for the improvement of professional and career development practice. Amid this diversity, however, emerge two unifying themes. The first is that every author is convinced of the critical importance of professional development in educational improvement efforts. For some, if these efforts are to result in significant and enduring positive change, high-quality professional development will be essential. For others, a far more critical perspective is called for. The second theme, and perhaps more important, is that the authors are optimistic about the likelihood of success in these efforts. At a time when many both inside and outside education are pessimistic about the prospects for improvement, these authors emphasize their strong belief that not only is improvement possible, but that we have specific and practical ideas about how it can be accomplished.

Our hope is that considering and evaluating these varied perspectives will be a stimulating, thought-provoking, and enlightening experience for readers. We also hope it will help guide the development of more thoughtful and more critically informed models of professional development that, in turn, will lead to more effective professional development activities for educators at all levels.

REFERENCES

Barth, R. S. (1991). Restructuring schools: Some questions for teachers and principals. *Phi Delta Kappan, 73*(2), 123–128.

Berman, P., & McLaughlin, M. W. (1978). *Federal programs supporting educational change: Vol. VIII. Implementing and sustaining innovations.* Santa Monica, CA: Rand Corporation.

Clune, W. H. (1991). *Systemic educational policy.* Madison, WI: Wisconsin Center for Educational Policy, University of Wisconsin–Madison.

Doyle, W., & Ponder, G. (1977). The practical ethic and teacher decision-making. *Interchange, 8*(3), 1–12.

Epstein, J. L., Lockard, B. L., & Dauber, S. L. (1988, April). *Staff development policies needed in the middle grades.* Paper presented at the annual meeting of the American Educational Research Association, New Orleans, LA.

Fullan, M. G. (1985). Change processes and strategies at the local level. *Elementary School Journal, 85,* 391–421.

Griffin, G. A. (Ed.). (1983). *Staff development. Eighty-second yearbook of the National Society for the Study of Education.* Chicago: University of Chicago Press.

Guskey, T. R. (1986). Staff development and the process of teacher change. *Educational Researcher, 15*(5), 5–12.

Joyce, B., McNair, K. M., Diaz, R., & McKibbin, M. D. (1976). *Interviews: Perceptions of professionals and policy makers.* Stanford, CA: Stanford Center for Research and Development in Teaching, Stanford University.

Joyce, B., & Showers, B. (1988). *Student achievement through staff development.* New York: Longman.

Lambert, L. (1988). Staff development redesigned. *Educational Leadership, 45*(8), 665–668.

Lawrence, G. (1974). *Patterns of effective inservice education: A state of the art summary of research on materials and procedures for changing teacher behavior in inservice education.* Tallahassee, FL: Florida State Department of Education.

Lieberman, A., & Miller, L. (1979). *Staff development: New demands, new realities, new perspectives.* New York: Teachers College Press.

Mann, D. (1978). The politics of training teachers in schools. In D. Mann (Ed.), *Making change happen* (pp. 3–18). New York: Teachers College Press.

Mann, D. (1986). Authority and school improvement: An essay on "Little King" leadership. *Teachers College Record, 88*(1), 41–52.

Massarella, J. A. (1980). Synthesis of research on staff development. *Educational Leadership, 38*(2), 182–185.

McLaughlin, M. W. (1990). The Rand change agent study revisited: Macro perspectives and micro realities. *Educational Researcher, 19*(9), 11–16.

McLaughlin, M. W., & Marsh, D. D. (1978). Staff development and school change. *Teachers College Record, 80*(1), 70–94.

Orlich, D. C. (1989). *Staff development: Enhancing human potential.* Boston: Allyn & Bacon.

Sparks, G. M. (1983). Synthesis of research on staff development for effective teaching. *Educational Leadership, 41*(3), 65–72.

Tye, K. A., & Tye, B. B. (1984). Teacher isolation and school reform. *Phi Delta Kappan, 65*(5), 319–322.

Wade, R. K. (1984). What makes a difference in inservice teacher education? A meta-analysis of research. *Educational Leadership, 42*(4), 48–54.

Waugh, R. F., & Punch, K. F. (1987). Teacher receptivity to systemwide change in the implementation stage. *Review of Educational Research, 57*(3), 237–254.

Weatherley, R., & Lipsky, M. (1977). Street-level bureaucrats and institutional innovation: Implementing special education reform. *Harvard Educational Review, 47*(2), 171–197.

Wise, A. E. (1991). On teacher accountability. In *Voices from the field* (pp. 23–24). Washington, D.C.: William T. Grant Foundation Commission on Work, Family and Citizenship and Institute for Educational Leadership.

Wood, F. H., & Thompson, S. R. (1980). Guidelines for better staff development. *Educational Leadership, 37*, 374–378.

Wood, F. H., & Thompson, S. R. (1993). Assumptions about staff development based on research and best practice. *Journal of Staff Development, 14*(4), 52–57.

PART I

The Role of Personal Bases and Characteristics

Professional development is viewed by the authors in this part as a dynamic and highly personal endeavor. As such, its meaning and worth are based largely on individual interpretations and adaptations.

In Chapter 1 the importance of social and moral purposes in professional development, and in teachers' work generally, is emphasized by Andy Hargreaves of the Ontario Institute for Studies in Education. Despite the lip service currently being granted teacher professionalism, Hargreaves argues that both initial teacher training and inservice professional development overlook and undermine the place of purpose and goals in teachers' work. As a result, ends are separated from means. Efforts are made to equip teachers with appropriate skills and secure from them loyalty and motivation that will enable and encourage them to deliver the goals of others. Instead, Hargreaves argues that we should concentrate on matters of social motivation and commitment derived from the personal meaning and understandings individual teachers bring to teaching.

The need to consider what individuals bring to the social dynamics of teaching is also reflected in Chapter 2, by Hilda Borko of the University of Colorado and Ralph T. Putnam of Michigan State University. Based on principles of cognitive psychology, Borko and Putman set forth a conceptual model from which the complexities of teaching and the professional development of teachers are viewed. From this perspective, teaching is seen as a complex cognitive skill determined in large part by the nature of teachers' knowledge and belief systems. Professional development, in turn, is viewed as a "developmental process" that allows teachers to expand and elaborate their professional knowledge base.

1

Development and Desire
A Postmodern Perspective

ANDY HARGREAVES

For many years now, I have worked with teachers across the world in the context of professional development and have also devoted much of my research effort to studying the cultures and conditions of teachers' work that help or hinder such development (A. Hargreaves, 1986; 1994). In this chapter, I try to define and locate my understanding of teacher development in relation to my own biographical influences and theoretical preferences. While policy rhetoric stresses knowledge and technique as central to good teaching, I draw attention to the importance of purpose, passion, and desire. Seeing teacher development in this light, I argue, highlights the central place of moral, political, and emotional issues in the field. The nature and implications of these moral, political, and emotional dimensions of teacher development are explored in the remainder of the chapter.

It makes little sense to analyze, still less to prescribe forms of teacher development without first establishing what it is that needs to be developed, what teachers and teaching are for. My own position on teacher development is therefore closely associated with basic principles of what for me stands at the heart of teaching. This has roots in my own experiences of teachers and teaching and reference points in particular theoretical traditions.

In part, my views of teacher development derive from my own experiences of teachers and teaching, my own "apprenticeship of observation" (Lortie, 1975) as a student. Although research suggests that many teachers were good students for whom schooling was a positive experience (Lindblad & Prieto, 1992), my own experience as a working-class student in a selective English grammar school was more distanced and marginal. For me, secondary school—and everything it represented culturally, with its didactic pedagogies, seemingly irrelevant curricula, religious assemblies, organized games, and regimented uniforms—was not an institution to embrace but a place to socialize and an instrument for credentials and success (A. Hargreaves, 1989).

This school-based cultural marginality has created in me a strong impulse to reform, repair, and make amends in education. When my school sent me a questionnaire about my future plans upon university graduation, I remember writing rather piously that I wished to enter teaching and eventually train a better generation of teachers than that which had taught me! Though modified and moderated in later years, this impulse to reform and repair still stays with me in my research and practice concerning teacher development. Teacher development for me is not only an item of detached intellectual curiosity but also a focus of missionary purpose and passionate desire.

Over time, I have come to understand that the teachers who taught me were not personally unskilled or uncaring, but rather people of a particular time and place, shaped and constrained as much by the structures and traditions of secondary schooling as were their students. As Waller (1932) recognized, this institutional life of schooling makes the teacher as much as it makes the student. It therefore became increasingly important for me to work with teachers from a standpoint of understanding rather than one of condemnation and to do so with all kinds of teachers, not just enthusiastic innovators or exemplary teachers in exemplary schools but stalwarts, cynics, and sceptics as well. By broadening the range of teachers with whom I work, to include even diffident and disagreeable ones, I have learned a lot. This learning has often led me to be critical of common claims about teacher development that prevail in the literature. Generally, I think, I have come to understand many sorts of teachers and why they do what they do, with sympathy but without undue sentiment.

In theoretical terms, my position on teacher development is somewhat eclectic. The celebrated Canadian geologist J. Tuzo Wilson, whose "brilliant theory" of continental drift "provided a unifying model for all of the large scale dynamics evident at the earth's surface," confessed before his death to having "always been rather eclectic in my interests" ("Celebrated Geologist," 1993, p. 16). Eclecticism is often a thinly veiled term of abuse, implying inferior scholarship or lack of rigour. Paradigms are purity. Eclecticism is danger. As Wilson's example shows, though, eclecticism can sometimes forge creative connections across paradigms and push the boundaries of understanding further. Within my own eclectic orientation, three theoretical perspectives have become prominent: symbolic interactionism, critical social theory, and theories of postmodernity.

Symbolic Interactionism. This perspective helps clarify why teachers (and others) do what they do. It addresses practical realities rather than holding people to prescriptive ideals or moral exhortations concerning human change and development. It does not condone people's actions but certainly sets out to appreciate them (D. Hargreaves, 1978). Built upon the work of George Herbert Mead (1934) and developed extensively by Herbert Blumer (1969) and others, symbolic interactionism addresses how people's selves are formed and transformed through the meanings and language (symbols) of human interaction (Woods, 1992). These socially constructed selves attach meanings to the contexts in which they work and act on the basis of them. In symbolic interactionism, teaching is more than a set of technically learnable skills: It is given meaning by teachers' evolving selves, within the realistic contexts and contingencies of their work environments.

Symbolic interactionism affords insights into teachers' *selves*, their meanings and purposes—which are frequently overlooked or overridden in reform efforts (Nias, 1989). It helps us see how less-than-perfect teacher actions are, in fact, rational, *strategic* responses to everyday, yet often overwhelming, constraints in teachers' workplaces (D. Hargreaves, 1978). Symbolic interactionism also points to the importance of shared *cultures* of teaching, common beliefs and perceptions among subgroups of teachers rooted in different subjects or sectors that develop in response to commonly faced problems and provide ready-made solutions and sources of learning for new entrants to the occupation (A. Hargreaves, 1986; D. Hargreaves, 1980). Lastly, symbolic interactionism alerts us to patterned human differences among teachers in terms of such things as age and career stage (Becker, 1952; Sikes, Measor, & Woods, 1985), gender (Acker, 1992), and race (Troyna, 1993). Not all teachers respond to innovation, commit to collaboration, or construe the purposes of education, for instance, in quite the same way. Symbolic interactionism helps identify and explain these important differences. Symbolic interactionism, in short, helps us see teaching and teacher development as humanly constructed and constrained processes in all their imperfection and complexity.

Critical Social Theory. Symbolic interactionism tends to confine itself to the immediate settings of social interaction, such as schools, classrooms, staffrooms, and communities, that are clearly bounded in time and space. Yet there are worlds beyond these settings that we capture in aggregates and abstractions, such as states and economies, that powerfully shape the work of teaching, the aspirations that people hold for it, and the conditions under which it can be accomplished. To understand the world of teaching properly, we must therefore move to some extent beyond it. Some symbolic interactionists regard this macro-theorizing as legitimate business, but one that is not theirs (Goffman, 1975; Woods, 1977). Other symbolic interactionists see such efforts at macro-theorizing as unachievable, a futile pursuit of conceptual ghosts that have no substance in immediate interaction (Denzin, 1991, 1992).[1] Another discourse is therefore needed in which the macro-social influences on teacher development can be explored.

Little of the teacher development literature addresses macro-level issues (but see Smyth, 1994). Research and writing on teaching more generally, however, have pointed to the societally generated constraints and dilemmas under which teachers work (McNeil, 1986), the ways in which teachers' work varies according to the social-class and gender relations in which it is located (Connell, 1985; Metz, 1990), and the changing nature of the labor process in modern societies together with its implications for whether teachers' work, like the work of other semiprofessionals, is becoming increasingly deskilled (Apple, 1986; Smyth, 1991).

Critical social theory is sensitive to the contexts of human interaction and the power relationships that comprise and surround it. It prompts us to consider the place of power, control, equity, justice, patriarchy, race, bureaucracy, and so forth in teaching and teacher development; to see teaching and teacher development as more than internal, institutional matters.

Theories of Postmodernity. A third perspective addresses the *particular kinds* of contexts and changes that teachers and other people are encountering and experiencing at this specific moment in history. It adds a dynamic element to understanding the contexts of teacher development.

Theories of postmodernity point to the characteristics and consequences of what is coming to be called the postindustrial, postmodern age. In this period, old factory systems of mass production and consumption in an age of heavy manufacturing—and the standardized schooling systems that served it—are being replaced by flexible technologies in smaller units of enterprise (Harvey, 1989; S. Robertson, 1993). These flexible economies are calling for more flexible skills among future workforces—and flexible patterns of teaching, learning, and schooling through which such skills can be developed (Reich, 1992; Schlechty, 1990).

Organizationally, the need for flexibility and responsiveness is increasingly reflected in decentralized decision making along with flatter decision-making structures, reduced specialization, and blurring of roles and boundaries (Leinberger & Tucker, 1991). In postmodern organizations, fixed rules and segregated roles are replaced by a focus on tasks and projects, utilizing whatever skills are collectively available for their completion (Kanter, Stein, & Jick, 1992). Self-managing schools (Caldwell & Spinks, 1988; Smyth, 1993) and professional development networks (Lieberman & McLaughlin, 1992) are realizations of these emerging tendencies.

Culturally and politically, the postmodern age is witnessing a collapse of moral, political, and scientific certainties. Advances in telecommunications along with more rapid dissemination of information are placing old ideological and scientific certainties in disrepute (Giddens, 1991). Patterns of migration and international travel are diversifying beliefs and multiplying voices in our culture. Old missions are collapsing, giving rise to struggles to build new ones—hence all the emphasis on mission and vision building in schools (Barth, 1990; Louis & Miles, 1990). With the decline of singular certainties, more voices are able to make themselves heard throughout the culture—the voices of women, visible minorities, the disabled, and so forth—and our schools are becoming more politicized as a result (Elbaz, 1991; Goodson, 1992).

To UNDERSTAND teacher development at the turn of the millennium is to understand it in a peculiarly exhilarating and terrifying time of accelerating change, intense compression of time and space, cultural diversity, economic flexibility, technological complexity, organizational fluidity, moral and scientific uncertainty, and national insecurity (A. Hargreaves, 1994). Only when we know what learning is for or what people think it is for can we know and imagine what teacher development might be for. This is why critical judgments about the changing social context of learning are so central to the teacher development agenda.

DIMENSIONS

For most people, good teaching is a matter of teachers mastering the skills of teaching and the knowledge of what to teach and how to teach it. Teacher development, in this view, is about knowledge and skill development. This kind of teacher development is well known and widely practiced. It can be neatly packaged in courses, materials, workshops, and training programs.

Success in knowledge- and skill-based endeavours in teacher development remains insufficient and elusive, however. When exposed to or trained in new knowledge and skills, teachers often resist or reject them, select only the bits that suit them, or delay until other innovations supersede them. They reject knowledge and skill requirements when:

1. They are imposed. As McLaughlin (1990) notes, "we cannot mandate what matters to effective practice" (p. 15).
2. They are encountered in the context of multiple, contradictory, and overwhelming innovations (Werner, 1988).
3. Most teachers, other than those selected for design teams, have been excluded from their development (Fullan, 1991).
4. They are packaged in off-site courses or one-shot workshops that are alien to the purposes and contexts of teachers' work (Little, 1993b).
5. Teachers experience them alone and are afraid of being criticized by colleagues or of being seen as elevating themselves on pedestals above them (Fullan & Hargreaves, 1991).

Not surprisingly, the reason that knowledge about how to improve teaching is often not well utilized by teachers is not just that it is bad knowledge (though sometimes it is), or even badly communicated and disseminated knowledge. Rather, it does not acknowledge or address the personal identities and moral purposes of teachers, nor the cultures and contexts in which they work (Hultmann & Horberg, 1993). The false certainties of much knowledge and skill development are too inflexible for the practical complexities of the postmodern age. They reside in the preoccupations and obsessions of modern times with eliminating ambiguity, suppressing spontaneity, taming chaos, and putting order in its place (Bauman, 1992). Clearly there is and should be much more to teacher education and development than knowledge and skill development. In this chapter, I want to draw attention to three additional dimensions of teacher development that help make good teaching. These are the moral, political, and emotional dimensions of development.

Moral Purpose

What do we find in teaching when we acknowledge that there is more to it than technique? What lies beyond expertise (Olson, 1991)? As Fenstermacher (1990) reflects and regrets, in debates about the knowledge base of teaching, "very little is heard about the fundamental purposes of teaching" (p. 131). In particular, literature that analyzes and advocates professionalization in teaching

> is nearly devoid of talk about the moral nature of teaching, the moral duties and obligations of teachers, and the profound importance of teachers to the moral development of students. It is as if the moral dimensions of teachings were lost, forgotten about or . . . simply taken for granted. (p. 132)

Teaching is inescapably a "moral craft" (Tom, 1984). It is "a profoundly moral activity" (Fenstermacher, 1990). Schoolteaching is moral, firstly, because it contributes to the creation and re-creation of future generations (Durkheim, 1961). In the societies of classrooms are the future societies of adults. By design or default, teachers cannot help but be involved in preparing these generations of the future. Children spend too many hours in their charge for them to escape this obligation.

Second, teaching is moral because of the small but significant judgments that teachers make in their innumerable interactions with children, parents, and one another. As Goodlad (1990) puts it, "full recognition of teaching in schools as a profession depends on teachers, individually and collectively, demonstrating their awareness of and commitment to the burdens of judgment that go with a moral enterprise" (p. 30).

The broad moral purposes of schooling and teaching are frequently implicit and unexamined, guided by comfort, convention, history, and habit. As Pratt (1983) argues, though, in a society that is technologically complex, environmentally ravaged, culturally diverse, and often socially unstable in its rapidly changing structures of family and community, these purposes and the subjects and learnings that flow from them are ripe for fundamental revision.

One of the central challenges to teachers in the postmodern age is that of working within contexts of pervasive moral uncertainty. Because of growing multicultural migration, international travel, global economies, and reconstructed polities, the fundamental moral assumptions of the Judeo-Christian tradition and common schooling upon which Western educational systems have been based are collapsing (A. Hargreaves, 1994). In the face of this moral collapse, some educators have sought to retreat to old moral certainties and restore "traditional" values in a singular way (Holmes, 1984). It is as well to remember, however, as Lasch (1991) notes, that such nostalgia for the past is "the abdication of memory" (p. 82). Indeed, he says, "nostalgia does not entail the exercise of memory at all, since the past it idealizes stands outside time, frozen in unchanging perfection" (p. 83). Others have imposed such moralities legislatively in the form of culturally loaded national curricula that reinvent notions of national identity (Goodson, 1990; A. Hargreaves, 1989). But in many other cases, individual schools and systems are energetically trying to construct their own missions and visions together. Teacher and school development are, in this respect, closely related features of the changing moral contours of schooling.

Teachers may or may not have conscious moral intent in their work, but almost all of that work has consequences that are moral. There is no escaping this. Acknowledging these unavoidable moral dimensions of teaching has powerful implications for teacher education and development. For some, it is a question of identifying and grappling with moral absolutes, however uncomfortable or inconvenient they might be. It is a matter of knowing and respecting the difference between right and wrong and adopting the right course with good conscience, whatever the consequences (Campbell, in press). In a postmodern world of immense cultural and religious diversity, however, such moral absolutes are almost impossible to pin down.

Attending to the moral dimensions of teaching usually involves distinguishing between better and worse courses of action, rather than right and wrong ones. There are no clear rules of thumb, no useful universal principles for deciding what to do. Unlike university philosophers of education, classroom teachers do not have the ethereal privilege of proclaiming their virtue from the high ground. They must live their moral lives in the swamp (Schön, 1983), especially when moral certainties grounded in tradition or science are collapsing and people must rely on their own reflective resources as a basis for moral judgment (Giddens, 1991). The considered moral life of teaching then becomes a matter of resolving multiple dilemmas (Berlak & Berlak, 1981), of making optimal moral decisions that are ethically defensible and practically workable within the teacher's particular contingencies of time and place.

Teacher development can help teachers articulate and rehearse resolving these moral dilemmas in their work. By reflecting on their own practice, observing and analyzing other teachers' practice, or studying case examples of practice, teachers can clarify the dilemmas they face and develop principled, practical, and increasingly skillful and thoughtful ways of dealing with them (Groundwater-Smith, 1993). This approach to teacher development elevates the principles of thoughtful, practical judgment above personal prejudice, misleading moral absolutes, or the false certainties of science as a guide to action and improvement (Louden, 1991).

Teacher development can also help create the conditions of work and cultures of collaboration in which teachers can develop, clarify, review, reflect on, and redefine their purposes, missions, and visions together. In discussion, as team partners, or as peer coaches, colleagues can serve as mirrors for teachers to view their own practice. Teachers can also find or be offered "critical friends" who will talk to them, observe them, give them feedback, offer other perspectives, provide access to readings and research—all of which will help teachers probe more deeply and critically into the moral grounds and consequences of their classroom actions (Day, Whitaker, & Johnston, 1990).

However, while the moral purposes of teacher development are important, more than moral exhortation is required for realizing them. Morality is not just a personal issue. It is also a political one—especially in a postmodern world where the boundaries between what is personal and what is political are becoming increasingly blurred (Denzin, 1992). The political aspects of teacher development must therefore also be attended to.

Political Awareness, Adeptness, and Acuity

If moral philosophy attracts those who seek after virtue, politics often draws together those who suspect duplicity and vice. Political pursuits and concerns have often been seen as diametrically opposed to moral ones. Indeed, politics is often regarded as immensely *immoral* in nature—shot through with artifice, self-interest, opportunism, and corruption. Not surprisingly, therefore, those teachers who sometimes seem to care most for their children, whose classroom commitments seem most intense, are precisely the ones most likely to see educational politics as irrelevant to or even counterproductive for their own teaching. Art teachers often exemplify this pattern, for instance (Bennett, 1985). Politics for such teachers is about careerism, committee work, or collective bargaining. Politics is tainted. Teaching is pure. Politics has no meaning or obvious benefits for their classroom work.

This common view of politics as organized politics is misleading, however. Politics is not specifically about organization and representation. It is about power in general. And power in education is everywhere. It is not extraneous to the classroom but always right there within it. Teachers exercise power over their students all the time. Most experience power being exercised over them by administrators. Many know equally well how to manipulate or maneuver around their principals (Blase, 1988).

When topics or project work are structured more around the interests of boys than girls, this is political (Delamont, 1980). When teachers support practices of tracking that systematically consign Native American and African-American students to lower tracks, poorer instruction, and lesser opportunities than their high-track fellows, this is political (Oakes, 1992). When teachers in classrooms characterized by cultural diversity do not address the many distinctive learning styles of their students, this is political. It is political when teachers hustle and lobby for extra resources and attention that will benefit their students, and equally political when they refrain from doing so. When teachers give parents' voices no hearing or when students' classroom voices are silenced or suppressed, this is political, too (A. Hargreaves, Leithwood, Gerin-Lajoié, Cousins, & Thiessen, 1993).

Many seemingly moral judgments in education are therefore inescapably political. What are some of the things that might be encompassed by a more politicized view of teaching and teacher development? What role can teacher development play beyond the obvious domains of organized politics, unionism, and committee work?

In general, being more political means being not merely reflective, but *critically* reflective about one's work, about the social conditions, contexts, and consequences of one's teaching, as well as about one's skill, efficiency, or kindliness in performing it (Carr & Kemmis, 1986; Liston & Zeichner, 1990). Critical reflection can be undertaken alone or together with colleagues. It can be actively provoked by seeking out "critical friends" to offer searching but supportive analyses of one's practice (Day et al., 1990). Once this *stance* of critical reflection begins to be taken in teaching and teacher development, other actions and consequences flow from it.

First, being a more political and critically reflective teacher means learning about the micro-political configurations of one's school. It means developing the capacity to discern who has formal and informal power, how this power is exercised, how resources are allocated, and how they can be secured beyond straight rational argument by influence, persuasion, assertiveness, diplomacy, trading favors, influencing power brokers, building coalitions, involving others, lobbying for support, planting seeds of an idea or proposal before presenting it in exhaustive detail, and so forth. Schools are micro-political worlds as well as moral ones (Ball, 1987; Blase, 1991). To pursue one's moral purposes without reference to the micro-political realities of schooling is to pursue them to the point of frustration, failure, and futility. Very few proposals get accepted simply because they are good ideas! Moral martyrs, as Fullan (1993) terms them, might soldier on for a while aside from those political realities, but ultimately when they become burned out or embittered, they do little good for students or themselves.

Teachers who have been introduced to the micro-politics of schooling in relation to their own institutions can achieve breakthroughs in insight, action, and effectiveness that help them secure support and resources for their students (Goodson & Fliesser, 1992). This perspective should be a key component of teacher preparation and inservice development on-site, in schools, where teachers can come to understand the micro-political contours of their own workplaces, then take appropriate action as a result. Bringing together on-site teacher education and inservice development around political agendas and concerns, as well as the more customary moral and technical ones, remains one of the key and controversial challenges of school-based teacher education, teacher development, and school improvement.

Second, being a more politically aware and developed teacher means empowering and assisting others to reach higher levels of competence and commitment. This is what Blase (1987) calls "positive politics." Student empowerment, for instance, can be fostered by creating more active and cooperative groupwork in classrooms, where students work not merely side-by-side *in* groups but also collectively together *as* groups (Galton & Simon, 1980; Slavin, 1988). Teachers can also do more to explain upcoming innovations to students and involve students actively in developing them (Rudduck, 1991). Additionally, students can be partners in as well as customary targets for assessment, through self-assessment, peer assessment, and periodic individual conferencing with their teachers (Broadfoot, James, McMecking, Nuttall, & Stierer, 1988; Hargreaves et al., 1993). Asking teachers to empower students more thoroughly is partly a matter of moral exhortation and increased awareness. It is also a demand that teachers feel requires additional training—in one-to-one conferencing skills, for instance (Hargreaves et al., 1993).

Parent empowerment can be fostered by building partnerships with parents in implementing and developing innovations, rather than informing parents about them once teachers have made all the decisions (Swap, 1993). Elsewhere, Michael Fullan and I have argued for greater *interactive professionalism* among communities of teachers (Fullan & Hargreaves, 1991). However, when this collaboration excludes parents and is confined to teachers alone, interactive professionalism runs the risk of becoming *incestuous professionalism*. Indeed, the language and discourse of teacher professionalism can be so specialized and self-enclosed as to exclude and alienate many parents, especially in the guarded terminology of school reports. Teachers are trained extensively in how to communicate with children. They receive little or no training and inservice development in how to communicate openly, honestly, and accessibly with parents (Alexander, 1992).

Empowerment is a responsibility that teachers also owe their colleagues. I have written extensively about these issues elsewhere (A. Hargreaves, 1994; Fullan & Hargreaves, 1991). What my own and other research on professional collaboration suggests is that teachers who work collaboratively rather than individually take more risks (Little, 1987), commit to continuous rather than episodic improvement (Rosenholtz, 1989), tend to be more caring with students and colleagues alike (Nias, Southworth, & Yeomans, 1989; Taafaki, 1992), have stronger senses of teaching efficacy (Ashton & Webb, 1986), are more assertive in relation to external pressures and demands (A. Hargreaves, 1994), experience greater opportunities to learn and improve from one another (Woods, 1990), and have access to more feedback (Lortie, 1975) and opportunities for reflection (Grimmett & Crehan, 1991).

Teacher collaboration and shared leadership (Barth, 1990) are not gifts that should be awaited from administrators. They are something that teachers can and should also actively create themselves in ways that connect to and communicate with their colleagues. Constructing and participating in such professional communities (Little & McLaughlin, 1993) in schools is itself a vibrant form of teacher and school development that is built into rather than extraneous to the ongoing life of the school as a "learning organization" whose members are constantly searching for ways to improve their practice (Senge, 1990). Leadership can help by creating and sustaining the conditions in which teacher-led collaboration can flourish (Leithwood, 1992) and by avoiding more superficial and administratively controlled forms of "imposed" or contrived collegiality (Grimmett & Crehan, 1991; A. Hargreaves, 1994). Placing and training beginning teachers within such positive cultures of collaboration and continuous improvement should also be a high priority in teacher education (Fullan, 1993).

Third, being more political means acknowledging and embracing, not avoiding, human conflict. One of the drawbacks of many teacher cultures, especially at the elementary level, is that their members are often inclined to move to early acquiescence and consensus (Nias, 1989) rather than risk the hurt and disconnection that conflict and disagreement might bring. Yet, as Lieberman, Darling-Hammond, & Zuckerman (1991) argue, conflict is a necessary part of the change and improvement process. Change threatens existing interests and identities and, in larger schools in particular, the interests embedded in different subject departments, for instance, will often be competing (Ball, 1987; A. Hargreaves et al., 1992). Indeed, if change does not involve conflict, the change being attempted is probably superficial, not threatening enough to be deep and significant (Louis & Miles, 1990).

The postmodern world increases possibilities for conflict because of greater cultural diversity, higher levels of moral uncertainty, flattened structures of decision making, and increasing attempts to hear and actively solicit the voices of different, dissonant, and even dissident groups throughout social and organizational life. Conflict is a necessary, normal, and perhaps even desirable feature of this complex and uncertain postmodern world. Indeed, within postmodernity, politics is less and less an issue of representative conflicts between large modernistic collectivities—between labor and capital, unions and employers, schools and states. Politics expresses itself more and more in particular issues and local contexts within decentralized systems. School-based management is exemplifying and heightening this tendency toward greater local politicization in education. It puts teachers right in the front lines of decision making. In postmodern society, politics permeates every part of institutional life (Denzin, 1992).

Teachers need to be better prepared to deal with personal and political conflicts in their work—not to avoid or even endure them, but to embrace them as positive forces for change. Bringing differences into the open, being sensitive to one another's interests and positions, working for clarity and compromise, being encouraged to express feelings and frustrations, moving beyond initial and often inaccurate fears about one's threatened interests, expressing one's own voice and giving voice to others—all these are vital components of a productive and emancipatory process of continuous learning and improvement (A. Hargreaves et al., 1993). New and experienced teachers need to be trained in and prepared for these processes of conflict acceptance and resolution, for without them change will be superficial, missions and goals will be boring and bland, and the disagreements and resentments that always accompany improvement efforts will be driven underground and lead to frustration, martyrdom, and intolerable guilt (A. Hargreaves, 1994).

Fourth, for teacher developers themselves, being more political means recognizing that many typical training efforts in knowledge and skill development falsely treat the techniques in which teachers are being trained as universal, generic, neutral, and equally applicable to all students irrespective of race, gender, and other distinctions. Yet H.-J. Robertson (1992) summarizes the research on gender differences in instruction to conclude that teachers distribute attention, praise, and opportunities unequally between boys and girls. Even in seemingly learner-centered cooperative group projects, boys tend to be dominant. Yet, she notes, efforts at improving instruction tend to be treated as "gender-neutral." Staff developers need to be more sensitive to how patterns of instruction and teachers' training in them impact upon students differently according to gender, race, and so forth.

Fifth, it is important to be reflective about the long-term political and social consequences of one's classroom work, to develop a principled (which does not mean pious) stand in relation to them, to build active support for the principles embodied in that stand, and to defend one's classroom ground, one's workplace culture, and one's whole profession against political and administrative assaults and intrusions upon those principles. This, too, is an important priority for teacher development. Although many teacher developers may be afraid to rock this particular boat, in their hearts, beneath the comforts of expediency, perhaps they really should.

Like it or not, teacher development *is* a political activity, especially in the emerging postmodern world. Building more awareness, adeptness, and acuity among teachers so that they can pursue positive politics inside and beyond their schools for the benefit of their students must therefore become a much more salient and explicit part of the teacher development agenda.

Emotional Involvement

While reflection is central to teacher development, the mirror of reflection does not capture all there is to see in a teacher. It tends to miss what lies deep inside teachers, what motivates them most about their work. However conscientiously it is done, the reflective glance can never quite get to the emotional heart of teaching.

Beyond technique and moral purpose, what makes good teaching is *desire.* According to the *Shorter Oxford English Dictionary, desire* is "that emotion which is directed to the attainment or possession of some object from which pleasure or satisfaction is expected; longing, craving, a wish." Desire is imbued with "creative unpredictability" (Lash, 1990) and "flows of energy" (Deleuze & Guattari, 1977). In desire is to be found the creativity and spontaneity that connects teachers emotionally and sensually (in the literal sense of feeling) to their children, their colleagues, and their work. Such desires among particularly creative teachers are for fulfilment, intense achievement, senses of breakthrough, closeness to fellow humans, even love for them (Nias, 1989; Woods, 1990). Without desire, teaching becomes arid and empty. It loses its meaning. Understanding the emotional life of teachers, their feelings for and in their work, and attending to this emotional life in ways that positively cultivate it and avoid negatively damaging it should be absolutely central to teacher development efforts.

Yet most teacher development initiatives, even the most innovative ones, neglect the emotions of teaching. The whole push toward creating more reflective practice tends to do this in rational, calculative, cognitive ways. Reflective practice is usually presented as being about thinking, analyzing, and inquiring, not about feeling, intuiting, and engaging. Indeed, Liston and Zeichner (1990) argue for the importance of "rational deliberation" and "giving of good reasons" when teachers reflect on moral value claims, rather than resorting to the "doctrine" of "emotivism" and its claim that all moral judgments are nothing but expressions of preference, attitude, or feeling.[2]

Action research, even critical action research, has been criticized for similar reasons. While often predicated on the pursuit of dispassionate inquiry, Chisholm (1990) argues that action research should instead reject "deceptive rational coolness in favour of explicit commitment . . . in favour of passionate scholarship" (p. 253; also Dadds, 1991). Dadds (1993) points out that in one action-research relationship she examined, "far from the experience being initially, coolly cerebral and analytical for the researcher, it is emotive, disturbing and judgmental" (p. 294). Thus action research that does not attend to the feelings of teachers—and to creating situations of safety and security in which observation, inquiry, and criticism can take place—may actually reverse or retard teacher development by making teachers vulnerable, exposed, and even ashamed about what transpires (Dadds, 1991).

Similarly, in the education and induction of new teachers, while the strains of becoming a new teacher are often viewed as ones of competence, mastery, developing routines, building a repertoire, establishing a reputation, and so forth, Tickle (1991) has found, in a study of beginning teachers, that "learning how to handle the emotional responses was . . . as important as learning how to conduct tasks, meet new experiences, make judgments, build relationships, or assimilate new knowledge" (p. 320). For Tickle, these emotional aspects of the beginning teacher's self are inextricably linked to acquiring and using classroom techniques and to applying professional judgment.

Outside the classroom, in the domain of teachers' relations with their colleagues, there has been a tendency among researchers to value forms of collaboration that are more intellectual, inquiry-based, and task-centered over ones that are organized more informally around principles and purposes of care, connection, and storytelling (e.g., Little, 1990). Taafaki (1992), however, shows that in their exchange of narratives and stories, teachers are not merely "gossiping" for amusement or moral support. They are learning about the moral principles that guide one another's work and that, if sufficiently shared, might provide a basis for further associations among them. These "communal caring" cultures are most likely to be found in the feminine, feminized, though not necessarily feminist, world of elementary teaching (Acker, 1993). Such cultures may not operate like rational seminars of rigorous intellectual inquiry, but alongside and within the practices of care and connection, they do incorporate inquiry and reflection in more implicit, informal, and incidental ways.

Much of the writing on and practice of teacher development has tended to emphasize its rational, intellectual, cognitive, deliberative, and strategic qualities. Even those views of teacher development that have paid attention to teachers' emotions and selves have tended to rationalize and intellectualize their treatment in calculative, managerial ways. The self is regarded as something to be "managed" (Woods, 1981), interests are things to be "juggled" (Pollard, 1982), personal and professional growth have to be "planned" (Day, 1993). Selves, like actions and careers, it seems, are subject to strategic definition and redefinition (Nias, 1989; Woods, 1983). Yet as Crow (1989) points out, not all social actions can be usefully construed in terms of strategies. Some actions are spontaneous or traditional in nature. Commenting on conceptualizations of teachers' careers, Evetts (1994) argues that

> For many individuals, but particularly women, career actions would fit more appropriately into a category of traditional action since career decisions illustrate reference to the past, continuity and lack of calculation, rather than the instrumentality and rationality that are implied by the term strategy. (p. 16)

Indeed, Evetts concludes, "it might be the case that strategy, like career, is a gendered concept" (p. 17).

In short, whether they are supportive or critical of existing systems, the dominant paradigms of teacher development research and practice tend to be rational, calculative, managerial, and somewhat masculine in nature. The professorial values of rational debate and analysis in the seminar room are imposed upon the pedagogical practices of intuition and improvisation in the classroom.[3] The turbulence, excitement, and unpredictability of teachers' emotions are either ignored in much teacher development work or reinscribed within rational frameworks where they can be planned and managed in dispassionate ways.

Purposive rationality and reasoned reflection are not irrelevant to teaching or to other parts of our lives. Indeed, they remain extremely important as sources of technical, moral, and political deliberation. But they must be placed in proper perspective. Problem solving, reflection, and rational discussion are not hierarchically or developmentally superior or preferable to care, connection, and emotional engagement. There is a need for greater equity, integration, and balance between the two. This remains a real and unrealized challenge for teacher development work.

Exploring the emotions is the exception in teacher development (see Salzberger-Wittenberg et al., 1983, for one such exception). But even where the affective aspects of teaching *are* acknowledged and encouraged, only certain emotions are made visible or portrayed as positive, while others are portrayed negatively or omitted altogether. What matters here is not that teachers' emotions are represented in evaluative ways but that these representations are asserted or assumed rather than argued through in considered and explicit detail. Implicitly, the discourse of teacher development has come to value particular forms of emotional being among teachers and to devalue others. Jennifer Nias's important work, which has done more than almost any other to bring emotions and the self to the forefront of teacher development, nonetheless reveals patterns of preference for particular kinds of emotional expression and development among teachers. In her book on primary teachers, for example Nias (1989) argues that

> the warmth, patience, strength and calm required by tradition and circumstances cannot eradicate teachers' fiercer and more negative emotions: for teaching is, in Connell's words an "emotionally dangerous occupation" (Connell, 1985:121). . . . For example, Jackson (1968:139–141) gives a sensitive and insightful account of American elementary teachers' 'love' and 'respect' for their pupils. The intensity of such emotions is balanced by anger . . . and by the shame which accompanies the uncontrolled expression of this rage. (p. 194)

Toward the end of her book, Nias concludes that

> Although much of this book focuses on teachers' socially regulated 'selves', their own descriptions of their feelings about pupils, and their relationships with them and with their colleagues, reminds us that the regressive, passionate and unruly aspects of human nature are always present in the classroom and may sometimes escape from rational control. (p. 203)

In Nias's writing and elsewhere, there is a tendency, when the emotions of teaching are acknowledged, to rate them on a seemingly singular scale of desirability and appropriateness. Carefully regulated and tempered emotions such as warmth, patience, strength, calm, caring, concern, building trust, and expressing vulnerability are preferred and privileged over anger, rage, passion, and sometimes even love; over emotions that are portrayed as fiercer, more negative, intensive, regressive, and unruly in nature.

Emotional states, though, are not simply positive or negative, good or bad, in some universal sense. They can only be evaluated *in context*. Anger, for instance, can be surprisingly positive in some contexts, even educational ones, as in the North American Native Indian Medicine Way Path of Learning's positive valuation of "anger at injustice" as something worth developing among one's students.[4] This program also values "noble passions" among its desirable outcomes. Emotions and their legitimate expression, that is, are *culturally loaded*. Particular emotions and their expression are accorded different value within different cultural, racial, and ethnic groups (Gordon, 1990; Montandon, 1992).

Intense human emotions and passions are often at the very heart of teacher commitment and desire. Accepting, even accentuating, these kinds of emotion in teaching—moving beyond the emotional codes of polite society to ones that embrace the vigor and vitality of working-class inheritance, Mediterranean or Latin American cultural styles, or African-American forms of experience, for instance—remains an important challenge for practice and research in teacher development. It is important, in this respect, that teacher developers do not merely cultivate the emotional lives of teachers, but that they do so in ways that extend beyond white, middle-class norms of quiet caring and cultural politeness.

Reason and purposive rationality have enjoyed preeminence for centuries. In the postmodern age, this preeminence is drawing to a close. Purposive rationality was integral to the modern age and its concern with control, regulation, ordering, and centralization of power on the one hand, or the pursuit of emancipation through intellectual enlightenment and application of scientific knowledge on the other (Bauman, 1992). The uncertainties, complexities, and rapid change of the postmodern age, along with growing awareness of the perverted realizations of science in war, weaponry, and environmental disaster, have brought about disillusionment with this purposive rationality (Smart, 1992). Practical rationality (Toulmin, 1990), practical reasoning (Schwab, 1971), and personal knowledge (Polanyi, 1958) have been brought out of the shadows cast by purposive rationality. The pride of place occupied by purposive rationality among all other forms of rationality, which have tended to be viewed as lesser or derivative versions of it, has been questioned. Max Weber (1947), who wrote extensively and influentially on the nature of rational action, argued that

> For the purposes of a typological scientific analysis, it is convenient to treat all irrational, affectually determined elements of behavior as factors of deviation from a conceptually pure type of rational action. (p. 88)

However, away from the world of ideal categorization, in reality, when it is compared to the pervasive presence of creative action, traditional action, and the like, purposive rationality is actually something of a minority form in our culture (Joas, 1993). In the postmodern world, multiple rather than singular forms of intelligence are coming to be recognized (Gardner, 1983), multiple rather than singular forms of representation of students' work are being advocated and accepted (Eisner, 1993). Many ways of knowing, thinking, and being moral—not just rational, "logical" ones—are coming to be seen as legitimate, not least the knowledge and moral judgment of women (Belenky, Clinchy, Goldberger, & Tarule, 1986; Gilligan, 1982).

Postmodernity is pressing us to accept complexity, diversity, and uncertainty as central to our professional and personal lives. In an increasingly postrational society, emotions that cannot easily be managed, regulated, planned, or controlled will become increasingly prominent and problematic features of our workplaces. In one sense, passion, desire, and other intense emotions have always been central to teaching. But governments, bureaucracies, and even professional developers have ignored them, driven them underground, or sought to tame and regulate them in pursuit of the technical efficiency, planned change, and rational reform that have characterized the modern mission. As a result, care has been cast aside when busy teachers coping with multiple innovations have no longer been able to give it (Neufeld, 1991). Joy has been planned away by meetings, mandates, and school development or professional growth plans (A. Hargreaves, 1994). Anxiety, frustration, and guilt have become widespread consequences, burnout and cynicism their legacies to the classroom (A. Hargreaves, 1994). Emotions are pivotal to the quality of teaching. Teacher developers ignore them at their peril.

CONCLUSIONS

The practice and research of teacher development, I have argued, should address the technical competence of teaching, the place of moral purpose in teaching, political awareness, acuity, and adeptness among teachers, and teachers' emotional attachments to and engagement with their work. None of these dimensions alone capture all that is important or all there is to know about teacher development. What really matters is the interactions among and integration between them.

Focusing on technical competence in isolation can make teacher development into a narrow, utilitarian exercise that does not question the purposes and parameters of what teachers do. All the glitziness of stage-managed workshop presentations, all the "bells and whistles" in the world, are no substitute for the openness and rigor of this moral and political questioning. Such workshops may even seduce teachers into sidestepping such questioning (Hargreaves & Dawe, 1990). Even when new techniques have demonstrable merit, training in them may be ineffective when it does not address the real conditions of teachers' work, the multiple and contradictory demands to which teachers must respond, the cultures of teachers' workplaces, and teachers' emotional relationships to their teaching, to their children, and to change in general.

Focusing on moral purpose and moral virtue alone also has its limitations. Teachers and teacher developers who do this can become pious and grandiose in their pursuit of moral virtue. If they are in positions of teacher leadership, their missionary fervor can blind them to the differences in values, competence, working conditions, or levels of emotional security among their colleagues. Such leaders have the visions. Their colleagues are merely expected to share them! By comparison, when their positions are more marginalized within the school, teachers motivated by a singular moral purpose, however laudable it is, can become moral martyrs, isolated in enclaves of sacrificial self-righteousness. Stigmatized teachers of stigmatized students—teachers of special education or of low-status practical subjects, for instance—are particularly vulnerable to this syndrome. It is almost impossible for moral martyrs to influence the colleagues who reject them, and in their increasing isolation, it becomes more and more likely that they will suffer from burnout or cynicism as a result (Little, 1993a).

Political strategies pursued in isolation raise different problems. In the absence of sensitivity to the emotional needs of others, they can make teachers carping and hypercritical. Teachers of this kind can monopolize endless staff meetings and consume vast quantities of office paper for memoranda that ritually oppose any and all proposals for change. Without sincere moral purpose that is connected to the well-being of students, even those politicized teachers who ostensibly embrace positive change can also fall into the trap of careerism and opportunism, playing school politics mainly to feather their own nests.

Finally, problems can arise if exclusive emphasis is placed on the emotions of teacher development. Approaching teacher development predominantly or exclusively as a process of self-development can create real difficulties when moral frameworks or senses of context are weak. Under these conditions, teacher development can become disturbingly narcissistic and self-indulgent. The rhetoric of personal change is one of human empowerment. However, when the contours and conditions of teaching are being massively restructured all around them, retreating to an enclosed world of the personal and the practical, withdrawing exclusively into stories of the self, creates in teachers exactly the opposite effect—political quiescence and professional disempowerment.

So the different dimensions of teacher development must in practice be addressed together. If desire is a pivotal point of focus here, it can be properly stimulated and supported only through the holistic integration of all the dimensions of teacher development. Quick shots of desire can be administered through single workshops, but their benefits are rarely permanent. If passion and desire are to be stimulated and supported among many teachers over long periods of time, they must be attended to in the ongoing conditions and cultures of teachers' working lives. Increasing competence and mastery both fuels and is fueled by teacher desire. Moral purpose gives a focus to desire, can channel it in worthwhile directions. Political action and awareness can help combat the conditions of isolation, poor leadership, imposed and escalating demands, narrow visions, and disheartening working conditions that can otherwise dampen teachers' desire. Creating collaborative environments of continuous learning and working with "critical friends" can enhance this project of resistance and reconstruction even further.

What we want for our children, we should also want for their teachers—that schools be places of learning for both of them and that such learning be suffused with excitement, engagement, passion, challenge, creativity, and joy. Meeting such goals is not only a challenge for teacher development but also fundamentally a challenge to our beliefs about and commitments to the kinds of schools and education we want in the postmodern world. The issue for those of us who care about teaching and teacher development is whether technically, morally, politically, and emotionally, we are up to that broader challenge.

NOTES

1. My own refutation of this attempt to deny the possibility or relevance of macro-theorizing is argued in detail in A. Hargreaves (1985).
2. Close inspection of Liston and Zeichner's (1990) text reveals deceptiveness in the discourse through which they compare emotivism and rational deliberation. Emotivism is characterized as invoking "*nothing but*" expressions of preference, attitude, or feeling. By contrast, "*it is possible*" for rational deliberation over value claims to occur (emphases added). Liston and Zeichner thereby rhetorically dismiss the emotions by rejecting an exaggerated position wherein moral judgment involves *nothing but* emotions. The more reasonable partial claim that *it is possible* for rational deliberation to occur then becomes the total, and only, claim. The discourse thereby elevates rational deliberation above the emotions in teacher reflection, and the possibility of an integrated, balanced rapprochement between thinking and feeling, cognition and emotion, is discursively dismissed.
3. It is important to acknowledge here that, ironically, professorial cultures outside the seminar room, in other parts of the workplace, often operate on very different principles than those that are valued within it.
4. The Medicine Way Path of Learning as a guide for curriculum planning is produced by and available from Children of the Earth Secondary School, Winnipeg, Manitoba, Canada.

REFERENCES

Acker, S. (1992). Creating careers: Women teachers at work. *Curriculum Inquiry, 22*(2), 141–163.
Acker, S. (1993). *Women teachers working together.* Unpublished paper. Toronto: Department of Sociology in Education, Ontario Institute for Studies in Education.
Alexander, R. (1992). *Policy and practice in primary education.* London: Routledge.
Apple, M. (1986). *Teachers and texts.* London and New York: Routledge.
Ashton, P., & Webb, R. (1986). *Making a difference: Teachers' sense of efficacy and student achievement.* New York: Longman.
Ball, S. (1987). *Micropolitics of the school.* London: Methuen.
Barth, R. (1990). *Improving schools from within.* San Francisco: Jossey-Bass.
Bauman, Z. (1992). *Intimations of postmodernity.* London and New York: Routledge.

Becker, H. (1952). The career of the Chicago public school-teacher. *American Journal of Sociology, 57,* 470–477.

Belenky, M. F., Clinchy, B. M., Goldberger, N. R., & Tarule, J. M. (1986). *Women's ways of knowing.* New York: Basic Books.

Bennett, C. (1985). Paints, pots or promotion?: Art teachers' attitudes towards their careers. In S. Ball & I. Goodson (Eds.), *Teachers' lives and careers* (pp. 120–137). New York: Falmer.

Berlak, H., & Berlak, A. (1981). *Dilemmas of schooling: Teaching and social change.* London: Methuen.

Blase, J. (1987). Political interactions among teachers: Sociocultural context in the schools. *Urban Education, 22*(3), 286–309.

Blase, J. (1988). The teachers' political orientation vis-a-vis the principal: The micropolitics of the school. *Politics of Education Association Yearbook* (pp. 113–126). New York: Taylor & Francis.

Blase, J. (Ed.). (1991). *The politics of life in schools.* New York: Corwin.

Blumer, H. (1969). *Symbolic interactionism.* Englewood Cliffs, NJ: Prentice-Hall.

Broadfoot, P., James, M., McMecking, S., Nuttall, D., & Stierer, B. (1988). *Records of achievement: Report of the National Evaluation of Pilot Schemes.* London: Her Majesty's Stationery Office.

Caldwell, B., & Spinks, J. (1988). *The self-managing school.* London and New York: Falmer.

Campbell, E. (in press). Raising the moral dimension of school leadership. *Curriculum Inquiry.*

Carr, W., & Kemmis, S. (1986). *Becoming critical: Education, knowledge and action research.* London and New York: Falmer.

Celebrated geologist, J. Tuzo Wilson, 84. (1993, April 17). Toronto *Star*, p. 16.

Chisholm, L. (1990). Action research: Some methodological and political considerations. *British Educational Research Journal, 16*(3), 249–257.

Connell, R. (1985). *Teachers' work.* Sydney and New York: George Allen & Unwin.

Crow, G. (1989). The use of the concept of strategy in recent sociological literature. *Sociology, 23*(1), 1–24.

Dadds, M. (1991, April). *Passionate inquiry: The role of the self in teacher action research.* Paper presented to the Classroom Action Research Network Conference, Bromsford.

Dadds, M. (1993). The feeling of thinking in professional self-study. *Educational Action Research, 1*(2), 287–303.

Day, C. (1993, September). *Personal development planning: Towards a lifelong development model of teacher growth.* Paper presented to the second Professional Actions and Cultures of Teaching (PACT) conference, London, Canada.

Day, C., Whitaker, P., & Johnston, D. (1990). *Managing primary schools in the 1990s: A professional development approach.* London: Chapman.

Delamont, S. (1980). *Sex roles and the school.* London: Methuen.

Deleuze, G., & Guattari, F. (1977). *Anti-Oedipus: Capitalism and schizophrenia.* New York: Viking.

Denzin, N. (1991). *Images of postmodern society.* London and Newbury Park, CA: Sage.

Denzin, N. (1992). *Symbolic interactionism and cultural studies*. Oxford, UK, and Cambridge, MA: Blackwell.

Durkheim, E. (1961). *Moral education*. New York: Free Press.

Eisner, E. (1993). Forms of understanding and the future of educational research. *Educational Researcher, 22*(7), 5–11.

Elbaz, F. (1991). Research on teachers' knowledge. *Journal of Curriculum Studies, 23*(1), 1–19.

Evetts, J. (1994). *Becoming a secondary school headteacher*. London: Cassell.

Fenstermacher, G. (1990). Some moral considerations on teaching as a profession. In J. Goodlad, R. Soder, & K. Sirotnik (Eds.), *The moral dimensions of teaching* (pp. 130–151). San Francisco: Jossey-Bass.

Fullan, M. (1991). *The new meaning of educational change*. New York: Teachers College Press; Toronto: OISE Press; and London: Cassell.

Fullan, M. (1993). *Change forces: Probing the depths of educational reform*. London and New York: Falmer.

Fullan, M., & Hargreaves, A. (1991). *What's worth fighting for?: Working together for your school*. Toronto: Ontario Public School Teachers Federation; Andover, MA: The Network, North East Laboratory; Milton Keynes, UK: Open University Press; and Melbourne: Australian Council for Educational Administration.

Galton, M., & Simon, B. (Eds.). (1980). *Progress and performance in the primary classroom*. London: Routledge.

Gardner, H. (1983). *Frames of mind: The theory of multiple intelligences*. New York: Basic Books.

Giddens, A. (1991). *Modernity and self identity*. Cambridge, UK: Polity Press.

Gilligan, C. (1982). *In a different voice*. Cambridge, MA: Harvard University Press.

Goffman, E. (1975). *Frame analysis*. Harmondsworth, UK: Penguin.

Goodlad, J. (1990). The occupation of teaching in schools. In J. Goodlad, R. Soder, & K. Sirotnik (Eds.), *The moral dimensions of teaching* (pp. 3–34). San Francisco: Jossey-Bass.

Goodson, I. (1990). Nations at risk and national curriculum: Ideology and identity. In *Politics of Education Association Yearbook* (pp. 219–252). New York: Taylor & Francis.

Goodson, I. (1992). Sponsoring the teacher's voice. In A. Hargreaves & M. Fullan (Eds.), *Understanding teacher development* (110–121). London: Cassell and New York: Teachers College Press.

Goodson, I., & Fliesser, C. (1992). Exchanging gifts: Collaborative research and theories of context. In I. Goodson & M. Mangan (Eds.), *History, context and qualitative methods in the study of education*, RUCCUS, Occasional Papers, Vol. 3, Faculty of Education, University of Western Ontario.

Gordon, S. L. (1990). Social structural effects on emotions. In T. Kemper (Ed.), *Research agendas in the sociology of emotions* (pp. 145–179). New York: State University of New York Press.

Grimmett, P., & Crehan, P. (1991). The nature of collegiality in teacher development: The case of clinical supervision. In M. Fullan & A. Hargreaves (Eds.), *Teacher development and educational change* (pp. 56–85). London and New York: Falmer.

Groundwater-Smith, S. (1993, February). *Introducing dilemmas into the practicum curriculum.* Paper presented to the 5th National Practicum Conference, Macquarie University, Sydney, Australia.

Hargreaves, A. (1985). The micro-macro problem in the sociology of education. In R. Burgess (Ed.), *Issues in educational research* (pp. 21–47). London and New York: Falmer.

Hargreaves, A. (1986). *Two cultures of schooling.* London and New York: Falmer.

Hargreaves, A. (1989). *Curriculum and assessment reform.* Milton Keynes, UK: Open University Press and Toronto: OISE Press.

Hargreaves, A. (1994). *Changing teachers, changing times: Teachers' work and culture in the postmodern age.* London: Cassell; New York: Teachers College Press; and Toronto: OISE Press.

Hargreaves, A., Davis, J., Fullan, M., Wignall, R., Stager, M., & Macmillan, R. (1992). *Secondary school work cultures and educational change.* Final report of a project funded by the Ontario Ministry of Education Transfer Grant. Toronto: Department of Educational Administration, Ontario Institute for Studies in Education.

Hargreaves, A., & Dawe, R. (1990). Paths of professional development: Contrived collegiality, collaborative culture and the case of peer coaching. *Teaching and Teacher Education, 4*(2), 227–241.

Hargreaves, A., Leithwood, K., Gerin-Lajoié, D., Cousins, B. L., & Thiessen, D. (1993). *Years of transition: Times for change.* Final report of a project funded by the Ontario Ministry of Education. Toronto: Queen's Printer.

Hargreaves, D. (1978). Whatever happened to symbolic interactionism? In L. Barton & R. Meighan (Eds.), *Sociological interpretations of schooling and classrooms: A reappraisal* (pp. 7–22). Driffield, UK: Nafferton.

Hargreaves, D. (1980). The occupational culture of teaching. In P. Woods (Ed.), *Teacher strategies* (pp. 125–148). London: Croom Helm.

Harvey, D. (1989). *The condition of postmodernity.* Cambridge, UK: Polity Press.

Holmes, M. (1984). *The victory and failure of educational modernism. Issues in Education, 2*(1), 23–35.

Hultmann, G., & Horberg, C. (1993, August). *Teachers informal rationality: Understanding about teachers utilization of knowledge.* Paper presented at the sixth conference of the International Study Association of Teacher Thinking, Gothenburg, Sweden.

Jackson, P. (1968). *Life in classrooms.* New York: Holt, Rinehart & Winston.

Joas, H. (1993, August). *The creativity of action.* Paper presented to the sixth conference of the International Study Association of Teacher Thinking, Gothenburg, Sweden.

Kanter, R. M., Stein, B. A., & Jick, J. D. (1992). *The challenge of organizational change.* New York: Free Press.

Lasch, C. (1991). *The true and only heaven: Progress and its critics.* New York: Norton.

Lash, S. (1990). *Sociology of postmodernism.* London and New York: Routledge.

Leinberger, P., & Tucker, B. (1991). *The new individualists: The generation after the organization man.* New York: HarperCollins.

Leithwood, K. (1992). The move toward transformational leadership. *Educational Leadership, 49*(5), 8–12.

Lieberman, A., Darling-Hammond, L., & Zuckerman, D. (1991). *Early lessons in restructuring schools.* New York: National Center for Restructuring Education, Schools, Teachers and Teaching (NCRESTT).

Lieberman, A., & McLaughlin, M. (1992). Networks for educational change: Powerful and problematic. *Phi Delta Kappan, 73*(9), 673–699.

Lindblad, S., & Prieto, H. (1992). School experiences and teacher socialization. *Teaching and Teacher Education, 8*(5/6), 465–470.

Liston, D., & Zeichner, K. (1990). Reflective teaching and action research in preservice teacher education. *Journal of Education for Teaching, 16*(3), 235–254.

Liston, D., & Zeichner, K. (1991). *Teacher education and the social conditions of schooling.* New York: Routledge, Chapman & Hall.

Little, J. W. (1987). Teachers as colleagues. In V. Richardson-Koehler (Ed.), *Educators' handbook* (pp. 491–510). White Plains, NY: Longman.

Little, J. W. (1990). The persistence of privacy: Autonomy and initiative in teachers' professional relations. *Teachers College Record, 91*(4), 509–536.

Little, J. (1993a). Professional community in comprehensive high schools: The two worlds of academic and vocational teachers. In J. Little & M. McLaughlin (Eds.), *Teachers' work: Individuals, colleagues and contexts* (pp. 136–163). New York: Teachers College Press.

Little, J. W. (1993b). Teachers' professional development in a climate of educational reform. *Educational Evaluation and Policy Analysis, 15*(2), 129–152.

Little, J. W., & McLaughlin, M. (Eds.) (1993). *Teachers' work: Individuals, colleagues and contexts.* New York: Teachers College Press.

Lortie, D. (1975). *Schoolteacher.* Chicago: University of Chicago Press.

Louden, W. (1991). *Understanding teaching.* London: Cassell and New York: Teachers College Press.

Louis, K. S., & Miles, M. (1990). *Improving the urban high school.* New York: Teachers College Press.

McLaughlin, M. (1990, December). The Rand change agent study revisited: Macro perspectives and micro realities. *Educational Researcher,* pp. 11–16.

McNeil, L. (1986). *Contradictions of control: School structure and school knowledge.* New York: Routledge & Kegan Paul.

Mead, G. H. (1934). *Mind, self and society.* Chicago: University of Chicago Press.

Metz, M. (1990). How social class differences shape teachers work. In M. McLaughlin, J. E. Talbert, & N. Bascia (Eds.), *The contexts of teaching in secondary schools* (pp. 40–107). New York: Teachers College Press.

Montandon, C. (1992). La socialisation des émotions: un champ nouveau pour la sociologie de l'éducation. *Revue Francaise de Pedagogie, 101*, Octobre–Novembre–Décembre, 105–122.

Neufeld, J. (1991). Curriculum reform and the time of care. *Curriculum Journal, 2*(3), 285–300.

Nias, J. (1989). *Primary teachers talking.* London: Routledge.

Nias, J., Southworth, G., & Yeomans, A. (1989). *Staff relationships in the primary school.* London: Cassell.

Oakes, J. (1992). *Restructuring the opportunity structure: Detracking schools.* Paper presented to International Conference on Restructuring Education: Choices and Challenges, Toronto, Ontario Institute for Studies in Education.

Olson, J. (1991). *Understanding teaching: Beyond expertise.* Milton Keynes, UK: Open University Press.

Polanyi, M. (1958). *Personal knowledge.* Chicago: University of Chicago Press.

Pollard, A. (1982). A model of coping strategies. *British Journal of Sociology of Education, 3*(1), 19–37.

Pratt, D. (1983, Winter). Curriculum for the 21st century. *Education Canada,* pp. 41–47.

Reich, R. B. (1992). *The work of nations.* New York: Random House.

Robertson, H.-J. (1992). Teacher development and gender equity. In A. Hargreaves & M. Fullan (Eds.), *Understanding teacher development* (pp. 43–61). London: Cassell and New York: Teachers College Press.

Robertson, S. (1993). *Teachers' labour and post-Fordism: An exploratory analysis.* Deakin, Australia: Deakin University Press.

Rosenholtz, S. (1989). *Teachers' workplace: The social organization of schools.* New York: Longman.

Rudduck, J. (1991). *Innovation and change.* Milton Keynes, UK: Open University Press.

Salzberger-Wittenberg, I., et al. (1983). *The emotional experience of teaching and learning.* London: Routledge and Kegan Paul.

Schlechty, P. (1990). *Schools for the twenty-first century.* San Francisco: Jossey-Bass.

Schön, D. (1983). *The reflective practitioner.* San Francisco: Jossey-Bass.

Schwab, J. (1971). The practical: Arts of eclectic. *School Review, 79,* 493–542.

Senge, P. (1990). *The fifth discipline.* New York: Doubleday.

Sikes, P., Measor, L., & Woods, P. (1985). *Teacher careers: Crises and continuities.* London: Falmer.

Slavin, R. E. (1988). Cooperative learning and student achievement. *Educational Leadership, 46*(2), 31–33.

Smart, B. (1992). *Modern conditions, postmodern controversies.* London: Routledge.

Smyth, J. (1991). International perspectives on teacher collegiality: A labour process discussion based on the concept of teachers' work. *British Journal of Sociology of Education, 12*(3), 323–346.

Smyth, J. (Ed.). (1993). *The socially critical self-managing school.* London and New York: Falmer.

Smyth, J. (Ed.). (1994). *Critical discourses in teacher development.* London: Cassell.

Swap, S. M. (1993). *Developing home–school partnerships: From concept to practice.* New York: Teachers College Press.

Taafaki, I. (1992). *Collegiality and women teachers in elementary and middle school settings: The caring relationship and nurturing interdependence.* Unpublished doctoral dissertation, University of Massachusetts, Amherst.

Tickle, L. (1991). New teachers and the emotions of learning teaching. *Cambridge Journal of Education, 21*(3), 319–329.

Tom, A. (1984). *Teaching as a moral craft.* New York: Longman.

Toulmin, S. (1990). *Cosmopolis: The hidden agenda of modernity.* New York: Free Press.

Troyna, B. (1993, August). *Deracialized teachers*. Paper presented to the sixth conference of the International Study Association of Teacher Thinking, Gothenburg, Sweden.

Waller, W. (1932). *The sociology of teaching*. New York: Wiley.

Weber, M. (1947). *The theory of social and economic organization*. New York: Free Press.

Werner, W. (1988). Program implementation and experienced time. *Alberta Journal of Educational Research, 34*(2), 90–108.

Woods, P. (1977). Teaching for survival. In P. Woods and M. Hammersley (Eds.), *School experience* (pp. 87–108). London: Croom Helm.

Woods, P. (1981). Strategies, commitment and identity: Making and breaking the teacher role. In L. Barton & S. Walker (Eds.), *Schools, teachers and teaching*. Lewes, UK: Falmer.

Woods, P. (1983). *Sociology and the school*. London: Routledge.

Woods, P. (1990). Teaching and creativity. In P. Woods (Ed.), *Teacher skills and strategies* (pp. 18–35). London and New York: Falmer.

Woods, P. (Ed.). (1990). *Teacher skills and strategies*. London and New York: Falmer.

Woods, P. (1992). Symbolic interactionism: Theory and method. In M. LeCompte, W. Millroy, & J. Preissle (Eds.), *The handbook of qualitative research in education* (pp. 337–404). New York: Academic Press.

2

Expanding a Teacher's Knowledge Base

A Cognitive Psychological Perspective on Professional Development

HILDA BORKO AND RALPH T. PUTNAM

This chapter presents a perspective on teachers' professional growth that is grounded in the discipline of cognitive psychology. More specifically, our perspective is based on the premise that one important component of teachers' ongoing learning is the expansion and elaboration of their professional knowledge base. The chapter begins by building a case for a focus within professional development programs on teachers' knowledge and beliefs, based on themes in cognitive psychological research on teaching and implications of current efforts to reform educational practice. We next present a model of the knowledge base of teaching that can serve as a framework for professional development, and we describe three professional development programs that reflect many components of that model. The chapter concludes with a summary of features of professional development programs that seem to be successful in helping teachers to expand and elaborate their professional knowledge base. Many of our examples are drawn from the domain of mathematics teaching, due in part to our interests and expertise as researchers and in part to the prominent role that mathematics educators have played in the overall education reform movement.

FOCUSING ON TEACHERS' KNOWLEDGE AND BELIEFS

A Cognitive Psychological Perspective on Teachers and Teaching

There is no single cognitive psychological perspective on teachers and teaching, nor is there a single model of learning to teach. Although cognitive psychologists use a variety of models to describe and investigate teachers' ideas and practices, however, their work shares a number of assumptions and focal issues. This section explores several of these commonalities that are particularly relevant to designing professional development programs for teachers.[1]

Individuals and Their Mental Lives. The central focus of cognitive psychology is individuals and their mental lives. The discipline is concerned primarily with the contents of the human mind (e.g., knowledge, perceptions, beliefs) and the mental processes in which people engage (e.g., thinking, problem solving, planning). As Lauren Resnick (1985) noted, "The heart of cognitive psychology is the centrality given to the human mind and the treatment of thinking processes as concrete phenomena that can be studied scientifically" (p. 124).

The Structure of Knowledge. *Knowledge* is a key construct in cognitive psychological research, and one that is particularly relevant to understanding and changing classroom practice. Cognitive psychologists agree that "the essence of knowledge is structure. Knowledge is not a 'basket of facts'" (R. Anderson, 1984, p. 5). They have developed a number of models for the representation and organization of knowledge in human memory. Some models are general in nature; the structures and systems they propose are meant to be applicable to all domains of knowledge. According to schema theory (R. Anderson, 1984), for example, people store knowledge about objects and events in their experiences as schemata—abstract knowledge structures that summarize information about many particular cases and relationships among them.

Other models propose organizational systems for specific knowledge domains. For example, Shulman's theoretical model of components of teachers' professional knowledge (e.g., Grossman, Wilson, & Shulman, 1989; Shulman & Grossman, 1988) focuses on knowledge related to the teaching profession. Shulman and his colleagues hypothesized that teachers draw from seven domains of knowledge (or sets of cognitive schemata) as they plan and carry out instruction: general pedagogical knowledge, knowledge of students, knowledge of subject matter, pedagogical content knowledge, knowledge of other content, knowledge of the curriculum, and knowledge of educational aims. Because this model explicitly addresses the content and structure of the professional knowledge base of teaching, it can provide a useful conceptual framework for designing professional development programs for teachers. Later in the chapter, we explore in more detail several of the domains that are particularly relevant to understanding and changing teachers' classroom practices.

Knowledge, Thinking, and Actions. Virtually all cognitive psychologists share a fundamental assumption that an individual's knowledge structures and mental representations of the world play a central role in perceiving, thinking, and acting (Putnam, Lampert, & Peterson, 1990). Teachers' thinking is directly influenced by their knowledge. Their thinking, in turn, determines their actions in the classroom. Thus, to understand teaching, we must study teachers' knowledge systems; their thoughts, judgments, and decisions; the relationships between teachers' knowledge systems and their cognitions; and how these cognitions are translated into action. Similarly, to help teachers change their practice, we must help them to expand and elaborate their knowledge systems.

Professional Development and Educational Reform Efforts

Professional development programs that focus on expanding and elaborating teachers' knowledge systems are particularly important in today's climate of educational reform. Current efforts to reform educational practice, which are originating from a variety of sources within and outside the education community, are calling for teachers to teach in new ways—ways that differ substantially from how they were taught and how they learned to teach. For example, the National Council of Teachers of Mathematics (NCTM) published the *Curriculum and Evaluation Standards for School Mathematics* (NCTM, 1989), which contains standards for mathematics curricula in kindergarten through grade 12 and for evaluating both the curriculum and student achievement. A companion document, the *Professional Standards for Teaching Mathematics*, "promotes a vision of mathematics teaching, evaluating mathematics teaching, the professional development of mathematics teachers, and responsibilities for professional development and support" (NCTM, 1991, p. vii). Together, these documents provide a framework to guide efforts to reform school mathematics. Professional organizations in other subject areas are working on similar projects. Within the United States, many individual states are developing curriculum frameworks to guide instruction (e.g., California State Department of Education, 1991). At the national level, reform efforts include specification of six national education goals to be achieved by the year 2000 (National Education Goals Panel, 1991). Virtually all reform efforts are calling for changes in our educational system that will help students to develop rich understandings of important content, think critically, construct and solve problems, synthesize information, invent, create, express themselves proficiently, and leave school prepared to be responsible citizens and lifelong learners.

Achieving these ambitious goals will require enhancing, and perhaps in some cases supplanting, the kinds of experiences provided by the "direct instruction" models that are so prevalent in today's public school classrooms. These models are based on the views—pervasive in our society and schools—of teaching as the presenting of information and learning as the practicing and retention of presented knowledge and skills. The instructional formats and strategies of direct instruction clearly can be effective for teaching factual information and well-defined skills, but educators have long questioned their usefulness for promoting critical thinking or deeper levels of understanding that are accessible in other settings (e.g., Collins, Brown, & Newman, 1989; Dewey, 1938). The ambitious educational goals of current reform efforts will require instructional approaches that enable students to take more active roles in their learning and to work independently and collaboratively to construct more powerful and flexible knowledge and understanding. Examples of promising alternative instructional models include small-group problem solving, reciprocal teaching, and cooperative learning. Brophy (1989) suggests that the expression "teaching for meaningful understanding and self-regulated learning" (p. 346) captures several of the important common elements in these new conceptions of teaching.

For many teachers, such approaches, and the new roles for teachers and students they entail, represent a substantial departure from current practice. To use these approaches well, teachers will need to think in new ways about students, subject matter, and the teaching–learning process. Such changes in thinking will require new kinds of knowledge and beliefs on the part of teachers as well as a willingness to become more "adventurous" in their practice, for the details of these richer visions of instruction cannot readily be prescribed (Cohen, 1989). Thus, to help teachers change their practice, we must help them to expand, enrich, and elaborate their knowledge systems. At the same time, however, teachers' existing knowledge and beliefs act as lenses or filters through which they view calls for change (Cohen & Ball, 1990; Putnam, Heaton, Prawat, & Remillard, 1992). Their knowledge systems are simultaneously the objects of change and factors that support or constrain the change process. This situation adds to the complexity of the change process and to the need for powerful professional development programs.

THE PROFESSIONAL KNOWLEDGE BASE OF TEACHING

We turn now to a conceptual framework for the knowledge base of teaching that can be used to guide the design of professional development programs. The framework is based loosely on the categories of teachers' professional knowledge proposed by Shulman and his colleagues (e.g., Grossman et al., 1989; Shulman & Grossman, 1988). It is organized around three domains of knowledge that are particularly relevant to teachers' instructional practices: general pedagogical knowledge, subject-matter knowledge, and pedagogical content knowledge. For each domain, we address the question of what teachers need to know and believe in order to teach for understanding, examine research evidence on novice and experienced teachers' knowledge and beliefs, and suggest implications for professional development.

Before proceeding with this analysis, a caveat is in order. The domains of teachers' professional knowledge are not discrete entities but are highly interrelated. A teacher's knowledge and beliefs about how students learn, for example, are intertwined with his or her knowledge of instructional strategies. A teacher's knowledge of a subject per se is related to his or her knowledge about how to teach that subject. Furthermore, the distinctions among the various categories are somewhat arbitrary. This fuzziness of boundaries is apparent in our discussion of the conceptual framework. It does not, however, negate the framework's usefulness as a heuristic device for helping us to think about the content and structure of teachers' knowledge and implications for professional development programs.

General Pedagogical Knowledge

The domain of general pedagogical knowledge encompasses a teacher's knowledge and beliefs about teaching, learning, and learners that transcend particular subject-matter domains. It includes knowledge of various strategies for creating learning environments and conducting lessons; strategies and arrangements for effective classroom management; and more fundamental knowledge and beliefs about learners, how they learn, and how that learning can be fostered by teaching.

Learning Environments and Instructional Strategies. Cognitive psychological conceptions of teaching and learning emphasize teaching for student understanding and self-regulation, and learning as the active construction of meaning. Much of the research on teaching conducted from this perspective has focused on specific subject-matter domains. The instructional approaches described in this research, however, share a number of common elements (L. Anderson, 1989a; Brophy, 1989). Knowledge of these elements (e.g., teacher's role, instructional strategies, learning environments) constitutes a major component of the general pedagogical knowledge that teachers must have in order to teach for student understanding and self-regulation.

Although these approaches do not rule out direct instruction or presentation, they deemphasize the teacher's role as a provider of information, emphasizing instead his or her role as mediator of student learning. As Resnick (1987) has argued, instruction is viewed not simply as the direct presentation of knowledge to be learned, but as the creation of environments in which students can construct their own powerful understandings. One important form of mediation during interactions with students is instructional scaffolding, through which teachers, in order to facilitate the students' construction of meaning, provide assistance and guidance when students are having difficulty completing a task. Assistance is gradually removed as students internalize problem-solving strategies and become capable of completing tasks on their own. For example, in a "cognitive apprenticeship" model of scaffolded instruction (Collins et al., 1989), teachers use modeling, coaching, and then fading to promote students' development of expertise. In order to support students in their efforts to understand a topic or solve a problem, they decide what information to present and when to present it.

Teachers also facilitate meaningful learning by engaging students in academic tasks that promote active cognitive processing about academic content. The nature of tasks that a teacher selects and the manner in which they are presented are crucial to ensuring the quality of students' cognitive processing. Tasks must require problem solving and critical thinking, not just recall or reproduction of specific information. They should involve questions that do not have a single correct answer. And the teacher must adjust task difficulty levels for individual students, for example, by providing appropriate scaffolding.

Teachers must create an environment within the classroom that fosters learning for understanding and self-regulation. L. Anderson (1989a) identified three social conditions necessary in such a learning community. Because academic tasks that require problem solving and self-regulated learning are characterized by ambiguity and some initial failure, the environment must be one in which the costs associated with failure are not too high. Independent decision making must be valued. And classroom discourse must be characterized by students' talking about their thinking and valuing each other's contributions to discussions.

Brophy (1989) added to this list the issue of student evaluation. Teachers must have methods of assessing student learning that probe their understanding of the content and their ability to apply what they learn to new situations. Paper-and-pencil tests consisting of multiple-choice recognition items are not sufficient. More appropriate strategies include extended interviews, observation of group problem-solving tasks, and assessments that involve recording and scoring student performance on complex assignments.

Brophy (1989) suggested that these elements—teacher as mediator of student learning, academic tasks that promote active processing, supportive learning environments, methods of assessment that reveal students' thinking—constitute key features in a model or theory of effective classroom teaching. Unfortunately, many of these elements do not characterize current classroom practice (L. Anderson, 1989a; Brophy, 1989). They are thus an important focus for professional development. More specifically, professional development activities must help teachers acquire or develop instructional strategies and techniques that promote students' active construction of meaning and self-regulated learning (L. Anderson, 1989a).

Classroom Management. One of the most prominent aspects of general pedagogical knowledge is teachers' knowledge of classroom management—how to keep a group of 20 to 35 students working together and oriented toward classroom tasks. New teachers cite classroom management as one of their top concerns (Veenman, 1984). And for effective experienced teachers, establishing management procedures and routines is a major goal during the first few weeks of the school year (Evertson, 1987).

The conception of classroom management offered by Doyle (1986) is compatible with a cognitive psychological perspective on teaching and with the features of effective teaching proposed above. According to Doyle, classroom teaching has two major tasks—promoting learning and order. The task of promoting order is primarily one of establishing and maintaining an environment in which learning can occur. This conception shifts the primary focus of classroom management away from individual children and the control of misbehavior to the orchestration of classroom activities.

Each type of classroom activity has a different program of action. These programs of action vary along dimensions such as group structure, rules and procedures, and appropriate teacher and student actions. Classroom management entails the establishment, maintenance, and repair of programs of action. To accomplish these management tasks, teachers must have strategies for establishing rules and procedures, organizing groups, monitoring and pacing classroom events, and reacting to misbehavior. Most experienced teachers have repertoires of management strategies that work well for various instructional activities they use often. As Doyle (1983) pointed out, however, academic tasks that promote student thinking and reflection are usually accompanied by increased ambiguity and uncertainty. If teachers are to move toward these more discussion- and activity-oriented academic tasks, they must learn new management strategies as well. And they must establish programs of action in their classrooms that create an environment in which students can effectively work at more open-ended tasks.

Knowledge of Learners and Learning. We have described teachers' knowledge and beliefs about how to create powerful learning environments and manage classrooms primarily in terms of strategies and routines that they should know how to carry out. This sort of procedural and strategic knowledge is supported by and intertwined with knowledge and beliefs about how children think and learn, and about how teachers can foster that learning. Recent research and theory characterize learning as a student-mediated process, one that occurs when the learner acts upon incoming information by relating it to existing knowledge, imposing meaning and organization on experience, and monitoring his or her understanding throughout the process. In this *cognitive-mediational* conception of learning, learners are characterized as active problem solvers who construct their own knowledge. The teacher is considered to be responsible for stimulating students' cognitive processes that are necessary for learning (L. Anderson, 1989b). The cognitive-mediational conception of learners and learning is compatible with instructional models such as reciprocal teaching (Palincsar & Brown, 1984) and cognitive apprenticeship (Collins et al., 1989). It is very different from the view of learners often implicit in direct instruction models of teaching—a *receptive-accrual* view (L. Anderson, 1989b), in which the learner's role is to receive and practice information and skills presented by the teacher. To adopt a cognitive-mediational view, then, represents a substantial shift in beliefs for many experienced teachers.

When teachers try to adopt new instructional activities or textbooks intended to promote more thoughtfulness and understanding, their existing views of learners and the learning process can have a profound effect on the kinds of changes they actually make. In discussing case studies of California teachers teaching mathematics in the context of state and district press for change, Putnam, Heaton, Prawat, and Remillard (1992) described several beliefs about learning that shaped the way these teachers interpreted new textbooks and calls for change in their teaching practice. Beliefs in teaching as a process of telling or presenting information resulted in teachers sometimes "announcing" important ideas and assuming that children made sense of them. And a belief that understanding can be acquired only after mastering basic, factual information, or that young students are not developmentally ready to understand, sometimes led to teaching that emphasized facts and procedures over thoughtfulness and understanding. As part of the same project, Cohen (1990) described a teacher whose existing beliefs about learning led her to use manipulatives in a highly proceduralized and directive fashion. In all these instances, teachers were trying to create more meaningful learning experiences for their students—by using more problem-solving oriented textbooks, more discussion-oriented classroom activities, or more powerful instructional materials (i.e., manipulatives). But their use of these things was shaped by what they already knew and believed about learning and teaching, resulting in changes that may have been quite superficial.

If teachers seriously adopt a cognitive-mediational conception of learners and learning, they will also need different knowledge about learners than they do within a receptive-accrual conception. According to the cognitive-mediational view, two types of cognitive characteristics are central to the learning process: knowledge and capacity for self-regulation. Knowing about these characteristics and their role in learning and teaching is an essential component of the professional knowledge base of teaching. For example, teachers must be aware of learners' prior knowledge about particular topics and how that knowledge is organized and structured. They must understand basic characteristics of metacognitive knowledge and experience, and how learners use metacognition to regulate their cognitive processes during learning. And they must understand the role that motivation plays in the self-regulation of learning.

Subject-Matter Knowledge

Few people would disagree with the statement that having a flexible, thoughtful, and conceptual understanding of subject matter is critical to effective teaching for understanding. Yet just as subject matter is the "missing paradigm" in research on teaching (Shulman, 1986a), it has only recently become a central focus in research on teachers' professional development. Early investigations found little or no relationship between teachers' knowledge of their subjects and student achievement, in part because of the ways in which teacher knowledge was defined (e.g., number of courses taken in college, teachers' scores on standardized tests; see Byrne, 1983). More recent studies, however, have explored the elements of subject-matter knowledge that are important for teaching for understanding; these studies suggest that there are important relationships between teachers' subject-matter knowledge and their instructional practices.

The Knowledge Growth in a Profession project conducted by Shulman and colleagues was one of the first research programs to study systematically the relationship between subject-matter knowledge and teaching practices. Drawing from the work of Schwab (1964), Shulman and colleagues defined subject-matter knowledge to include knowledge of the content of a discipline, as well as the substantive and syntactic structures of the discipline (Grossman et al., 1989). Our consideration of the role of subject-matter knowledge in teachers' professional development addresses these three overlapping dimensions.

Knowledge of Content and Substantive Structures. Content knowledge refers to teachers' knowledge of the facts, concepts, and procedures within a discipline and the relationships among them. Substantive structures are the explanatory frameworks that affect both the organization of content knowledge within a discipline and the questions that guide further inquiry (Grossman, 1990). Although it is possible to make an analytic distinction between content and substantive structure, in practice the distinction is difficult to maintain. In fact, a number of researchers combine the two in their conceptual frameworks. Some researchers, for example, use the construct, knowledge *of* subject matter (Ball, 1990), to include an understanding of particular topics, procedures, and concepts, as well as the organizing structures and connections within a discipline. Ball (1990) argues that to teach mathematics for understanding, teachers' knowledge of mathematics must meet three criteria:

(1) teachers' knowledge of concepts and procedures must be correct; (2) teachers must understand the principles and meanings that underlie mathematical procedures; and (3) teachers must appreciate and understand the connections among mathematical ideas. These criteria are applicable to teaching for understanding within other disciplines as well.

A number of recent studies document the role of teachers' content knowledge in shaping their instructional practices. Stein, Baxter, and Leinhardt (1990) examined a sequence of lessons on functions and graphing taught by an experienced fifth-grade teacher. The teacher lacked knowledge of several key mathematical ideas about functions and graphing, and his knowledge was organized in a superficial way that did not include deep connections among ideas. These limitations led to an overemphasis on rules and procedures and missed opportunities for fostering meaningful connections between key concepts and representations. Similarly in science, Hashweh (1987) found that teachers teaching outside areas of their own expertise (physics and biology) tended to treat material in the science textbooks mechanically and missed errors in the texts.

Case studies by Heaton (1992) and Putnam (1992), drawn from the California Study of Elementary Mathematics, show that as teachers try to make instruction more problem-based and situated in real-world tasks, and as they move away from straightforward coverage of content in textbooks, limitations in their knowledge of subject-matter content can become even more problematic. For example, Heaton's case documents difficulties resulting from a teacher's weak knowledge of the measurement of volume. Students in a fifth-grade class were working on a project to design and order materials for a park. In trying to decide how much sand they would need for a sandbox, they attempted to figure out how much sand an actual sandbox in their schoolyard held. Neither students nor teacher knew the procedure for calculating volume, so the teacher looked up the definition of volume in a dictionary (a positive instance of a teacher modeling the seeking out of information). The students then computed the volume of the sandbox by multiplying the measurements they had obtained for its length, width, and depth: 46 yards x 10 yards x 1 foot. The resulting number, 460, was a measure of neither cubic yards nor cubic feet, but no one noticed that this was a problem. This episode, although it had considerable potential for helping students see the usefulness of mathematics, likely left students with misconceptions about the mathematical content.

Research that has attempted to look more systematically at teachers' substantive knowledge has yielded equally troubling results. At the preservice stage, "considerable evidence suggests that many prospective teachers, both elementary and secondary, do not understand their subjects in depth" (McDiarmid, Ball, & Anderson, 1989, p. 199). The most extensive set of evidence comes from the Teacher Education and Learning to Teach (TELT) research program conducted through the National Center for Research on Teacher Education (NCRTE). TELT researchers concluded that many prospective teachers complete their preservice programs with an understanding of their subjects that is inadequate for teaching. For example, few prospective teachers—either elementary or secondary—increased or deepened their understandings of mathematics or their beliefs about the nature of mathematics during preservice teacher education. Many completed their programs still having difficulty with ideas such as place value and division of fractions (NCRTE, 1991). Their difficulties with content can only be exacerbated when they attempt to teach unfamiliar mathematical content (e.g., statistics and probability or discrete mathematics) being called for by reformers.

TELT investigators reached similar conclusions about experienced teachers. They found, for example, few differences between preservice and experienced teachers' mathematical knowledge, with many of the experienced elementary teachers lacking understandings of the meanings underlying mathematical procedures (NCRTE, 1991). Although there was substantial variation in the teachers' substantive knowledge, researchers concluded that many of them would benefit from learning additional content.

Syntactic Structures. Syntactic structures are the canons of evidence and proof that guide inquiry in a discipline—the ways of establishing new knowledge and determining the validity of claims. The construct is similar to knowledge *about* a discipline, as used by Ball (1990). Again focusing on the discipline of mathematics, Ball described knowledge about mathematics as an understanding of the nature of mathematical knowledge—where it comes from, how it changes, how truth is established, and what it means to know and do mathematics.

Grossman, Wilson, and Shulman (1989) noted tremendous variation in novice teachers' knowledge of the syntactical structures of their disciplines. In the subject area of history, this variation was associated with the teachers' disciplinary perspectives; these perspectives influenced the teachers' views of the roles of factual knowledge, evidence, and interpretation in history (Wilson & Wineburg, 1988). For example, Jane, a history major as an undergraduate, saw history as both narrative and interpretation and viewed interpretation as a central task of the historian. Fred, a political science major, also recognized the importance of interpretation in social science. In contrast to Jane, he viewed history as limited to facts and interpretation as the purview of political scientists. Although this project focused on variations rather than limitations in syntactic knowledge, findings suggest that teachers could benefit from professional development programs designed to broaden their understandings of the nature of inquiry within their teaching fields.

The importance of professional development that focuses on knowledge of syntactic structures is even clearer in the subject area of mathematics, in large part because the assumptions about this aspect of mathematics underlying most reform efforts stand in stark contrast to assumptions held by many teachers and underlying most school practices (NCTM, 1989; Romberg & Carpenter, 1986). Whereas in schools, mathematics is typically viewed as a collection of indisputable facts and procedures established by external authorities (mathematicians), reformers emphasize the processes of reasoning to construct mathematical knowledge, the use of knowledge in solving problems, and the flexible and changing nature of mathematical knowledge. This contrast is clearly evidenced by TELT researchers' examinations of teachers' understandings of what it means to know and do mathematics and how mathematical truth is established (e.g., Ball, 1990; NCRTE, 1991). Most novice and experienced teachers did not conceive of mathematics as a domain of human inquiry. They understood little about mathematical reasoning, and they looked to experts as authorities for establishing mathematical truth. For many of them, these understandings changed little over the course of teacher education programs.

Implications for Professional Development. As these few examples illustrate, there is substantial evidence that many experienced teachers do not have the kinds of subject-matter knowledge needed to support the teaching for understanding being encouraged through current reform efforts. To some extent, this situation is a result of the fact that the new standards for learning and teaching demand different and more extensive subject-matter knowledge. The National Council of Teachers of Mathematics (1991) described this demand well in its *Professional Standards for Teaching Mathematics*: "Given the nature of mathematics and the changes being recommended in the teaching of mathematics, teachers at all levels need substantive and comprehensive knowledge of the content and discourse of mathematics" (pp. 139–140). This level of knowledge was not as important when the focus of the curriculum was on memorization of rules, algorithms, and mathematical procedures; it is essential, however, for teaching in ways that promote understanding and flexible problem solving. As a result of these changing demands on teachers, there is a clear need for professional development programs to focus on subject matter knowledge.

Pedagogical Content Knowledge

Pedagogical content knowledge, or subject-specific pedagogical knowledge, consists of an understanding of how a subject area, and the topics and issues within it, can be organized and represented for teaching. Shulman

(1986b), in first bringing attention to the term, offered the following definition:

> Within the category of pedagogical content knowledge I include, for the most regularly taught topics in one's subject area, the most useful forms of representation of those ideas, the most powerful analogies, illustrations, examples, explanations, and demonstrations—in a word, the ways of representing and formulating the subject that make it comprehensible to others. . . . Pedagogical content knowledge also includes an understanding of what makes the learning of specific topics easy or difficult; the conceptions and preconceptions that students of different ages and backgrounds bring with them to the learning of those most frequently taught topics and lessons. (p. 9)

Grossman (1990) elaborated upon this definition by identifying and describing four central components of pedagogical content knowledge: overarching conception of teaching a subject, knowledge of instructional strategies and representations, knowledge of students' understanding and potential misunderstandings, and knowledge of curriculum and curricular materials. Our discussion of pedagogical content knowledge is organized around these four components.

Overarching Conception of Teaching a Subject. A person's overarching conception of what it means to teach a particular subject serves as a "conceptual map" for instructional decision making, as the basis for judgments about classroom objectives, instructional strategies and student assignments, textbooks and curricular materials, and the evaluation of student learning. Strong pedagogical content knowledge is characterized by a well-developed, overarching conception of what it means to teach a subject matter—a conception that is compatible with the most current thinking within a discipline and that guides the teacher in planning and carrying out instruction.

In today's climate of educational reform, teachers' overarching conceptions are a particularly salient component of the professional knowledge base. Many reform efforts call for approaches to teaching specific subject areas that are substantially different from past (or current) practice. Several research studies suggest that recent graduates of at least some teacher education programs have overarching conceptions that differ from those of their more experienced colleagues and their contemporaries who took alternative routes to teacher certification.

Grossman (1990) examined the influence of teacher education, particularly subject-specific coursework, on the development of pedagogical content knowledge in English. The three teachers in her study who entered teaching without formal pedagogical preparation made little distinction between English as an intellectual discipline and English as a subject for high school students. For them, the central goal of studying English is learning literary criticism and textual analysis. The recent graduates of teacher education saw English more as an opportunity to encourage self-expression and understanding through reading and writing. For them, the major purpose of high school English is teaching students how to express themselves in writing.

Wilson and Wineburg (1993) present findings from Stanford University's Teacher Assessment Project (TAP), which developed and field-tested performance assessments for teachers. Their article focuses on two teachers, one of whom graduated from Stanford's teacher preparation program and taught for 3 years prior to participating in the project; the other had 28 years of teaching experience. Differences in the teachers' performances on the TAP assessments suggest that they held different views of the nature of history as a school subject. The more experienced teacher believed, for example, that teaching history consists of imparting a set of facts about economic and political history. Learning of factual knowledge must precede learning of interpretation, and less able students may never get to the interpretive side. In contrast, and more in line with current thinking in academic circles, the less experienced teacher viewed factual knowledge and interpretation as inextricably interwoven; she believed that it is impossible to disentangle the two, either theoretically or pedagogically. Findings such as these suggest that professional development progams for teachers should include attention to their overarching conceptions of the disciplines they teach, particularly in the current climate of changing orientations to subject-matter teaching.

Knowledge of Instructional Strategies and Representations. A second component of pedagogical content knowledge is knowledge of instructional strategies and representations for teaching particular topics. This is the component that Shulman and other researchers studying knowledge use in teaching have addressed most extensively. Instructional representations—the models, examples, metaphors, simulations, demonstrations, or illustrations a teacher uses to foster students' understanding of specific topics—have received particular attention. Ball (1993) recently wrote about a related, but broader, concept, which she refers to as the "representational context." As she explained, the representational context

> encompasses the terrain for investigation and development opened by a particular representation as well as the meanings and discourse it makes possible. The representational context encompasses the ways in which teachers and learners use the particular representation, how it serves as a tool for understanding their work. (pp. 160–161)

Strong pedagogical content knowledge is characterized by an extensive repertoire of powerful representations and the ability to adapt these representations in multiple ways in order to meet specific goals for specific sets of learners; in other words, the ability to construct multiple representational contexts for a single representation.

There is a growing body of evidence that novice teachers do not have extensive repertoires of powerful representations for teaching in their subject areas. For example, Borko and colleagues found that student teachers had limited repertoires of instructional strategies. In one study, an elementary student teacher was unable to produce powerful representations for concepts such as counting numbers, prime factors, and division of fractions (Eisenhart et al., 1993). In another study, a secondary English teacher was unable to plan a good introduction to a unit on Shakespeare. He attributed his problems to a lack of teaching experience (Borko, Livingston, McCaleb, & Mauro, 1988).

There is also evidence suggesting that experienced teachers' repertoires are limited, particularly with respect to instructional approaches that reflect conceptions of subject-matter teaching promoted by current educational reform efforts. For example, elementary teachers in a study by Smith and Neale (1991) used few strategies associated with obtaining conceptual change in science prior to their participation in an inservice program. Researchers in the California Study of Elementary Mathematics found some teachers' knowledge of instructional representations to be limited (Putnam et al., 1992). Their case analyses included instances where teachers devised instructional representations to supplement or replace those used in their textbooks. But their repertoires of representations and their criteria for choosing them were based more on the representations' motivational features than on their fit with the mathematics being taught, possibly leading to misconceptions on the part of students.

Knowledge of Students' Understandings and Potential Misunderstandings. A third component of pedagogical content knowledge is knowledge of students' understandings and potential misunderstandings of a subject area. This component differs from general knowledge of learners by virtue of its focus on specific content. In the subject areas of science and mathematics, for example, researchers have identified preconceptions, misconceptions, and alternative conceptions commonly held by learners for topics such as division of fractions, negative numbers, heat energy and temperature, and photosynthesis (for a review, see Confrey, 1990). Teachers with well-developed pedagogical content knowledge understand how students typically learn a particular subject. They are aware of the topics within a field that students are likely to find difficult, know what the common difficulties are, and have strategies for addressing those difficulties in their representational and adaptational repertoires. And they typically report that they listen carefully to students, focusing on their ideas and understandings of the subject (Fennema,

Carpenter, Franke, & Carey, 1992; Simon & Schifter, 1991; Smith & Neale, 1991).

Novices frequently report that they do not know what their students know about particular subject areas and cannot predict where in the curriculum students are likely to run into problems. Such limitations can lead to difficulties in planning and carrying out appropriate instructional activities. For example, several student teachers in the study by Borko and colleagues (1988) discussed problems they encountered trying to present content in a way that would be appropriate for their students. The comments of a secondary mathematics student teacher are typical. He noted that he began student teaching by covering too much content, "not realizing that I'm teaching it to people who are learning it for the first time" (p. 72). He began slowing down his pace as he learned more about what his students did and did not know.

Experienced teachers vary in their pedagogical content knowledge related to students. Wilson and Wineburg (1993) asked the two teachers in their study to review a packet of primary and secondary source documents about the Battles of Lexington and Concord. Both teachers were aware of the difficulty of these materials. But the less experienced teacher pointed out that teachers as well as students would have trouble with these documents, whereas the more experienced teacher showed little awareness of the formidable challenges the documents present to able students. Thus simply having experience teaching students by no means ensures that teachers will develop knowledge of what their students know or sensitivity to what is difficult for them.

Knowledge of Curriculum and Curricular Materials. The fourth component of pedagogical content knowledge is knowledge of curriculum and curricular materials. Strong pedagogical content knowledge is characterized by in-depth knowledge about the curricular materials available for teaching a particular subject matter and about how the curriculum is organized and structured both horizontally (within a grade level or course) and vertically (across the K–12 curriculum) within one's own school system.

Prospective teachers have limited knowledge about the curricula they are to teach and limited familiarity with curricular materials. These limitations make it difficult for them to do long-range planning or make priority decisions about content coverage. Borko and Livingston (1989) compared the planning, teaching, and post-lesson reflections of three student teachers in the subject area of mathematics (two secondary and one elementary) with those of their cooperating teachers. The elementary student teacher noted that her cooperating teacher "just weeds things out. He doesn't give the slower group certain things. . . . And I can't make those decisions myself. I don't know enough about math to know what to include and what not to" (p. 486).

Although experienced teachers typically are familiar with the curriculum and curricular materials they use, there are a number of situations in which this is not the case. For example, one of the secondary teachers in Borko and Livingston's (1989) study reflected on her first experience teaching analytic geometry: "Last year I was much too rigid because I didn't see some of the relationships [across the curriculum] that I'm seeing now" (p. 490).

Teachers confronted with a situation in which they are expected to adopt new textbooks or curriculum frameworks are also likely to have limited pedagogical content knowledge of curriculum and curricular materials. The California Study of Elementary Mathematics (Cohen & Ball, 1990; Putnam et al., 1992) provides examples of teachers' experiences with a recently adopted curriculum framework for mathematics teaching. Teachers in that study differed substantially in their familiarity with the substance of the curriculum framework and in the extent to which their knowledge, beliefs, and practices were affected by the reform efforts. The example of one teacher's use of curricular materials illustrates limitations in some teachers' pedagogical content knowledge and the potential importance of professional development efforts (Peterson, 1990). Cathy Swift, like other teachers in her school district, received a kit of manipulatives along with the textbooks and materials in the new math program. She began to use the manipulatives regularly, particularly when introducing a new mathematical skill. But, rather than having children use manipulatives to develop their own strategies for solving problems, Swift used them to instruct children directly in the strategy that she wanted them to learn. In other words, she incorporated the manipulatives into her direct instruction procedures. Manipulatives were an add-on to her teaching of procedures, rather than an integral part of a new approach that emphasized teaching for understanding. At least in part, this situation was a function of Swift's limited pedagogical content knowledge of curricular materials. As she noted, she needed more than the three-hour introductory inservice workshop provided by the district to understand possible uses of manipulatives in teaching for understanding.

A COGNITIVE PSYCHOLOGICAL PERSPECTIVE
ON PROFESSIONAL DEVELOPMENT

In the remainder of the chapter, we explore implications of a cognitive psychological perspective on teaching and learning for professional development programs. We begin by examining the professional development component of the Cognitively Guided Instruction (CGI) approach to teaching mathematics—its characteristics and its impact on teaching and learning. We then briefly discuss two other professional development programs that are compatible with a cognitive psychological perspective. The section concludes with a discussion of common features of these professional development programs, features that seem to be associated with successful attempts to help teachers expand and elaborate their professional knowledge base.

We selected the CGI project as an illustration because its professional development component is based on principles of teaching, learning, and learning to teach derived from cognitive psychological research. In addition, because the project has a large research component, much more information is available about it than about other, equally noteworthy, professional development programs.

The Cognitively Guided Instruction Project

The Cognitively Guided Instruction project is a multiyear, multiphase program of curriculum development, professional development, and research conducted by Thomas Carpenter, Elizabeth Fennema, Penelope Peterson, and colleagues.[2] Our discussion is limited to the first three phases of the project, which explored the teaching and learning of addition and subtraction in first-grade classrooms.[3] We focus primarily on the second phase, which was designed to investigate whether professional development experiences based on knowledge derived from classroom-based research on teaching and laboratory-based research on children's learning would improve teachers' classroom instruction and students' learning.

The CGI Approach to Mathematics Teaching. The CGI approach to teaching mathematics is based on the premise that the teaching–learning process is too complex to specify in advance. As a consequence of this complexity, teaching is essentially problem solving; classroom instruction is mediated by teachers' thinking and decisions (cf. Clark & Peterson, 1986). Teachers are most effective when their decisions are informed by an in-depth knowledge of their subject matter and students. Particularly important in mathematics teaching is a knowledge of students' strategies for solving mathematical problems.

CGI project personnel believe that they can best bring about significant changes in mathematics instruction by helping teachers to make informed decisions. Thus professional development is a key component of the project. Professional development activities are designed to introduce teachers to knowledge from cognitive science about children's thinking and problem solving in mathematics, and to help them consider how to use that knowledge to design and carry out instruction.

The Professional Development Component of CGI. The professional development component for the initial phases of CGI was a four-week summer workshop for teachers designed in accordance with the assumption that both students and teachers are thoughtful learners who construct their own knowledge and understanding. The goals of the workshop were to help teachers understand how addition and subtraction concepts develop in children, provide them with opportunities to explore possible uses of those understandings in their mathematics instruction, and give them time to reflect on what happened as a result of using that knowledge.

Research-based knowledge of how addition and subtraction concepts develop in children (Carpenter & Moser, 1983) provided the substantive framework for the workshop. For the first one and a half weeks, teachers learned to classify addition and subtraction problems and to identify the solution strategies that children typically use to solve different types of problems. During the remaining two and a half weeks, they discussed principles of instruction that might be derived from the research, and they worked together and separately to design their own programs of instruction based on those principles.

Instead of prescribing specific instructional practices or providing instructional materials, workshop leaders provided a set of questions for the teachers to address in planning their instructional programs. These questions guided teachers to think about issues such as: (1) how instruction can build upon the informal counting and modeling strategies that children are already using by the time they enter first grade; (2) how formal mathematical symbols should be linked to children's informal knowledge of addition and subtraction; and (3) whether specific strategies, such as counting strategies, should be taught explicitly.

Workshop leaders also provided a variety of materials for the teachers' own learning and for their consideration as possible instructional tools. They prepared readings that presented the problem type taxonomy, synthesized research findings on children's solutions of addition and subtraction word problems, and examined potential classroom applications of the research. Videotapes of children solving problems were used to illustrate the different solution strategies, and teachers had the opportunity to interview one or two young children. Various textbooks, manipulatives, and enrichment materials were also available for the teachers to review.

The Research Component of CGI. Phase 1 of the CGI project was a descriptive study, conducted prior to the summer workshop, in which the researchers identified and described relationships among 40 first-grade teachers' knowledge and beliefs about students' mathematical knowledge and thinking, their reports of their approaches to teaching, and their students' achievement in mathematics (Carpenter, Fennema, Peterson, & Carey, 1988; Peterson, Fennema, Carpenter, & Loef, 1989). Although most teachers could make critical distinctions among different types of problems and were familiar with the primary strategies children use to solve problems, their knowledge generally was not organized into coherent structures in which distinctions among types of word problems, problem difficulty, and children's problem-solving strategies were related. Differences in the teachers' pedagogical content knowledge and beliefs were related to their self-reported teaching strategies and to student achievement. For example, teachers with more cognitively based perspectives had greater knowledge of their students' problem-solving strategies than did teachers with less cognitively based perspectives, and in the classroom they used word problems more extensively and placed less emphasis on the teaching of number facts. These findings provide additional evidence for the relationship between teachers' pedagogical content knowledge and their instructional practices, addressed earlier in the chapter.

Phase 2 was an experimental study designed to investigate the impact of the professional development workshop on the same 40 teachers' knowledge and beliefs, classroom instruction, and students' achievement (Carpenter, Fennema, Peterson, Chiang, & Loef, 1989; Peterson, Carpenter, & Fennema, 1989). Twenty were randomly assigned to an experimental group and participated in the CGI summer workshop. The remaining 20 teachers (the control group) participated in a half-day workshop on problem solving. Teachers and their students were observed for 16 days of mathematics instruction during the subsequent school year. Interviews and questionnaires, administered near the end of the year, assessed teachers' pedagogical content knowledge (e.g., knowledge of their children's knowledge, how they assessed and used that knowledge) and pedagogical content beliefs. Student achievement was assessed with standardized tests of computation and problem solving, experimenter-constructed problem-solving scales, and interviews about problem-solving strategies.

Experimental (CGI) teachers taught problem solving significantly more and number facts significantly less than did control teachers. CGI teachers also posed problems to students more often, encouraged students to use a variety of problem-solving strategies, and more frequently listened to the processes their students used to solve problems. They believed that instruction should build on students' existing knowledge to a greater extent than did control teachers, and they knew more about individual students' strategies for both number facts and problem solving. Experimental students exceeded control students in number fact knowledge and some tests of problem solving. They were also more confident of their abilities to solve mathematics problems and reported significantly greater understanding of the mathematics than did control students.

In phase 3, researchers conducted case studies of six teachers who had participated in the original CGI workshop, examining how the teachers gained an understanding of their students' thinking and how they used that understanding to build upon their students' informal knowledge during mathematics instruction (e.g., Fennema et al., 1992). A project assistant spent at least two hours per week observing mathematics instruction in each teacher's classroom and talking with her about how she used children's thinking. In addition, the six teachers participated with project assistants and senior researchers in monthly meetings to discuss the teachers' mathematics instruction. For the most part, teachers talked among themselves about problems and successes they had experienced, with researchers participating by sharing their thoughts about teaching or mathematics when asked by the teachers.

Key elements in successful CGI classrooms were that teachers listened to their students and built upon what they already knew. The researchers speculated that the specific knowledge about children's thinking in a clearly defined content domain was critical to the success of the program. The taxonomy of addition and subtraction problem types and children's solution strategies provided a rationale for teachers' selection of problems, guidance regarding what to listen for, and a context for interpreting students' responses. Teachers in successful CGI classrooms continually asked students to explain the processes they used to solve problems, and they encouraged students to describe alternative solutions. By engaging in these conversations about mathematics, children learned to reflect on how they solved problems and to articulate their solutions. The informal strategies that children used to solve problems became more accessible to their classmates, and children learned by listening to other children describe their strategies.

The Impact of Professional Development. Within the CGI project, teachers were asked to reconsider some of their fundamental beliefs about teaching and learning—that they are the source of knowledge and that they have a responsibility to cover a specified amount of content. The workshops alone did not change these teachers. It was listening to their own students solve problems that made the greatest difference in their instructional practices. Also, it took many of the teachers considerable time to adapt their teaching to the principles of CGI, and some only changed their practices to a limited extent. These caveats aside, the CGI project provides powerful evidence that experienced teachers' pedagogical content knowledge and pedagogical content beliefs can be affected by professional development programs and that such changes are associated with changes in their classroom instruction and student achievement.

Additional Professional Development Programs Based on a Cognitive Psychological Perspective

A number of other professional development programs have been created based on, or consistent with, recent theoretical and empirical work in cognitive psychology. Many of these programs are in the area of mathematics teaching, at least in part as a response to reforms called for by the mathematics education community through its curriculum and teaching standards (NCTM, 1989, 1991). We briefly discuss two programs, one in mathematics and one in science.

The SummerMath for Teachers Program. The SummerMath for Teachers program is an ongoing inservice program for elementary and secondary teachers of mathematics based on a constructivist view of learning and an assumption that fundamental change in teaching requires growth in teachers' conceptions of mathematics and learning (Schifter & Simon, 1992). The teacher is viewed as providing students with the opportunity and stimulation to construct mathematical ideas, by creating an environment in which they are consistently engaged in exploring mathematical problem situations, generating and verifying hypotheses, and communicating and justifying their ideas. The inservice program is guided by two principles: (1) that it is important to teach teachers as you want them to teach; and (2) that follow-up support and supervision are important to fostering teacher change.

Thus, in conducting their Educational Leaders in Mathematics (ELM) project, the SummerMath staff assumed that teachers must actively construct their own understandings of mathematics, mathematics teaching, and mathematics learning. Teachers participated in a two-week summer institute designed to provide them with an opportunity to learn mathematics in a setting where construction of meaning was valued and encouraged, reflect on these experiences and on the roles of teacher and students, and then design instructional sequences that would provide their own students with similar opportunities. As in the CGI project, participating teachers were not given a specific curriculum to be adopted.

The second stage of ELM provided participating teachers with extensive support and supervision throughout the year following the summer institute, in order to facilitate the integration of new learnings into their classroom practices. Staff members visited the teachers' classrooms on a weekly basis and provided feedback, demonstration teaching, and opportunities for reflection. The teachers also attended four workshops that provided opportunities for sharing efforts to change their teaching; further exploring issues related to mathematics, learning, and teaching; and participating in small-group planning sessions.[4]

Teachers' writings, their responses to structured interview questions, and their responses on the Assessment of Constructivism in Mathematics Instruction (ACMI) instrument revealed that the intervention had a substantial impact on participants' beliefs about learning and that the changes in their beliefs affected decisions they reported making in the classroom. For example, many teachers' views changed in the direction of seeing students as more active and responsible for their own learning. Participants expressed an increased commitment to teaching for student thinking and understanding. And many of them integrated teaching strategies learned during the summer institute into their existing instructional programs. The most commonly reported impact of the project on participants' teaching was that they began listening more to students, focusing on their ideas and understandings.

Institute for Chemical Education Workshop. Clermont, Krajcik, and Borko (1993) reported changes in physical science teachers' conceptions of science teaching and repertoires of chemical demonstrations after participation in a two-week summer institute. The central goal of the Institute for Chemical Education (ICE) Workshop B: Chemistry Supplements for Pre-High School Classes was to increase teachers' use of chemical demonstrations in their teaching of chemistry and physical science. The workshop had four major components: (1) instruction on the purposes and characteristics of effective chemical demonstrations; (2) demonstrations by workshop instructors to model appropriate demonstration techniques; (3) demonstrations by participants, with feedback by colleagues and workshop instructors; and (4) demonstrations by participants to groups of middle school students. More than 50 self-contained chemical demonstration kits addressing more than 30 different topics were available to institute participants. Practice and observation of these demonstrations provided participants with many opportunities to enrich their repertoires of content-specific instructional strategies and representations for demonstrating fundamental concepts in chemistry.

Participants' conceptions of effective chemical demonstration teaching were obtained through clinical interviews in which they thought aloud about effective chemical demonstration teaching as they critiqued videotapes of chemical demonstrations and responded to specific questions about the quality of the videotaped presentations. Responses suggested growth in the teachers' repertoires for demonstrating fundamental topics in chemistry and an increased awareness of the complexity of chemical demonstration teaching. For example, participants discussed a greater number of chemical demonstrations and demonstration variations on each of several targeted chemical concepts after the intervention. They also discussed the complexity of several demonstrations, how these complexities could interfere with learning, and how simplified versions of the demonstrations could promote science learning for understanding. Like the CGI and SummerMath for Teachers projects, this research suggests that experienced teachers' professional knowledge base can be elaborated and expanded through intensive summer inservice programs.

THOUGHTS ON SUCCESSFUL PROFESSIONAL
DEVELOPMENT PROGRAMS

In this final section we reflect on the programs we reviewed above and on the research reviewed throughout this chapter, in order to identify some key features of successful professional development efforts.

Patterns in Successful Professional Development Programs

The three professional development programs described in the previous section share a number of characteristics that are compatible with current educational reform efforts. These characteristics reflect common assumptions about both the substance and the process of teacher education.

The Substance of Professional Development. All three programs assume that fundamental change in teaching requires growth in teachers' conceptions of subject matter, pedagogy, and subject-specific pedagogy. Although the programs differ to some extent in the specific areas of knowledge that they highlight, all three feature the elaboration and expansion of a teacher's knowledge base as a central goal. Furthermore, the directions for expansion and elaboration they recommend are compatible with changes in the professional knowledge base of teaching that are embraced by current educational reform efforts. For example, one factor identified by both CGI and SummerMath for Teachers project leaders as essential to successful professional development is that teachers are helped to reconsider fundamental beliefs about teaching and learning. More specifically, professional development should encourage and support teachers to adopt a more constructivist or student-mediated view of the learning process. CGI researchers also concluded that professional development programs for mathematics teaching, if they are to be successful, must help teachers acquire specific knowledge of children's thinking in mathematics. The primary emphasis of the ICE workshop was on helping elementary and secondary school science teachers to expand their repertoires of instructional strategies for demonstration teaching.

The Process of Professional Development. A central message of all three projects is that the process of professional development should reflect the approach to teaching and learning that a project advocates for teachers to adopt in their own classrooms. In other words, a project's assumptions about how teachers learn should be compatible with its assumptions about how students learn. In each of our examples, project personnel advocated and followed a process that was compatible with the vision of teaching and learning promoted by current reform efforts. Teachers were viewed as active learners who construct their own knowledge, and they were encouraged to develop instructional approaches and strategies that facilitate students' knowledge construction.

CGI project leaders used the language of cognitive science to describe teachers as active problem solvers. According to this conception, teachers' instructional practices are guided by their ongoing pedagogical decision making. Efforts to change instructional practices will fail if they attempt to prescribe programs of instruction without taking into account teachers' decision making in implementing the programs. The SummerMath for Teachers program leaders used the language of constructivist theory to make a similar point: Like the students in their classrooms, teachers must be encouraged to act upon incoming information by relating it to existing knowledge and by imposing meaning and organization. Professional development should provide opportunities for teachers to construct knowledge of subject matter and pedagogy in an environment that supports and encourages risk taking and reflection. Change efforts based on an expectation that teachers will receive and practice information and skills presented by others are unlikely to succeed in fostering meaningful changes in the ways in which teachers interact with their students. Thus, although the two programs come from different perspectives, both highlight teachers' active participation and learning as essential ingredients in successful professional development.

A second message provided by the CGI and SummerMath for Teachers projects is that teachers benefit greatly from support and supervision as they attempt to integrate their new learnings into their ongoing classroom practices. Observations by workshop personnel and opportunities to share and receive feedback on their experiences help teachers to adapt their existing instructional strategies and routines and to solidify changes in their knowledge and beliefs.

The Dual Role of Teachers' Knowledge and Beliefs in Professional Development

A key theme that emerges from the research we have explored in this chapter is that teachers' knowledge and beliefs affect how they perceive and act on various messages about changing their teaching. It is through their existing knowledge and beliefs that teachers come to understand recommended new practices and activities. These understandings, in turn, determine how the instructional tools are actually used in their classrooms. For example, in some classrooms, small groups serve simply as a new arrangement in which students sit around tables, instead of at desks, while they listen to the teacher present information. In other classrooms, these groups become powerful sites for students to work together to solve problems and think through ideas. The teacher's understanding of cooperative groups and his or her more fundamental beliefs about teaching and learning play critical roles in determining how such groups actually play out in the classroom. Thus, just as students' existing knowledge and beliefs serve as the starting point for their learning, teachers' knowledge and beliefs are important resources and constraints on change. They serve as powerful filters through which learning takes place.

Furthermore, teachers' knowledge and beliefs cannot be circumvented by efforts to reform educational practice. Teaching for understanding, because it requires thoughtful interaction with students around important ideas, is especially dependent on teachers' knowledge and beliefs. Efforts to develop programmed instruction or "teacher-proof" curricula notwithstanding, thoughtful teaching cannot be completely predetermined or scripted. Thus any effort to help teachers make significant changes in their teaching practice must help them to acquire new knowledge and beliefs. The same knowledge and beliefs that function as filters through which change takes place are also critical targets of change. In other words, teachers become simultaneously the objects and the agents of change (Cohen, 1990; Cohen & Ball, 1990; Putnam et al., 1992). They must change; and the change must come, in part, from within. This situation makes the achievement of fundamental changes in teaching practices difficult, because a teacher's existing conceptions of learning and of subject matter can be quite resistant to change.

This line of reasoning leads us to the same conclusions about professional development that we reached by examining patterns in successful professional development programs. That is, persons who wish to reform educational practice cannot simply tell teachers how to teach differently. Teachers themselves must make the desired changes. To do so, they must acquire richer knowledge of subject matter, pedagogy, and subject-specific pedagogy; and they must come to hold new beliefs in these domains. Successful professional development efforts are those that help teachers to acquire or develop new ways of thinking about learning, learners, and subject matter, thus constructing a professional knowledge base that will enable them to teach students in more powerful and meaningful ways.

An Optimistic Final Thought

Although the instructional practices found in many of today's classrooms do not reflect the spirit of educational reform, our reading of the literature and writing of this chapter left us with a feeling of optimism for the future. There is substantial evidence that professional development programs for experienced teachers *can* make a difference—that teachers who participate in these programs can, and often do, experience significant changes in their professional knowledge base and instructional practices. When professional development programs create an environment that facilitates and supports teacher learning, and when they continue to support teachers in their endeavors to integrate new conceptions and instructional strategies into their ongoing educational programs, then teachers can expand and elaborate their professional knowledge base and can begin to teach in fundamentally different ways.

NOTES

Acknowledgments. Ralph Putnam's work on this chapter was supported in part by grants from the Pew Charitable Trust (Grant No. 91–04343–000), Carnegie Corporation of New York (Grant No. B 5638), and the National Science Foundation (Grant No. ESI-9153834). The views expressed in this chapter are those of the individual authors and are not necessarily shared by the grantors. Our thinking about teachers' learning and change has been greatly enriched by our conversations with Ralph Putnam's colleagues on the Educational Policy and Practice Study, a highly collaborative research group at Michigan State University. We also thank Renée Clift for her thoughtful comments on an earlier draft of this chapter.

1. For a more extensive discussion of themes in cognitive psychological research on teachers and teaching, see Eisenhart and Borko, 1993. The ideas in this section are adapted from Chapter 3 in that book, Contributions from Cognitive Psychology.

2. Our description of the Cognitively Guided Instruction project, particularly the sections presenting its research component, has been adapted from Eisenhart and Borko, 1993.

3. Current work in the CGI project has expanded to include mathematical content domains such as multiplication and division, fractions, place value, and geometry. For more information, a complete bibliography of writings about CGI is available from Thomas Carpenter or Elizabeth Fennema at the University of Wisconsin's Wisconsin Center for Education Research.

4. Stages 3 and 4, which were designed to provide participants with training to conduct inservice workshops in their schools, are not addressed here.

REFERENCES

Anderson, L. M. (1989a). Implementing instructional programs to promote meaningful, self-regulated learning. In J. Brophy (Ed.), *Advances in research on teaching: Vol. 1. Teaching for meaningful understanding and self-regulated learning* (pp. 311–343). Greenwich, CT: JAI Press.

Anderson, L. M. (1989b). Learners and learning. In M. C. Reynolds (Ed.), *Knowledge base for the beginning teacher* (pp. 85–99). Oxford: Pergamon Press.

Anderson, R. C. (1984). Some reflections on the acquisition of knowledge. *Educational Researcher, 13*(10), 5–10.

Ball, D. L. (1990). The mathematical understandings that prospective teachers bring to teacher education. *Elementary School Journal, 90,* 449–466.

Ball, D. L. (1993). Halves, pieces, and twoths: Constructing and using representational contexts in teaching fractions. In T. Carpenter, E. Fennema, & T. Romberg (Eds.), *Rational numbers: An integration of research* (pp. 157–196). Hillsdale, NJ: Erlbaum.

Borko, H., & Livingston, C. (1989). Cognition and improvisation: Differences in mathematics instruction by expert and novice teachers. *American Educational Research Journal, 26,* 473–498.

Borko, H., Livingston, C., McCaleb, J., & Mauro, L. (1988). Student teachers' planning and post-lesson reflections: Patterns and implications for teacher preparation. In J. Calderhead (Ed.), *Teachers' professional learning* (pp. 65–83). New York: Falmer.

Brophy, J. (1989). Conclusion: Toward a theory of teaching. In J. Brophy (Ed.), *Advances in research on teaching: Vol. 1. Teaching for meaningful understanding and self-regulated learning* (pp. 345–355). Greenwich, CT: JAI Press.

Byrne, C. J. (1983, October). *Teacher knowledge and teacher effectiveness: A literature review, theoretical analysis, and discussion of research strategy.* Paper presented at the 14th annual convention of the Northeastern Educational Research Association, Ellenville, NY.

California State Department of Education. (1991). *Mathematics framework for California public schools.* Sacramento: Author.

Carpenter, T. P., Fennema, E., Peterson, P. L., & Carey, D. A. (1988). Teachers' pedagogical content knowledge of students' problem solving in elementary arithmetic. *Journal for Research in Mathematics Education, 19,* 85–401.

Carpenter, T. P., Fennema, E., Peterson, P. L., Chiang, C., & Loef, M. (1989). Using knowledge of children's mathematical thinking in classroom teaching: An experimental study. *American Educational Research Journal, 26,* 499–531.

Carpenter, T. P., & Moser, J. M. (1983). The acquisition of addition and subtraction concepts. In R. Lesh & M. Landau (Eds.), *The acquisition of mathematics concepts and processes* (pp. 7–44). New York: Academic Press.

Clark, C. M., & Peterson, P. L. (1986). Teachers' thought processes. In M. C. Wittrock (Ed.), *Handbook of research on teaching* (3rd ed.; pp. 255–296). New York: Macmillan.

Clermont, C. P., Krajcik, J. S., & Borko, H. (1993). The influence of an intensive inservice workshop on pedagogical content knowledge growth among novice chemical demonstrators. *Journal of Research in Science Teaching, 30,* 21–43.

Cohen, D. K. (1989). Teaching practice: Plus ca change . . . In P. W. Jackson (Ed.), *Contributing to educational change: Perspectives on research and practice* (pp. 27–84). Berkeley: McCutchan.

Cohen, D. K. (1990). A revolution in one classroom: The case of Ms. Oublier. *Educational Evaluation and Policy Analysis, 12,* 311–329.

Cohen, D. K., & Ball, D. L. (1990). Relations between policy and practice: A commentary. *Educational Evaluation and Policy Analysis, 12,* 311–338.

Collins, A., Brown, J. S., & Newman, S. E. (1989). Cognitive apprenticeship: Teaching the craft of reading, writing, and mathematics. In L. B. Resnick (Ed.), *Knowing, learning, and instruction: Essays in honor of Robert Glaser* (pp. 453–494). Hillsdale, NJ: Erlbaum.

Confrey, J. (1990). A review of the research on student conceptions in mathematics, science, and programming. In C. B. Cazden (Ed.), *Review of research in education* (Vol. 16; pp. 3–56). Washington, DC: American Educational Research Association.

Dewey, J. (1938). *Experience and education.* New York: Collier.

Doyle, W. (1983). Academic work. *Review of Educational Research, 53,* 159–199.

Doyle, W. (1986). Classroom organization and management. In M. C. Wittrock (Ed.), *Handbook of research on teaching* (3rd ed.; pp. 392–431). New York: Macmillan.

Eisenhart, M., & Borko, H. (1993). *Designing classroom research: Themes, issues and struggles.* Needham Heights, MA: Allyn & Bacon.

Eisenhart, M., Borko, H., Underhill, R., Brown, C., Jones, D., & Agard, P. (1993). Conceptual knowledge falls through the cracks: Complexities of learning to teach mathematics for understanding. *Journal for Research in Mathematics Education, 24,* 8–40.

Evertson, C. M. (1987). Managing classrooms: A framework for teachers. In D. C. Berliner & B. V. Rosenshine (Eds.), *Talks to teachers* (pp. 54–74). New York: Random House.

Fennema, E., Carpenter, T. P., Franke, M. L., & Carey, D. (1992). Learning to use children's mathematics thinking: A case study. In R. Davis & C. Maher (Eds.), *Schools, mathematics and the world of reality* (pp. 93–117). Needham Heights, MA: Allyn & Bacon.

Grossman, P. L. (1990). *The making of a teacher: teacher knowledge and teacher education.* New York: Teachers College Press.

Grossman, P. L., Wilson, S. M., & Shulman, L. S. (1989). Teachers of substance: Subject matter knowledge for teaching. In M. C. Reynolds (Ed.), *Knowledge base for the beginning teacher* (pp. 23–36). New York: Pergamon.

Hashweh, M. Z. (1987). Effects of subject-matter knowledge in the teaching of biology and physics. *Teaching and Teacher Education, 3,* 109–120.

Heaton, R. (1992). Who is minding the mathematics content: A case study of a fifth-grade teacher. *Elementary School Journal, 93,* 153–162.

McDiarmid, G. W., Ball, D. L., & Anderson, C. (1989). Why staying ahead one chapter just won't work: Subject-specific pedagogy. In M. C. Reynolds (Ed.), *Knowledge base for the beginning teacher* (pp. 193–205). New York: Pergamon.

National Center for Research on Teacher Education (1991). *Final report: The Teacher Education and Learning to Teach Study.* East Lansing, MI: College of Education, Michigan State University.

National Council of Teachers of Mathematics. (1989). *Curriculum and evaluation standards for school mathematics.* Reston, VA: Author.

National Council of Teachers of Mathematics. (1991). *Professional standards for teaching mathematics.* Reston, VA: Author.

National Education Goals Panel. (1991). *The national education goals report: Building a nation of learners.* Washington, DC: Author.

Palincsar, A. S., & Brown, A. L. (1984). Reciprocal teaching of comprehension-fostering and comprehension-monitoring activities. *Cognition and Instruction*, *1*, 117–175.

Peterson, P. L. (1990). Doing more in the same amount of time: Cathy Swift. *Educational Evaluation and Policy Analysis*, *12*, 261–280.

Peterson, P. L., Carpenter, T. P., & Fennema, E. (1989). Teachers' knowledge of students' knowledge and cognition in mathematics problem solving. *Journal of Educational Psychology*, *81*, 558–569.

Peterson, P. L., Fennema, E., Carpenter, T. P., & Loef, M. (1989). Teachers' pedagogical content beliefs in mathematics. *Cognition and Instruction*, *6*, 1–40.

Putnam, R. T. (1992). Teaching the "hows" of mathematics for everyday life: A case study of a fifth-grade teacher. *Elementary School Journal*, *93*, 163–177.

Putnam, R. T., Heaton, R., Prawat, R. S., & Remillard, J. (1992). Teaching mathematics for understanding: Discussing case studies of four fifth-grade teachers. *Elementary School Journal*, *93*, 213–228.

Putnam, R. T., Lampert, M., & Peterson, P. (1990). Alternative perspectives on knowing mathematics in elementary schools. *Review of Research in Education*, *16*, 57–150.

Resnick, L. B. (1985). Cognition and instruction: Recent theories of human competence. In B. L. Hammonds (Ed.), *Master lecture series: Vol. 4. Psychology and learning* (pp. 123–186). Washington, DC: American Psychological Association.

Resnick, L. B. (1987). Constructing knowledge in school. In L. S. Liben (Ed.), *Development and learning: Conflict or congruence?* (pp. 19–50). Hillsdale, NJ: Erlbaum.

Romberg, T. A., & Carpenter, T. P. (1986). Research on teaching and learning mathematics: Two disciplines of scientific inquiry. In M. C. Wittrock (Ed.), *Handbook of research on teaching* (3rd ed.; pp. 850–873). New York: Macmillan.

Schifter, D., & Simon, M. A. (1992). Assessing teachers' development of a constructivist view of mathematics learning. *Teaching and Teacher Education*, *8*, 187–197.

Schwab, J. J. (1964). The structures of the disciplines: Meanings and significances. In G. W. Ford & L. Pugno (Eds.), *The structure of knowledge and the curriculum* (pp. 1–30). Chicago: Rand McNally.

Shulman, L. S. (1986a). Paradigms and research programs in the study of teaching: A contemporary perspective. In M. C. Wittrock (Ed.), *Handbook of research on teaching* (3rd ed.; pp. 3–36). New York: Macmillan.

Shulman, L. S. (1986b). Those who understand: Knowledge growth in teaching. *Educational Researcher*, *15*(2), 4–14.

Shulman, L. S., & Grossman, P. (1988). *Knowledge growth in teaching: A final report to the Spencer Foundation* (Technical Report of the Knowledge Growth in a Profession Research Project). Stanford, CA: School of Education, Stanford University.

Simon, M. A., & Schifter, D. (1991). Towards a constructivist perspective: An intervention study of mathematics teacher development. *Educational Studies in Mathematics*, *22*, 309–331.

Smith, D. C., & Neale, D. C. (1991). The construction of subject-matter knowledge in primary science teaching. In J. Brophy (Ed.), *Advances in research on teaching: Vol. 2. Teachers' knowledge of subject matter as it relates to their teaching practice* (pp. 187–243). Greenwich, CT: JAI Press.

Stein, M. K., Baxter, J. A., & Leinhardt, G. (1990). Subject-matter knowledge and elementary instruction: A case from functions and graphing. *American Educational Research Journal, 27,* 639–663.

Veenman, S. (1984). Perceived problems of beginning teachers. *Review of Educational Research, 54,* 143–178.

Wilson, S. M., & Wineburg, S. S. (1988). Peering at history through different lenses: The role of disciplinary perspectives in teaching history. *Teachers College Record, 84,* 525–539.

Wilson, S. M., & Wineburg, S. S. (1993). Wrinkles in time and place: Using performance assessments to understand the knowledge of history teachers. *American Educational Research Journal, 30,* 729–769.

PART II

Social-Psychological and Institutional Factors

Regardless of its form, professional development is a contextualized process. The authors in this part emphasize the strong influence of context factors, especially current societal conditions, organizational presses, and the demands of an ever-expanding professional knowledge base.

In Chapter 3, John Smyth of Flinders University of South Australia views professional development from the perspective of economics. He argues that the current interest in the work of teachers is directly linked to declining levels of economic performance in Western capitalist economies. Smyth further contends that this interest is neither accidental nor incidental, and affects the way professional development for teachers is both conceived and enacted.

The dynamic interaction of individual change and organizational change is the focus of Chapter 4, by Mark A. Smylie of the University of Illinois at Chicago. Drawing on theory and research concerning educational organizations, adult learning, and teacher professional socialization, Smylie argues that organizational contexts exert strong influence on teachers' professional growth needs and opportunities. He concludes by showing how the structural, social, and normative dimensions of teachers' work must be considered if professional development endeavors are to be effective.

In Chapter 5, Thomas R. Guskey of the University of Kentucky argues that the powerful and often ignored influence of context consistently thwarts efforts to find universal truths in professional development. Instead of searching for abstract elements that can be applied across contexts, Guskey suggests finding an "optimal mix" of processes and technologies that can then be adapted to unique context characteristics. Drawing from research on professional development and individual change, he then outlines a series of guidelines for adapting critical professional development components to vital context characteristics.

3

Teachers' Work and
the Labor Process of Teaching
Central Problematics in Professional Development

JOHN SMYTH

In this chapter I want to argue that we need a new philosophical, theoretical, and practical base upon which to begin to talk about the professional development of teachers. There are several reasons why a shift in perspective is necessary and timely, not the least of which is a persistent inability of existing conceptualizations to deliver on their promises. My central claim is that if we wish to both understand and influence the way in which teachers develop professionally, then we need to be prepared to canvass possibilities that might lie outside our current range of vision. For instance, I want to start from the premise that there is something fundamentally deficient about a view of professional development that is wedded to or construed merely as a technical act of focusing on what individual teachers do (or might do) to rectify problems in their teaching. We need to transcend the ensconced "culture of individualism" (Hargreaves, 1982) that has come to represent the dominant view of the way we characterize schools, with its singular emphasis on "humanistic child-centred and psychologistic conceptions of 'teaching' and 'learning'" (Sachs & Smith, 1988, p. 427).

The kind of theoretical and philosophical lens I wish to bring to bear is one that has its origins in the work of critical social theorists, political sociologists, and scholars who have studied the nature of teachers' work and the labor process of teaching. This amounts to "puncturing the images of normality" (Thompson & McHugh, 1990, p. 357) and developing ways of "extraordinarily re-experiencing the ordinary" (Shor, 1980, p. 37). The attempt is not to come up with new solutions for teachers, or even to reorganize the work of teaching, but rather to think about the work of teaching differently. This means starting from school practitioners' existing theories, lives, and practices and using them as a basis for "proclaim[ing] the limits of existing organizational forms and practices" (Thompson & McHugh, 1990, p. 361). This enables teachers to "survive, improve and transform [the] organization [of schooling]" (Thompson & McHugh, 1990, p. 358).

PHILOSOPHICAL AND THEORETICAL PREMISES

Regarding schools as workplaces and teaching as a form of work departs dramatically from the concept of teachers as professionals. A labor process view of teaching involves looking at the way the work of teaching is organized, whose interests are silenced or denied, how it came to be that way, and, indeed, how power and control are exercised. It takes seriously questions about the nature of skill and competence and how these are themselves continually in the process of being constructed, contested, and redefined according to competing ideologies. As Ozga (1988) put it, to look at the notion of professionalism critically in the context of the substantive work of teachers is to direct attention to a number of crucial issues, including the organization of teachers' work and the workplace context; teachers' formal and informal groupings and networks; the division of labor both by function and by gender; the role of management and supervision; performance appraisal and efficiency; strategies of compliance and resistance; and job design and quality control in educational work.

Teachers' Work

The notion of teacher as educational worker has multiple origins. Lawn and Ozga have expressed dissatisfaction with notions of professionalism portraying teachers simply as a group engaged in upward mobility and status seeking. For them, "the social reality of teaching, working and organizing with other teachers, seems to be lost in this dimension of the literature" (1981, p. 45). They argue for a view of teaching that acknowledges the changing nature of working conditions in schools that reflects an "increased proletarianization of teachers' work, de-skilling and re-skilling" (p. 52). Lawn and Ozga's claim is that the work of teachers is no different in one important respect to that of any other kind of work; namely, the existence of forces that act to fragment what teachers do, reducing complex problems to technical/rational/managerial solutions by controlling the technology of schooling.

Lawn and Ozga's theoretical roots come from Braverman's (1974) seminal work on the labor process and the writings of Braverman's various critics who have challenged the inevitability of his deskilling argument and added in different ways to the original arguments (see Burawoy, 1979; Edwards,

1979; Salaman, 1986; Thompson, 1983; Wood, 1989; Zimbalist, 1979). Ozga and Lawn have become embroiled in some arguments about the nature of the proletarianization thesis, the importance of history, and the crucial nature of active agency in the micro-politics of the school. Notwithstanding, they have reiterated their basic aim as being "to study teachers' work with attention to lived experience, collective actions, group cultures, strategies, struggles . . . [and] the active role of workers in controlling or resisting or adapting this process" (1988, p. 329).

Seddon and Connell (1989) argue that in many respects this alternative perspective has been spawned because of growing dissatisfaction with at least two areas of research on schools that have been "teacher blind"—organizational research on schooling and research on school improvement. Both have failed adequately to take account of the realities of teachers' work. For example, there are those like Denscombe (1980), Gitlin (1983), Hargreaves (1989), and Tipton (1985) who critique the *organizational research* on schools and who argue that educational organizations are workplaces in which teachers have historically been treated as invisible, in which goals are notoriously unclear, and where there is much uncertainty and contestation about processes and technology. The bottom line for these people is the need to know much more about the work organization of schooling as well as the importance and self-understandings teachers as insiders attach to the nature of the workplace and what it is they do.

There are those who argue that teachers' work has never been an *apolitical activity* (see Bigelow, 1990)—that choices are continually being made about what to include and exclude from the curriculum, how to connect (or not) with the lives of students outside of classrooms, and how to respond to the increasing intervention by the state in terms of imposing mandates and goals aimed at redesigning and "increasing control over our *and* our colleagues work" (Ginsburg, 1988, p. 360). The argument is that education and teaching have always been political work and that we must therefore treat teachers as educational workers and political actors (Carlson, 1987; Stevens, 1987; J. White & White, 1986). The challenge, according to Ozga (1988), is to begin to "understand changes in the control and structure of teaching work using the organizing principles of teaching as *work* and teaching as a labor process" (p. 3).

Current amputated views of teacher professionalism tend to be long on rhetoric about teacher autonomy and short on reality. We need to address the fundamental ways in which the structure of schooling inhibits the autonomy of teachers; in other words, recognize the ways in which teaching is a labor process and, as such, *the way in which work is organized.* For example, the overall shape of teachers' work and what are deemed "acceptable end products" are increasingly coming to be determined by forces outside of schools (especially with moves to expand statewide testing and introduce performance appraisal measures); the intensity and pace at which teachers' work (i.e., the number of classes they teach, the students per class, and the scheduling of those classes) are dictated by exogenous budgetary constraints and the demand of "value for money"; many of the routines imposed upon teachers—including prescribed curriculum frameworks, adherence to required state and federal guidelines and policies, recommended curriculum packages, and time to be spent on particular curriculum content—have their origins beyond the classroom and bear an uncanny resemblance to the kind of constraints that place limits around the nature of work in industry generally. Therefore, to speak of "professionally developing" teachers while significant constraints of this kind remain unacknowledged and even unchallenged is to adopt a head-in-the-sand view of professional development. Such changes can amount to little more than tinkering with the technical skills of teaching, while the broader issues are defined and determined elsewhere.

Arguing from a *historical perspective*, Seddon (1988) claims that teachers' status as employees of the state, the implicit nature of their work relationships in teaching, and hence teachers' understandings and sense of professionalism have all been set in place through contested settlements that have a long legacy. This goes some way toward explaining, Connell (1985) says, why teachers have been assumed until fairly recently "to be more or less well controlled agents of the capitalist system" (p. 2). For this reason, studies like Connell's are important because of the way in which they revive interest in "teachers as key actors in the social processes affecting education" (p. 3). Studying the work of teaching, he says, not only enables us to see more clearly the labor process of teaching and the importance of gender relations, in particular, but also enables us to bring together three levels of analysis that have hitherto remained separate—teachers' life histories, the study of the institutional life of the school, and the large-scale structural factors affecting schooling.

Characterizing teaching as a form of work (Seddon, 1990) raises a number of interesting questions not only about teachers' status as employees, but also about the way in which what teachers do is structured, framed, and constrained by "salary scales, avenues for promotion, and status hierarchies" (Seddon & Connell, 1989). Examining the restructuring of teachers' work in Australia, Ashenden (1990) has argued that the scope for increased productivity in teaching is severely circumscribed because "teachers suffer from very badly designed and managed jobs" (p. 7) and that "the very low division of labor . . . and the limited use made of technology or of students themselves in the teaching process, makes jobs ill-defined and unrewarding" (p. 3). Ashenden claims that teaching is the last of the "mass cottage industries" and that the reality of the classroom for most teachers is a schizoid one—"pride in their finely honed repertoire of tactics with which they tame the jungle life . . . [but] an endless frustration in their work" (p. 13). He likens teachers'

work to that of "backyard mechanics—always out in the shed tinkering, trying out new bits and pieces" (p. 14), and it is this continuing desire for experimentation that has paradoxically resulted in teachers' promoting the survival of the classroom as an outmoded model of production. Unions have, he
says, bolstered this model by carefully codifying who will do the work, who
has access to teaching, the hours within which it will be performed, the length
of teaching periods, and the size of the educational group. By implication,
Ashenden is saying, these features have combined to ossify the nature of teachers' work and make it impervious to any structural change. He is also arguing
that claims about the low productivity of teachers may be due as much to the
workflow and the organization of the work as it is to any idiosyncracies of
individual teachers. In addressing the implications of all this for teacher education, Hatton (1987, 1988, 1991) has likened teachers' work to that of
bricoleurs, who employ indirect means, the influences of which lie consider-
ably beyond the workplace in prior experiences and other forms of socialization. Denscombe (1980) has similarly argued that routine teacher activity
constitutes a practical response to the exigencies of particular organizational
arrangements. In other words, from the perspective of the sociology of work,
styles of teaching are not so much an outcome of "pedagogic choice" as they
are a response to the environmental circumstances in which teachers find themselves. Hargreaves (1989) has provided evidence showing that "time" is the
major element in the construction of teachers' work: "Time is a fundamental
dimension through which teachers' work is constructed and interpreted—by
themselves, by their colleagues and by those who administer and supervise
them" (p. 1). He argues that time and how it is used is a very effective instrument by which to enhance central control over curriculum and assessment and
to generally widen the breach between administrators and teachers, policy and
practice, by regulating, routinizing, and rationalizing its use.

   Another strand of teachers' work has been picked up by critics of the school
improvement literature as they have struggled with issues of who controls the
work of teaching. Harris (1990a, 1990c), for example, argues that contrary
to current rhetorical claims that teachers have more control than ever before
over educational processes, what schools are being sold is "management
dogma" under the rubric of market-driven and market-managed approaches
to schooling. The imposition of forms of managerialism, far from giving teachers more control, is severely circumscribing their opportunities. The consequence, he says, is "decreased status, loss of autonomy, worsening conditions,
lowering morale, and subjugation to increasing external control of schooling
and curricula" (p. 21). Overall, the thrust toward school reform appears to be
predicated on a degradation of the work of teachers, with the craft of teaching being replaced by a panoply of technical rational procedures (Seddon &
Connell, 1989).

Labor Process of Teaching

The year 1974 marks a watershed, because that was the year in which Harry Braverman published his now celebrated *Labor and Monopoly Capital: The Degradation of Work in the Twentieth Century*. Although Braverman drew his inspiration from Marx, it was *he* who sought to retrieve many of Marx's ideas and place them in a context that took account of modern management techniques, particularly what he saw as the separation of "conception" (management) from "execution" (labor). Since 1974 there has been a burgeoning growth of theoretical and practical works that both discuss and critique the labor process, although few have taken education and teaching as their focus. Essentially, analyses of the labor process are interested in exposing how, in various historical periods, workers have been forced to surrender their labor for wages and the effects of giving up their "labor power." Without complicating matters, the focus in the study of the labor process is on the "concealment of the process of valorisation" (Knights & Willmott, 1990, p. 4)—that is to say, the method by which workers get less than a full wage return in selling their labor. So, labor process theory is basically concerned with the relationships and forms of organization that are involved at the point of production. The argument is that in the process of production, capital unfairly appropriates an increasing share of the final value of the product, turning workers into mere "wage labourers" (Knights & Willmott, 1990, p. 3) receiving less in wages than they add in value of production. It is the manner in which the true value of labor is concealed that is the key concern. The logic behind this is that once labor is subordinated in this way (compared, say, with the way in which autonomous craftsmen operated in the past), then it becomes possible to make further inroads by cutting real wages, by increasing the length of the working day, by developing more intense methods of working, by replacing labor with machinery, and so on (see Brecher [1978] for the broader arguments). Because the capitalist system is continually in a state of flux due to its need to continually keep adjusting to externally driven market circumstances, continual adjustments are occurring in the labor process through the fragmenting of work into smaller and smaller tasks.

What Braverman (1974) saw as most significant was the increasing concentration of conception into smaller and smaller groups (today we call it forms of corporate management) through the increasing subdivision of tasks—or what has become known as Taylorism, in which skills are destroyed and labor marginalized. There are three basic themes that come through *Labor and Monopoly Capital*:

1. Deskilling, or how the nature of skills changes
2. Management and control, or the strategies of how the labor force is controlled

3. The influence of the labor market, or how fluctuations in the demand for labor along with changes in technology can shape the nature of the labor force.

To adopt a labor process view is, therefore, to accept that a number of key constructs come into play (Smyth, 1992):

1. Work, organization, and change ought to be considered from the vantage point of those who live and experience them, thus opening up the possibility that outside factors (such as economic and social structures) both influence work and in turn are influenced by it (Aungles & Parker, 1988).
2. Work is not simply an abstract ahistorical process, but rather has cultural, political, ideological, and historical dimensions to it that speak to its socially and historically constructed nature (Joyce, 1987).
3. Work is a gendered, power-laden, and fragmented activity; as such, it represents a central expression of the way in which different skills are continually being constructed and reconstructed (Knights & Willmott, 1990).
4. Interventions made into the workplace by outsiders, rather than merely being determinants, actually amount to point-of-production possibilities for workers to reconstruct the nature of the relationship between the state and the economy (Burawoy, 1985).
5. Examining the changing forms of intensification and control over work is to see the way in which the relations among legitimation, consent, coercion, and resistance are played out in rapidly changing work contexts (Thompson, 1983).
6. Current changes in the way work is organized go well beyond Fordist and post-Fordist ideas to reveal the underlying manner in which continuities persist in change (Knights, Willmott, & Collinson, 1985).

These are not ideas and perspectives from within which it has been customary in the past to analyze the work of teachers. But if we are to make sense of the contradictions that are coming to plague teachers' lives, then it will be necessary to access as well as to monitor changes in teachers' lives and work practices while validating the means by which teachers make changes in their self-understandings.

In relation to teaching, there are a number of pertinent observations that can be made about the way in which the labor process of teaching is organized. Connell (1985) maintains that as a labor process, teaching is characterized first and foremost by a task orientation that, at best, is "so intangible— the minds of kids, or their capacity to learn—that it cannot be specified in any but vague and metaphorical ways" (p. 70). The tasks of a teacher are so many and vary so much from context to context that they almost defy specification. Even straight "chalk and talk" (or what Hoetker & Ahlbrand [1969] label the "persistence of recitation") involves complex interactions of events that include:

> Keeping order; dealing with conflicts between kids; having a joke with them from time to time and building up some personal contact; discussing work with them individually; planning sequences of lessons; preparing handouts and physical materials; collecting, using and storing books and audiovisual aids; organizing and marking tests and major exams; keeping records; liaison with other teachers in the same subject. Most of that has to be done separately for each class (Connell, 1985, p. 71).

In the final analysis it is this "labour process without an object" that leaves teachers' work open to "limitless intensification" (p. 72) but which, at the same time, leads to it being shaped by "circumstances and demands both immediate and remote" (p. 73).

Second, as a mode of work, teaching is characterized by what Miles (1969) labeled a high degree of "role performance invisibility"—or as Connell (1985) put it somewhat more starkly: "A great deal of teaching is done with one adult and twenty or thirty kids in a fairly bare room together, with the door shut" (p. 73). The consequence is not only that this produces a high degree of individualism in teachers' ideology but also that the "classroom separates teachers from each other in the ordinary course of their work" (p. 73) to produce a "blatantly non-collaborative" culture (Liston & Zeichner, 1991, p. 97).

Third, the actual craft of teaching, when based on this idea of "collective instruction" fragments, fractures and paces the work of teachers and students through 40 minute periods in which the timetable becomes the major framing and governing mechanism. This administrative "carving up of the total learning effort" and the highly political question of "who does the dishing out" (Connell, 1985, p. 82) have important and lasting implications for the division of labor, sexually as well as experientially. What we have between teachers and students in these circumstances is a situation of "controlled rapport" (p. 78), as teachers respond to the imposition of orchestrated control of their work.

Fourth, teaching has also been described as an "emotionally infused . . . emotionally diffuse labor process" (Liston & Zeichner, 1991, pp. 98–99). Jackson (1968/1990) makes the point rather well that classrooms are extremely crowded and intimate settings:

> There is a social intimacy in schools that is unmatched elsewhere in our society. Buses and movie theatres may be more crowded than classrooms, but people rarely stay in such densely populated settings for extended periods of time, and while there, they are usually not expected to concentrate on work or to interact with each other. Even factory workers are not clustered as close together as stu-

dents in a standard classroom. In all likelihood the unions would not allow it. Only in schools do 30 or more people spend several hours each day literally side by side. Once we leave the classroom we seldom again are required to have contact with so many people for so long a time. (p. 8)

Because of the high level of emotional management attaching to the job, teachers therefore typically "invest themselves in their work in a very personal way" (Liston & Zeichner, 1991, p. 98), a process that is especially poignant for neophyte teachers who are still trying to construct survival skills (Ryan, 1991).

WHAT DOES THIS MEAN FOR PROFESSIONAL DEVELOPMENT?

The evidence about "what works," or is likely to in respect of the professional development of teachers, is far from conclusive (see Smyth, 1991a,b). There has been much effort over the past decade at proclaiming the alleged virtues of collaborative forms of professional development for teachers. However, despite the well-meaning nature of much of this effort, it is by no means clear that such processes are necessarily efficacious for teachers or, indeed, sustainable, given what we are beginning to learn about the culture of teachers' work. In other words, the empirical base for the merits of collaborative forms of professional development is more fugitive and uncertain, at least in the research literature. For now, then, I am less inclined to openly advocate this line of reform until we have a clearer understanding about the nature of teachers' work and teachers' lives that is likely to make this possible, or not, as the case might be.

In a general sense I concur with Harris's (1990b) assessment that what is happening is that:

The technical job of teaching will, and has already, become deskilled and devalued as labour power . . . [and that teachers] can expect to do more controlling and less curricular instructing . . . and in the process, find their instruction function deskilled; they are likely, globally, to lose aspects of control over the content they teach and the conditions under which they work. (p. 195)

There is a deal of evidence around to substantiate this (Apple, 1983, 1986; Ball & Goodson, 1985; Harris, 1982, 1990a; Popkewitz & Lind, 1989), although, as Hargreaves (1994) has noted, it is by no means clear yet that the intensification and proletarianization thesis applies universally or operates in the same way with all teachers. Notwithstanding that the evidence is not yet in on particular cases, as R. White (1983) argues, "proletarianisation of teachers' labour . . . [is a] generalized phenomenon occurring throughout advanced

capitalist societies" (p. 45). In Larson's (1980) terms, it is concretely mani-
fested in three tendencies: "a tendency towards intensification (increased
volume of work); a tendency to increase and rigidify the division of labor;
and the tendency towards routinization of high level tasks (expert intervention and codification of existing tasks)" (pp. 163–164). The introduction in
England and Wales recently of a National Curriculum (through the 1988
Education Reform Act), despite protestations to the contrary that it is "not
an educational straitjacket" (National Curriculum Council, 1989, p. 1), is an
interesting case in point. Despite "ringed binders for each subject containing
Statutory Orders, which gave details of programmes of study, attainment targets and aged-based levels of attainment expected" (Acker, 1990, p. 258), there
is still not universal agreement on what this means. Acker, for example, through
her ethnographic study of two English primary schools in the period of the
1988 reforms, makes it clear that not only did teachers feel that "so little of
what [they] were accomplishing was appreciated by the politicians or the
public" (p. 268), but that the reforms "themselves limit the extent of teachers' professional judgement and autonomy" (p. 269). At the same time, however, she also admits to not being able to find evidence *yet* of teachers experiencing their work as "deskilled" or of the emergence *yet* of "teacher proof
curriculum packages" (p. 270).

   Once we can begin to see the bigger picture of the way in which teachers'
work as a phenomenon is being restructured as a consequence of broader
changes in the nature of capitalism, it becomes much easier to see how the
professional development of teachers is being used as a policy option. My
argument is that the issue of professional development of teachers is back on
the educational horizon in a way we could not have imagined a few years ago.
After several decades of benign neglect, teachers are suddenly in the spotlight.
While this new-found attention to teachers is laudable, the revival of interest
in teachers worldwide at this particular historical juncture is directly linked
to the declining levels of economic performance. This renewed interest in
teacher development reaches deep into the way in which professional development for teachers is being conceived and enacted. What we have come to
experience as age-old forms of muscular, authoritarian, and hierarchical forms
of surveillance are breaking down, and in their place are being posited collegial forms of site-based management, participation, and other forms of devolution.

   The widespread interest in teacher collaboration is a particular case in
point. The rekindled interest in collegiality is not accidental; it is part of a
broader strategy (deliberate or otherwise) to harness teachers more effectively
to the work of economic reconstruction. The irony is that while teachers and
schools worldwide are being sold the idea that they should be more autonomous and responsive to local needs, they are also being told what their out-

comes must be and how they must strive to meet *national priorities* and en-hance *international competitiveness*. Teachers, therefore, are supposedly being given more autonomy at the school level at precisely the same time as the parameters within which they are expected to work, and against which they will be evaluated, are being tightened and made more constraining. Hargreaves and Dawe (1989) describe this as the peculiar paradox in which teachers "are apparently being urged to collaborate *more*, just at the moment when there is *less* for them to collaborate about" (p. 3). What is occurring, then, is a change in the "pedagogic codes" (Bernstein, 1977) of supervision, evaluation, and professional development from ones that were *visible* and *strongly framed* to ones that are *invisible* and *weakly framed*. The emphasis is upon "building a professional culture of teaching which is more responsive and receptive to change [and this has become] an important managerial priority" (Hargreaves & Dawe, 1989, p. 2). My argument is that coupled with moves toward in-creased centralization of our educational systems, we are starting to see forms of pedagogic control that are sedimented into the work of teaching; collegial-ity is a good example of that.

The notion of collegiality as an expression of professional development is, therefore, a much more complex notion than we might think at first blush. It is not simply a matter of teachers conferring with one another. Rather, what we have emerging are forms of central control in the guise of local autonomy. This kind of "indirect rule," as Lawn and Ozga (1986) call it, is most often resorted to in conjunction with measures aimed at increased central control over selection, certification, and the content of teacher education programs—which is precisely what has occurred in England and Wales. Hartley (1985) comes closest to my point, when, in speaking of teachers in Scotland, he said that they are becoming

> little more than narrowly trained technicians, albeit more skilled in pedagogical practice, but largely bereft of an ability to analyse the institution of education itself . . . [in a context characterized by] the quickening pace of bureaucratiza-tion within . . . a rhetoric of collaboration between teachers and officialdom. (p. 108)

The dilemma confronting educational policy makers hinges around want-ing to develop collaborative structures but using them for essentially manage-rial ends. This is what I describe as the "hanging on while letting go" syn-drome, and it is a "solution" characteristic, generally speaking, of the wider economic crisis facing Western countries at the moment. Put in labor pro-cess terms, what this means is that "within capitalism there is a perpetual ten-sion between treating workers as a commodity to be hired and fired"—hence the lack of regard for teachers' capacity to conceptualize their work and the need for people other than teachers to do that—"and harnessing their ingenuity and co-operativeness" (Littler, 1982, p. 34)—thus the trend toward an apparent relaxation of control and allowing teachers the flexibility to make decisions collaboratively about their work. Management has always wanted to control the work process by prescribing knowledge and action, but at the same time realizing that they are unable to maximize output unless they successfully appropriate workers' knowledge (see Brecher, 1978). This is especially so in periods of protracted international crisis when profits are falling, competitiveness is declining, and there is a need to significantly restructure the nature of work.

My argument is that the notion of collegiality, as with other forms of teacher development, is coming to be intricately bound up with the nature of teachers' work and questions about who exerts the predominant influence in shaping it at particular historical moments. Collegiality is, therefore, much more than a desirable teacher-to-teacher relationship. It is a policy option being wielded to dramatically redefine what is meant by the notion of skill and competency in teaching. We need to focus discussion, therefore, on explanations that cast light on why it is that collegial and cooperative processes are being so widely touted as an attractive policy option.

In Australia, to take an example, what is beginning to emerge are partnerships that claim to provide collegial forms of professional development for teachers, but in a context in which the steerage and policy directions are unquestionably being framed from outside of schools. This is consistent with Little's (1987) view of U.S. teachers, whom she sees as having generally been excluded from curriculum policy decisions—a view that serves to further underscore the view of teachers' knowledge as being unimportant. While there is much discussion about collegiality in Australia in official educational reports, the reality is that the majority of teachers are excluded from the substance of policy decisions affecting them. This fits with what Hargreaves & Dawe (1989) argue is a "contrived" form of collegiality characterized by

> administrative contrivances designed to get collegiality going in schools where little has existed before. They are meant to encourage greater association among teachers; to foster more sharing, learning and improvement of skills and expertise. Contrived collegiality is also meant to assist the successful implementation of new approaches and techniques from the outside into a more responsive and supportive school culture. (p. 19)

Grimmett (1990) pinpoints the problem as being one that emphasizes "fulfilling the form of collegiality without regard for the spirit or underlying assumptions of interdependence. It is as if it has become mandatory that practitioners collaborate voluntarily" (p. 1). Instead of teachers engaging in a process of critiquing "the purposes and processes inherent in the required actions" (p. 2)—or as Harris (1979) put it, exploring "an ensemble of particular lived ideologies each of which [represents] a socially constructed set of practices, rituals and behaviours inter-related with one another and with certain concepts and images" (p. 87)—what we have, instead, is a process in which participation is construed as a "co-requisite of responsible professionalism" (Grimmett, 1990, p. 2). To become involved with one's colleagues in observation, talk, and sharing is to become implicated in "impression management" (Grimmett, 1990) in order simply not to be labeled as unprofessional.

What we are witnessing at the moment, then, is a resurgence of the idea that to act professionally, teachers must be prepared to enter a *partnership* with the state in return for varying degrees of "limited or licensed professionalism" (Lawn & Ozga, 1986, p. 225). This "mock partnership," in which "teamwork" (Lawn, 1988, p. 164) and "co-operation" (p. 162) are becoming central expressions of the new work relations, amounts, in effect, to an ideological form of control over how teachers relate to others in the course of their work. To display "collegiality" means to be able to work as "part of groups and teams" in the policy and decision-making process in schools and amounts to a form of "indirect rule" that is increasingly coming to characterize discussion about the management of schools. Within education this has meant a gradual "rejection of direct prescriptive controls" (Lawn and Ozga, 1986, p. 226) and putting in its place a process that is much more reliant on engineering broad forms of consensus. Lawn and Ozga (1988) note that emancipation is only for parts of the system—it does not mean endangering "real tactical control" (p. 88), but rather dispensing with some of the more burdensome aspects of unnecessary central power.

Schemes that purport to employ collegiality are being pushed in the United States under such labels as lead teacher, although also under various other names such as consulting teacher, team leader, mentor, learning strategist, support teacher, peer coach, teacher trainer, and clinical resident teacher (Academy for Educational Development, 1989, p. 15). This form of "contrived collegiality" (Hargreaves, 1990) is posited as an enlightened alternative to telling teachers what to do and is an approach designed to "empower" teachers and make them "majority shareholders in efforts to *push* public schooling ahead in the 21st century" (Berry, 1988, p. 20). According to Berry (1988):

> This conceptualization of school reform and teacher professionalism posits that teachers establish the standards of teaching while administrators (primarily principals)—as school stewards—facilitate and nurture collegiality and experimentation to create the time and space for professionalism to develop. (p. 20)

We are further told that

> lead teachers are a vehicle for rewarding excellent teachers, retaining them as
> classroom teachers, and empowering other teachers to act independently, to
> collaborate with others, and render critical judgement. . . . [They] will assume
> new responsibility for curriculum, student discipline, and community relations
> . . . [and] will be paid comparably to other professional managers. (p.10)

As Lawn (1988) put it, schemes like this that preach collegiality can often be
about new forms of delegated management in which teachers take on jobs
"which make them supervisors of other staff" (p. 166). Under these circumstances, collegiality and teamwork actually come to mean "the spread of management and supervision and its fragmentation so that an element of it is now
included in [the teacher's] job description" (p. 167). Rather then becoming
equal collegial peers, teachers become agents charged with policing one
anothers' oppression.

Teachers' own motivations and attitudes to collegiality are not inconse-
quential. As Nias, Southworth, and Yeomans (1989) have documented in
England, teachers both value collegial approaches to their work and frequently
use them as forms of covert resistance against the prescriptions of national
and local educational authorities, principals, and headmasters. There are still
considerable reservations in that country about the general applicability of the
notion of collegiality, especially in contexts where it is recommended by those
outside schools to be applied by those *inside* schools.

In searching for answers to what the notion of collegiality as a form of
professional development actually means, we need to watch and listen to the
ways in which teachers themselves seek to attach significance to what it is they
do and how they individually and collectively struggle to contest and redefine the work of schooling.

WHAT CAN BE DONE THEORETICALLY, EMPIRICALLY, AND PRACTICALLY ?

As Demaine (1988) argues, we first need to be sensitive to the quite dramatic shift in control over teachers' work away from a form of "producer
capture" (which was supposedly characterized by laxity, an ascendancy of the
"soft subjects," teacher control over the curriculum, declining standards, and
the like) and toward a form of "consumer capture" (which places much greater
emphasis on rigor, accountability, common standards, stringent appraisal,
assessment and evaluation)—in short, a shift to forms of privatization of education based on a culture of competitive and possessive individualism (Sachs

& Smith, 1988). This has become typified by the situation in Britain, where professionalism has come to mean "cooperativeness" and where teamwork and cooperation have been coopted as part of the new work relations. Involvement of teachers in the policy-making process and the surveillance of their colleagues will come to be just another "part of the formal organization of schoolwork . . . described as the 'corporate development' of the school" (Lawn, 1988, p. 164). The shift in emphasis from *direct* to more *participative* forms of control has been an extremely deft slip of the hand. What has occurred is that in moving from one form of professionalism characterized by classroom-based isolation, we have come to embrace another form of professionalism that involves collective schoolwide responsibility "based on narrowly defined though complex tasks within a context of shared management functions, clearly defined and appraised" (Lawn, 1988, p. 166). In Australia, if western Australia is anything to go by, the tendency has been one in which the state has certainly not given to schools the power to determine what the ends of education should be. In decidedly candid terms for a senior educational bureaucrat, Angus (1990) stated:

> Quite the opposite. Underpining the paradigm is the belief that better performance will result from *sharper focusing on systemic priorities*. What is being devolved to schools is the actual authority (and capacity) to determine the way in which the school will achieve the agreed outcomes. (p. 5; emphasis added)

The situation is much the same in the United States, where, according to the Carnegie Forum on Education and the Economy (1986), teachers will be free only to "decide how best to meet state and local goals for children while [being held] accountable for their progress" (O'Neil, 1990, p. 6).

Needless to say, while many (perhaps even the majority) of schools and school systems still rely heavily on directive, prescriptive, and oppressive forms of control, it is also true that the work of teachers is coming to be increasingly controlled through the orchestration of quite explicit meanings attaching to such notions as professionalism, cooperation, and teamwork. Expressed in these terms, professionalism becomes a measured response to the need to structurally rework the relationship between the economy and schooling in periods of legitimation and motivational crisis in capital accumulation. Professionalism thus becomes a way of "controlling teachers ideologically . . . by means of finely tuned tactical control in a system which now need[s] guiding not directing" (Lawn & Ozga, 1988, p. 88).

A poignant illustration of this can be seen in Hartley's (1986) discussion of the inservice education of teachers in Scotland in what he calls "guided volunteering" within a style of "consultative centralism." In that instance the collaborative model of staff development being mandated was regarded by the policy makers as being preferable to the directive model, but as Hartley points out "consultation" and "collaboration" occurred in that case "only between contiguous strata of the educational bureaucracy . . . [and] in the last analysis, the needs of officialdom will prevail over those of teachers" (p. 233). In what is becoming an all-too-common scenario, he cites from a government document on inservice education which makes it clear that the "collaborative, consultative staff development strategy *only* permits the discretion of teachers within the broad parameters of its educational policy: central government defines the premises and sets the agenda for action, the teachers 'develop' professionally within that framework" (p. 233). In the words of the document:

> The strength of personal professional development is that it generates enthusiasm and commitment among teachers who are doing things which they themselves have chosen. Its weakness is that teachers may not be channeling their energy and enthusiasms in directions which seem important. . . . It therefore does *not guarantee that the most important needs of the school or the authority are being met.* (Hartley, 1986, p. 233; emphasis in original)

We need, therefore, a very different starting point. Our vantage point needs to be one in which teaching is construed as a complex, value-laden, social activity that deserves (indeed requires) forms of analysis that open up for debate the nature of the interests served by having education and schooling the way it is. As Apple (1981) put it, we need "to illuminate the problematic character of the commonsense reality most educators take for granted" (p. 79). Teachers, and those of us interested in working with them, need ways to theorize about the social practices of teaching in a way that acknowledges its political and moral dimensions. We need to rely less on the language of technique, which locks us into a preoccupation with practical suggestions and questions of "what works," and instead to ask questions about "why things are the way they are and how they got to be that way" (Simon, 1988, p. 2). It is, after all, only by revealing how and in what ways particular teaching and professional development practices and proposals for their reform have come about, that the real interests can be unmasked, debated, and transformed. Doing this involves what Apple (1975) describes as

> a painful process of radically examining our current positions and asking pointed questions about these positions and the social structure from which they arise. It also necessitates a serious in-depth search for alternatives to these almost unconscious lenses we employ and an ability to cope with an ambiguous situation for which answers can now be only dimly seen and will not be easy to come by. (p.127)

In all of this I want to make the point that I am not arguing *only* for a more democratic approach to professional development in which teachers have

a greater say over what happens. To restrict myself to this would be too limiting and would be to overlook what Pratte and Rury (1988) label the "myth
of professionalism," in which:

> The message seems to be that if administrators would only treat teachers with
> greater respect and allow them the freedom to run their classes without nettlesome
> interference, everyone would feel good and teaching and learning would be
> enhanced. . . . The result will be "autonomy for the school as a whole" and good
> relations among the staff. (p. 72)

The problem with this amputated view of professionalism (and the views of
professional development that it encapsulates) is that it relies on the misguided
view that all that is required for professional development is that teachers be
left to their own devices. What it fails to address are the "fundamental ways
in which the structure of schooling inhibits the autonomy of teachers" (Pratte
& Rury, 1988, p. 72).

Rather, what we need are ways for teachers as a professional community
to ask and answer questions that go beyond conventional reactions to policy
initiated by people outside of schools. We need systematic ways in which teachers as a group are better able to pursue questions about their work and the
political factors shaping it—questions such as:

What is happening here?
Who says this is the way things ought to happen?
Who is it that is defining the work of teaching?
How is that definition being fought over and resisted in various ways?
What concessions and accommodations are being made?
How are issues of skill, competency, professionalism and autonomy being
    expressed in the social relations of teaching?
Whose interests are being served in the change process?
What new forms of power relations are being used to focus power rela-
    tions in teaching?
How are the redefined labor relations of teaching being played out?

All of this is only possible in contexts in which teachers regard themselves not as civil servants but as political actors capable of formulating as
well as actively pursuing a public position on educational issues. In the process, teachers and their professional associations need to see themselves, first
and foremost, as part of an extended collegial community that has a *right* as
well as a *responsibility* to articulate a coherent position on where education
in this country is headed. They need to be more forceful than they have been
in the past at trumpeting the virtues of what is happening in schools and

classrooms, and they need to be more adept at finding ways of linking up with other community groups so that their voices can be better heard (see Bigelow, 1990).

As a starting point, I want to suggest that teachers might want to develop systematic ways of describing their teaching so as to articulate the nature of hard-won experiential theories implicit in that teaching, while at the same time confronting and developing defensible positions on where their pedagogical principles come from biographically and historically, with a view to being able to construct a coherent public position on how teaching should be reconstructed differently (Smyth, 1989).

I would suggest that in the process they might need to develop a ten-point manifesto of professional development that goes something like this:

1. Professional development ought not to be restricted to examining the technical skills of effective teaching; it should equally be concerned with the ethical, social, and political context within which teaching occurs.
2. Professional development ought not be restricted to teachers reflecting individually upon their teaching, but ought to have a collective and collaborative dimension to it as well.
3. Professional development, as currently enacted, serves certain political interests while denying others—both ought to be disclosed.
4. Professional development ought to be about giving educational values preference over administrative and hierarchical values.
5. Professional development should be about challenging dominant myths, assumptions, and hidden message systems in the way teaching and schooling are currently organized.
6. Professional development should be concerned with creating improvements in educational practice and the social relationships that underlie those practices.
7. Professional development ought to be about crafting and living out mutual forms of accountability among teachers, administrators, parents, and students.
8. Professional development practices must regard knowledge about teaching as being in a tentative and incomplete state, continually being modified by practice.
9. Professional development must go beyond simple cause-and-effect connections and seek to situate or locate pedagogy in ways that uncover constraints that block wider educational and social reform.
10. Professional development occurs best when it begins with the experiences of school practitioners as they describe, inform, confront, and reconstruct their theories of practice (Smyth, 1991c).

Thus conceptualized, the purpose of teacher development becomes not one of shaping teachers according to some vaguely defined instrumental ends or national goals, but rather a process of exposing and highlighting contradictions in experience and intervening to assist teachers in reconstructing experiences—both within practice and between theory and practice. Professional development for teachers *then* becomes a form of intervention that has *liberating* rather then *domesticating* ends.

CONCLUSION

This chapter has argued that the increased international interest in teacher professional development through the various school-based professional approaches currently in vogue is not what it seems at first glance. What we are experiencing is a worldwide phenomenon not dissimilar to earlier moves that restructured control over teachers' work through the redefinition of professionalism. The strategy is one that gives the outward appearances of participative and collaborative ways of working but that on closer inspection amounts to a policy option that is cooptive of teachers and that gives them little more than control over the implementation aspects of teaching in a context of rigidly formulated centrally prescribed educational guidelines. If processes like collegiality are in fact being used as a managerial tool in the guise of a professional development process to coerce teachers into doing the bland work of economic reconstruction, then we should not be altogether surprised if the majority of teachers shun the processes. On the other hand, if we are prepared to institute processes of genuine participation that enable teachers to become real partners in education by allowing them to reflect upon the social, economic, and political factors that shape and reshape their work, then it may be possible to wind up in quite a different place.

Acknowledgment. Research in this chapter was made possible by funding from the Australian Research Council and the Flinders University Board of Research.

REFERENCES

Academy for Educational Development. (1989). *The profession of teaching in Pennsylvania: A report on lead teachers.* New York: Author.

Acker, S. (1990). Teachers' culture in an English primary school: Continuity and change. *British Journal of Sociology of Education, 11*(3), 257–273.

Angus, M. (1990, April). *Making better schools: Devolution the second time around.* Paper presented to annual meeting of American Educational Research Association, Boston.

Apple, M. (1975). Scientific interests and the nature of educational institutions. In W. Pinar (Ed.), *Curriculum Theorizing* (pp. 120–130). Berkeley: McCutchan.

Apple, M. (1981). The process and ideology of valuing in educational settings. In R. Bates (Ed.), *Organizational evaluation in schools* (pp. 79–102). Geelong, Australia: Deakin University Press.

Apple, M. (1983). Work, gender and teaching. *Teachers College Record, 84*(3), 611–628.

Apple, M. (1986). *Teachers and texts: Political economy of class and gender relations in education.* Boston: Routledge & Kegan Paul.

Ashenden, D. (1990). Award re-structuring and productivity in the future of schooling. *Victorian Institute for Educational Research Bulletin,* No. 64, 3–32.

Aungles, S., & Parker, S. (1988). *Work, organization and change; Themes and perspectives in Australia.* Sydney: Allen & Unwin.

Ball, S., & Goodson, I. (Eds.). (1985). *Teachers' lives and careers.* Lewes, UK: Falmer.

Bernstein, B. (1977). *Class, codes and control* (2nd ed.; Vol. 3). Henley, UK: Routledge & Kegan Paul.

Berry, B. (1988). Creating lead teachers: A policy alternative for rewarding talented teachers. Columbia: South Carolina Educational Policy Center, University of South Carolina.

Bigelow, W. (1990). Inside the classroom: Social vision and critical pedagogy. *Teachers College Record, 91*(3), 437–448.

Braverman, H. (1974). *Labor and monopoly capital: The degradation of work in the twentieth century.* New York: Monthly Review Press.

Brecher, J. (1978). Uncovering the hidden history of the American workplace. *Review of Radical Political Economics, 10*(4), 1–23.

Burawoy, M. (1979). *Manufacturing consent: Changes in the labor process under monopoly capitalism.* Chicago: University of Chicago Press.

Burawoy, M. (1985). *The politics of production: Factory regimes under capitalism and socialism.* London: Verso.

Carlson, D. (1987). Teachers as political actors. *Harvard Educational Review, 57*(3), 293–306.

Carnegie Forum on Education and the Economy. (1986). *A nation prepared: Teachers for the 21st century* (Report of the Task Force on Teaching as a Profession). New York: Carnegie Corporation.

Connell, R. (1985). *Teachers' work.* Sydney: George Allen & Unwin.

Demaine, J. (1988). Teachers' work, curriculum and the New Right. *British Journal of Sociology of Education, 9*(3), 247–264.

Denscombe, M. (1980). The work context of teaching: An analytic framework for the study of teachers in classrooms. *British Journal of Sociology of Education, 11*(3), 278–292.

Edwards, R. (1979). *Contested terrain.* New York: Basic Books.

Ginsburg, M. (1988). Educators as workers and political actors in Britain and North America. *British Journal of Sociology of Education, 9*(3), 359–367.

Gitlin, A. (1983). School structure and teachers' work. In M. Apple & L. Weiss (Eds.), *Ideology and practice in schooling* (pp. 193–212). Philadelphia: Temple University Press.

Grimmett, P. (1990). Teacher development and the culture of collegiality—Part 2. *The Australian Administrator, 11*(6), 1–5.

Hargreaves, A. (1982). The rhetoric of school-centred innovation. *Journal of Curriculum Studies, 14*(3), 251–266.

Hargreaves, A. (1989, April). *Teachers' work and the politics of time and space.* Paper presented to the annual meeting of the American Educational Research Association, San Francisco.

Hargreaves, A. (1990). *Contrived collegiality: A sociological analysis.* Paper presented to the 12th meeting of the International Sociological Association, Madrid.

Hargreaves, A. (1994). *Changing teachers; Changing times, teachers' work and culture in the postmodern age.* London: Cassell.

Hargreaves, A., & Dawe, R. (1989). *Paths of professional development: Contrived collegiality, collaborative culture and the case of peer coaching.* Unpublished manuscript, Ontario Institute for Studies in Education, Toronto.

Harris, K. (1979). *Education and knowledge: The structured misrepresentation of knowledge.* London: Routledge & Kegan Paul.

Harris, K. (1982). *Teachers and classes: A Marxist analysis.* Sydney: Routledge & Kegan Paul.

Harris, K. (1990a). Empowering teachers: Towards a justification for intervention. *Journal of Philosophy of Education, 24*(2), 171–183.

Harris, K. (1990b). Teachers and proletarianization: A reply to Lauder and Yee. *Australian Journal of Education, 34*(2), 192–203.

Harris, K. (1990c). Teachers: Really taking control of schools. *Education Links, 38,* 21–25.

Hartley, D. (1985). Bureaucracy and professionalism: The new 'hidden curriculum' for teachers in Scotland. *Journal of Education for Teaching, 11*(2), 107–119.

Hartley, D. (1986). Structural isomorphism and the management of consent in education. *Journal of Education Policy, 1*(3), 229–237.

Hatton, E. (1987). Determinants of teacher work: Some causal complications. *Teaching and Teacher Education, 3,* 55–60.

Hatton, E. (1988). Teachers' work as bricolage: Implications for teacher education. *British Journal of Sociology of Education, 9*(3), 337–357.

Hatton, E. (1991). Teachers' work and teacher education. *Discourse: The Australian Journal of Educational Studies, 12*(1), 124–139.

Hoetker, J., & Ahlbrand, W. (1969). The persistence of recitation. *American Educational Research Journal, 6*(2), 145–167.

Jackson, P. (1990). *Life in classrooms.* New York: Teachers College Press. (Original work published 1968)

Joyce, P. (Ed.). (1987). *The historical meaning of work.* Cambridge, UK: Cambridge University Press.

Knights, D., & Willmott, H. (Eds.). (1990). *Labour process theory.* London: Macmillan.

Knights, D., Willmott, H., & Collinson, D. (Eds.). (1985). *Job re-design: Critical perspectives on the labour process.* Aldershot, UK: Gower.

Larson, M. (1980). Proletarianization and educated labour. *Theory and Society, 9*(2), 131–175.

Lawn, M. (1988). Skill in schoolwork: Work relations in the primary school. In J. Ozga (Ed.), *Schoolwork: Approaches to the labour process of teaching* (pp. 161–176). Milton Keynes, UK: Open University Press.

Lawn, M., & Ozga, J. (1981). The educational worker: A re-assessment of teachers. In M. Lawn & L. Barton (Eds.), *Schools, Teachers and Teaching* (pp. 45–64). London: Falmer.

Lawn, M., & Ozga, J. (1986). Unequal partners: Teachers under indirect rule. *British Journal of Sociology of Education, 7*(2), 225–238.

Lawn, M., & Ozga, J. (1988). The educational worker? A reassessment of teachers. In J. Ozga (Ed.), *Schoolwork: Approaches to the labour process of teaching* (pp. 81–98). Milton Keynes, UK: Open University Press.

Liston, D., & Zeichner, K. (1991). *Teacher education and the social conditions of schooling.* New York: Routledge.

Little, J. (1987). Teachers as colleagues. In V. Koehler (Ed.), *Educators' handbook: A research perspective* (pp. 491–518). New York: Longman.

Littler, C. (1982). *The development of the labour process in capitalist societies.* London: Heinemann.

Miles, M. (1969). Planned change and organizational health: Figure and ground. In F. Carver & T. Sergiovanni (Eds.), *Organizations and human behvior: Focus on schools* (pp. 375–391). New York: McGraw-Hill.

National Curriculum Council. (1989). *A framework for the primary curriculum.* York, UK: National Curriculum Council.

Nias, J., Southworth, G., & Yeomans, R. (1989). *Staff relationships in the primary school: A study of organizational cultures.* London: Cassell.

O'Neil, J. (1990). Piecing together the restructuring puzzle. *Educational Leadership, 47*(7), 4–10.

Ozga, J. (Ed.). (1988). *Schoolwork: An introduction to the labour process of teaching.* Milton Keynes, UK: Open University Press.

Ozga, J., & Lawn, M. (1988). Schoolwork: interpreting the labour process of teaching. *British Journal of Sociology of Education, 9*(3), 323–336.

Popkewitz, T., & Lind, K. (1989). Teacher incentives as reforms: Teachers' work and the changing control mechanisms in education. *Teachers College Record, 90*(4), 575–594.

Pratte, R., & Rury, J. (1988). Professionalism, autonomy and teachers. *Educational Policy, 2*(1), 71–89.

Ryan, C. (1991, September). *"She'll be right mate": The empowerment of a beginning teacher in a turbulent society.* Paper presented to the annual conference of the Australian Council for Educational Administration, Goldcoast, Queensland.

Sachs, J., & Smith, R. (1988). Constructing teacher culture. *British Journal of Sociology of Education, 9*(4), 423–436.

Salaman, G. (1986). *Working.* Chichester, UK: Ellis Horwood.

Seddon, T. (1988). The transition in New South Wales schooling: From federation to Keynesian settlement. *Education Research and Development, 15*(1), 60–69.

Seddon, T. (1990). Who says teachers don't work? *Education Links, 38,* 4–9.

Seddon, T., & Connell, R. (1989). Teachers' work. In T. Husen & T. Posthlewaite (Eds.), *The International Encyclopedia of Education* (Suppl. Vol. 1, pp. 740–744). Oxford: Pergamon.

Shor, I. (1980). Extraordinarily re-experiencing the ordinary: An approach to critical teaching. *New Political Science,* Winter, 37–56.

Simon, R. (1988). For a pedagogy of possibility. *Critical Pedagogy Networker, 1*(1), 1–4.

Smyth, J. (1989). A critical pedagogy of classroom practice. *Journal of Curriculum Studies, 21*(6), 483–502.

Smyth, J. (1991a). International perspectives on teacher collegiality: A labour process discussion based on teachers' work. *British Journal of Sociology of Education, 12*(4), 323–346.

Smyth, J. (1991b). Professional development and the re-structuring of teachers' work: The case of teacher collegiality. *Unicorn,* 17(4), 224–232.

Smyth, J. (1991c). *Teachers as collaborative learners: Challenging dominant forms of supervision.* London: Open University Press.

Smyth, J. (1992). *Advanced skills teachers and a labour process analysis of teachers' work.* Proposal to the Australian Research Council, Department of Employment, Education and Training, Canberra.

Stevens, P. (1987). Political education and political teachers. *Journal of Philosophy of Education, 21*(1), 75–83.

Thompson, P. (1983). *The nature of work: An introduction to debates on the labour process.* London: Macmillan.

Thompson, P., & McHugh, D. (1990). *Work organizations: A critical introduction.* London: Macmillan.

Tipton, F. (1985). Educational organizations as workplaces. *British Journal of Sociology of Education, 6*(1), 35–53.

White, J., & White, P. (1986). Teachers as political activists. In A. Hartnett & M. Naish (Eds.), *Education and society today* (pp. 171–182). London: Falmer.

White, R. (1983). On teachers and proletarianization. *Discourse: The Australian Journal of Educational Studies, 3*(2), 45–57.

Wood, S. (1989). *The transformation of work: Skill, flexibility and the labour process.* Boston: Unwin & Hyman.

Zimbalist, A. (Ed.). (1979). *Case studies on the labour process.* New York: Monthly Review Press.

4

Teacher Learning in the Workplace
Implications for School Reform

MARK A. SMYLIE

In, his recent book, *The Predictable Failure of Educational Reform*, Seymour Sarason (1990) confronts us with a simple yet extraordinarily provocative argument. He contends that we will fail, as we have failed so many times before, to improve schooling for children until we acknowledge the importance of schools not only as places for teachers to work but also as places for teachers to learn. He writes:

> From their inception our public schools have never assigned importance to the intellectual, professional, and career needs of their personnel. However the aims of the schools were articulated, there was never any doubt that schools existed for children. . . . It is virtually impossible to create and sustain over time conditions for productive learning for students when they do not exist for teachers. (pp. 144–145)

Increasingly, attention is being called to those conditions of schools and teachers' work that obstruct instructional improvement and student learning (Buchmann & Schwille, 1983; Feiman-Nemser & Buchmann, 1985; Lieberman & Miller, 1991; Murphy, 1991; Shulman, 1989). Our concern about these conditions lies at the heart of recent efforts to restructure schools and redesign teachers' roles (Carnegie Forum on Education and the Economy, 1986; Darling-Hammond & Berry, 1988; Elmore, 1990; Holmes Group, 1990).

The case for workplace reform proceeds from several different starting points. One point is organizational theory and literature from business and industry that identify institutional and work-role structures that presume to enhance employee productivity (Conley, 1991; Hart, 1990; Little, 1990). Another is ethical arguments for democratization of the workplace and teacher professionalization (Clark & Meloy, 1990; Darling-Hammond, 1988). Yet another starting point is the classroom. Here, workplace reform follows from visions and models of what is presumably required for effective teaching and student learning (Evertson & Murphy, 1992; Hannaway, 1992; Hawley, 1988; Newmann, 1991).

While these starting points have some merit, they ignore a critical issue. If schools are to improve, if instructional opportunities for students are to be markedly better, teachers must teach differently. In order to change practice in significant and worthwhile ways, teachers must not only learn new subject matter and new instructional techniques; they must alter their beliefs and conceptions of practice, their "theories of action" (Argyris & Schön, 1974; Elmore & Sykes, 1992; Richardson, 1990). In order to be successful, there-fore, workplace reform should also proceed from our understanding of how teachers learn and change.

Discourse on workplace reform has been virtually uninformed by theories of adult learning and change. Surprisingly, this literature has been applied infrequently to issues of teacher preservice and inservice education. Its curi-ously sparse application has pointed to improvements in preservice and inser-vice teacher education programs (Burden, 1990; Carter, 1990; Lanier & Little, 1986; Oja, 1991; Sparks & Loucks-Horsley, 1990; Sprinthall & Theis-Sprinthall, 1983). However, few analyses have gone further to suggest how these theories may speak to issues of workplace reform (Levine, 1989; Shulman, 1989).

My purpose in this chapter is to introduce a view of teacher learning in the workplace that is absent in current discussion about teacher professional learning and development and school reform. I step away from the traditional literature on learning to teach and present several theories of adult learning and change in organizations. These theories suggest relationships between specific dimensions of school workplace environments and teacher learning. This discussion is juxtaposed to a related discussion of learning outcomes for teachers. From my review of these theories, I propose what I consider an op-timal model of a school environment that may support teacher learning. I conclude with a brief discussion of the problems associated with implement-ing such a model in practice.

The literature on adult learning and change is voluminous. There are many different and not always compatible perspectives. My discussion is guided necessarily by several premises.

Different theories treat the concepts of "learning" and "environment" differently (Merriam & Caffarella, 1991; see also Schunk, 1991a; Tennant, 1988). Some view learning as a singular, broad-based concept. Others distin-guish different types or levels of learning. Likewise, some theories consider learning environment a vague, single-dimensional concept. Other theories define it according to specific dimensions. A few theories consider *both* learning and environment as multidimensional concepts. It is with this latter group of theories that I am most concerned. If we wish to improve schools as places for teachers to learn, we need to be able to identify those workplace conditions that promote or constrain learning. Furthermore, we need to specify which teacher learning outcomes we wish to promote. We should not assume that all teacher learning is necessarily conducive to promoting student learning and development. I will return to this issue later.

This chapter does not purport to be a comprehensive review of adult learning theory; nor does it claim to be a critical analysis of that theory. In addition, this chapter does not engage several key issues that run throughout this literature. One of these issues is what makes an adult learning theory a theory of adult learning as opposed to a theory of general human learning (Merriam & Caffarella, 1991). Another is whether these theories apply similarly to men and women, to persons of different cultures and ethnicities, and to persons of different ages or at different points of their careers (Boucouvalas & Krupp, 1989; Cytrynbaum & Crites, 1989; Dalton, 1989). Acknowledging possibilities for such variation (and leaving them for others to explore), we begin.

THE LEARNING PROCESS

Across different theories of adult learning, a relatively consistent view of the learning process emerges (Brookfield, 1991; Merriam & Caffarella, 1991). This view reflects Dewey's (1938) model of experiential learning. According to Dewey, learning begins with ambiguous situations that present a dilemma, problem, or felt difficulty for the individual. The individual locates and defines the dilemma and then analyzes alternative solutions. Analysis may involve observation and experimentation that lead to understanding and to a decision to act or not act on a particular solution.

Similarly, Argyris and Schön (1974, 1978) contend that learning in organizations takes place under conditions of surprise or nonroutine circumstances that require heightened attention, experimentation, and determination of the source of problems. Learning occurs as individuals confront and alter taken-for-granted assumptions to reframe problem situations. Jarvis (1987) also argues that the impetus for learning comes from conflict between personal "biography" and current experience. Conflict may arise from many sources, from daily living to formal, planned learning activities. When conflict is perceived, individuals will seek to reestablish balance by testing and possibly revising their biographies to accommodate new experiences (see also M. R. Louis, 1990; March & Simon, 1958).

Schein's (1969, 1988) model of individual change incorporates this view of the learning process. If change—learning—is to occur, it must be preceded by altering an existing cognitive–psychological equilibrium that supports present behavior and attitudes. Schein calls this alteration "unfreezing." Once equilibrium is challenged and upset, an individual will seek information to resolve the dilemma that is posed. Information may come from personal or impersonal sources in the individual's environment, from a single person or a number of other persons, from a short or prolonged search. Assessment of new information may begin a process of "cognitive redefinition." The individual integrates new information into the "ongoing personality." Integration leads to establishment of a new equilibrium and "refreezing." This process of cognitive redefinition does not usually occur spontaneously. It is influenced by a number of different factors, including the intensity of cognitive discrepancy, the social context, and opportunities for "safe" reconsideration and experimentation with new practice.

These theories reflect a constructivist view of learning (Chapman, 1988; Gold, 1987; Moll, 1990) and suggest several propositions about adult learning in the workplace (Brookfield, 1991; Brundage & Mackeracher, 1980; Darkenwald & Merriam, 1982; Knox, 1977; Smith, 1982). First, adults learn, or have the potential to learn, throughout their lives. Some debate exists about relationships of physiological and neurological aging to learning (Brookfield, 1991; Merriam & Caffarella, 1991) and about relationships between learning and phases or stages of adult cognitive, psychological, and career development (Boucouvalas & Krupp, 1989; Dalton, 1989). Nevertheless, it is generally acknowledged that learning continues throughout adulthood.

Second, adult learning may occur across settings and circumstances (Marsick & Watkins, 1990). For example, adults may learn from formal, collective learning activities planned by others. They may learn from informal, self-initiated, and self-directed activities. They may also learn incidentally and unintentionally from everyday experiences such as task accomplishment and interpersonal interaction (see also Nadler, 1982). Any experience, be it formal or informal, intentional or incidental, individual or collective, has the potential to educate.

Third, adults enter learning situations with accumulated knowledge, skills, and beliefs from past experiences (see Knowles, 1984). Prior knowledge and beliefs may affect current learning by serving as cognitive and normative schemata through which individuals perceive and interpret their situations, new information, and themselves as learners. These schemata may enhance or hinder learning (Moll, 1990).

Fourth, adult learning is problem-oriented and occurs when problems relate in meaningful ways to adults' life situations. This proposition relates directly to the concept of dilemma, disequilibrium, and conflict. It is unlikely that learning will take place unless problems implicate routine practice or taken-for-granted knowledge, beliefs, and assumptions. Problems may emanate from a number of different sources, including individuals' experiences, the social or organizational environments in which they work, or personal curiosity and self-initiated inquiry.

Finally, adults can play an active role in their own learning. They are not merely passive recipients of information. At minimum, the cognitive and normative schemata they carry into learning situations mediate perception and interpretation of those situations. Adults may also be proactive and self-directed in searching for new learning opportunities and resources to apply to those opportunities (Knowles, 1984).

LEARNING OUTCOMES

Several adult learning theories distinguish among different learning outcomes. One of the most detailed taxonomies is presented by Jarvis (1987). It distinguishes nine outcomes:

1. Habitual reaction based on presuppositions
2. Nonconsideration of the situation as a learning opportunity
3. Rejection of new learning
4. Preconscious learning
5. Behavioral change
6. Memorization of new information
7. Contemplation
8. Reflective practice
9. Experimental or scientific inquiry

The first three are nonlearning outcomes. The second three represent nonreflective learning. The last three represent higher-order reflective learning.

Others identify similar types of adult learning outcomes. Merriam and Caffarella (1991), for example, contrast task-specific, instrumental learning outcomes (e.g., Guthrie, 1952; Skinner, 1974; Thorndike, Bregman, Tilton, & Woodyard, 1928) with conceptual, reflective, self-empowering outcomes (e.g., Knowles, 1984; Maslow, 1954; Rogers, 1961). Argyris and Schön (1974, 1978) distinguish proactive, creative, critical, reflective learning from passive, reactive, unreflective learning (see also M. R. Louis, 1990; Marsick & Watkins, 1990; Schön, 1983). Kohn and Schooler (1982, 1983) suggest that learning can result in conformity or intellectual autonomy and flexibility. Finally, Van Maanen and Schein (1979) argue that learning can lead to conformity and perpetuation of work roles or to innovation in the content and conduct of those roles.

Acknowledging that not all outcomes of learning are alike, we confront an important question. If we seek to redesign schools to promote teacher learning, it seems that we should first examine what teacher learning we wish to promote.

In the mid-1980s, a conception of teaching emerged that portrays teaching as a complex, dynamic, interactive, intellectual activity (Carter, 1990; Leinhardt & Greeno, 1986). This view emphasizes comprehension, reasoning, and conceptual transformation (Richardson, 1990; Shulman, 1987). It stresses autonomy and self-directedness in learning and analytical, reflective thought and practice (Schön, 1983; Zeichner & Liston, 1987). It suggests that teacher learning aims to increase personal agency, innovation and creativity, critical analysis and reflection, and teaching "against the grain" (Cochran-Smith, 1991).

These outcomes are promoted not only on the basis of their consistency with this new conceptions of teachers' work. Their value is linked to demands for increased educational productivity (Smylie & Conyers, 1991). These learning outcomes are considered crucial if teachers are to deal with rapid changes in the characteristics, conditions, and learning needs of students and the explosion of subject-matter knowledge and knowledge about teaching and learning (Devaney & Sykes, 1988; Shulman, 1987).

If the teacher learning we wish to promote involves conceptual change, reflective thinking, experimentation, and innovation, how might we best redesign schools to promote these outcomes? I now turn back to theories of adult learning and change to identify relationships between specific aspects of learning environments, particularly workplace environments, and these learning outcomes.

LEARNING ENVIRONMENTS AND OUTCOMES

Most theories of adult learning describe a relationship between learners and their environments (Brookfield, 1991; Merriam & Caffarella, 1991; see also Bolger, Caspi, Downey, & Moorehouse, 1988; Bronfenbrenner, 1979; Lewin, 1935; Schunk, 1991a). Those most germane to this discussion are (1) social learning theory, (2) incidental learning theory, and (3) organizational socialization theory. These related theories address the range of learning outcomes identified above. They also point to specific aspects of workplace environments associated with those outcomes. These theories adopt an interactionist perspective of the relationship between learners and their environments (e.g., Bell & Staw, 1989; M. R. Louis, 1990; Marsick & Watkins, 1990). While mutual influence is an important dimension of these theories, I have chosen to focus primarily on the presumed effects of environments on individual learning.

Social Learning Theory

Social learning theory suggests that much human learning is grounded in social context. In his review, Schunk (1991b) contends that individuals develop knowledge, skills, strategies, beliefs, and attitudes by observing and interacting with others. Individuals also learn the functional value and appropriateness of beliefs, attitudes, and behaviors by assessing the consequences of others' actions as well as the consequences of their own actions. Individuals act, in turn, according to their learned beliefs about expected outcomes and value of actions.

Among the most comprehensive social learning theories is that of Bandura (1977, 1986). His theory is based on several assumptions (see Schunk, 1991b). One assumption is that human learning and functioning are explained in terms of triadic reciprocality. Individual behavior, cognitive and other personal factors, and environmental conditions operate as interacting determinants of one another. A second assumption is that learning can occur either enactively or vicariously. Enactive learning involves learning from doing and the consequences of one's actions. These consequences may act as sources of information and motivation for individuals to assess the likely outcomes of behavior and their own ability to achieve them. Vicarious learning involves observing or listening to others, who serve as models and referents. As with enactive learning, models' actions and consequences inform and motivate individuals' thinking and behavior.

According to Bandura's theory, two constructs mediate learning and behavior. Those constructs are outcome expectations and perceived self-efficacy. Outcome expectations refer to beliefs about relationships between actions and outcomes. Self-efficacy is belief in one's own capacity to organize and implement actions necessary to achieve desired outcomes. Both outcome expectations and self-efficacy beliefs are learned through social interaction and personal experience.

Outcome expectations and perceived self-efficacy function in several ways to influence subsequent learning and performance. According to Bandura (1986), individuals tend to select courses of action (including learning activities) for which they hold positive outcome expectations. They tend to select and sustain courses of action that they believe will result in particular valued outcomes. Perceived self-efficacy functions somewhat differently (see also Schunk, 1984; 1991a). Efficacy can influence an individual's choice of activities as well as task engagement and avoidance. For example, individuals with higher self-efficacy are more likely to select complex and challenging tasks than individuals with lower self-efficacy. They are more likely to take risks, experiment, and be more creative in their learning, thinking, and work. In addition, self-efficacy can influence the amount of effort an individual expends and persistence in task completion. When facing difficulties, persons who feel efficacious are likely to expend greater effort and persist longer than those who do not. Efficacy is considered a domain-specific construct (see Schunk, 1991b; Wylie, 1979). That is, individuals may consider themselves more efficacious in some tasks and subjects than in others.

Bandura (1986) argues that certain conditions in the individual's environment may influence the development of outcome expectations and self-efficacy. Outcome expectations are most readily developed when individuals have opportunities to observe the performances, successes, and failures of others who may serve as performance models. Models may occupy formally designated roles (e.g., mentors); they may be co-workers who serve as informal models. Expectations for what works (and what does not) develop through perceived patterns of others' actions and outcomes. They also develop from one's own experiences. Such enactive learning is enhanced if mechanisms exist for providing individuals specific feedback about performances and consequences.

Like outcome expectations, perceived self-efficacy is developed through both vicarious and enactive learning. Observation of successful models tends to enhance self-efficacy. Self-efficacy is further enhanced if models are similar in status to the individual and are observed coping successfully with similar problems (Schunk, 1991b). Higher-status mastery models are less effective. Development of self-efficacy through enactive learning is promoted through specific feedback related to individual performance and consequences, especially if consequences are successful. Making sense of the relationship between self and the consequences of one's actions is further enhanced by the presence of institutional goals. Individuals are more likely to develop a positive sense of self-efficacy in settings where there are challenging but attainable goals with specific standards against which to measure effort, performance, and accomplishments. The influence of goals is enhanced if they contain proximal as well as distal dimensions, so that individuals may obtain immediate rather than delayed reinforcement of efficacious performance. Similarly, self-efficacy is enhanced if goals are challenging but attainable and if others in the setting provide encouragement that the individual can achieve them.

Several other theories identify related aspects of environments that influence learning. For example, Jarvis (1987) contends that environments characterized by formal, bureaucratic, hierarchical power and authority relationships are more likely to lead to learned conformity in thought and practice. In contrast, settings characterized by egalitarian power and authority relationships increase the likelihood that individuals will feel and be freer to engage in reflective practice and experimental learning. Schein (1969) also suggests that egalitarian or shared power and authority relationships are likely to be associated with innovative thinking and conceptual learning and change. In addition, he suggests that autonomy and choice in work and the presence of multiple performance models encourage these outcomes.

Incidental Learning Theory

Incidental learning is defined as a by-product of some other activity, such as task engagement and accomplishment or interpersonal interaction (Cell, 1984; Marsick & Watkins, 1990; Nadler, 1982). It takes place in everyday experience and occurs without intention, from "doing" and from both successes and mistakes. People may not be conscious of it. Incidental learning differs from formal and informal learning in that it is unplanned and unintentional. Formal learning is typically institutionally sponsored, classroom-based, and highly structured. Informal learning is initiated and often directed by the individual. It may be classroom- or nonclassroom-based, highly or loosely structured; but it is nonetheless intentional.

Incidental learning theories, like other learning theories reviewed here, suggest that learning takes place under conditions of surprise and nonroutine circumstances. Marsick and Watkins (1990) argue that learning from these situations may be mediated two ways (see also March & Simon, 1958). The first is by the characteristics of the situation itself. These characteristics include the nature of the work or specific activity generating the problem, the broader situational context of the problem, and time for task completion and learning. The second is the individual's cognitive capacity to give meaning to the problem; to gather, interpret, and analyze information to apply to the problem; and to develop and select among alternative, potentially effective solutions.

These theories contend that learning is enhanced by the development of specific capacities. Marsick and Watkins (1990), for example, identify three such learning capacities: (1) proactivity, (2) critical reflection, and (3) creativity. Proactivity refers to the learner's cognitive and motivational readiness to confront, interpret, and "solve" problematic situations. Critical reflection refers to the learner's skill in and disposition for examining one's underlying premises, assumptions, and schemata for learning and acting. Finally, creativity refers to thinking beyond the views one generally holds, generating new perspectives, and developing new courses of action. These capacities for learning are considered learning outcomes themselves.

Likewise, Argyris and Schön (1974) identify the capacity for critical reflection as an essential condition for productive learning. Their definition of critical reflection resembles that of Marsick and Watkins (1990)—digging below taken-for-granted assumptions so that the learner can reframe the learning situation. According to Argyris and Schön, critical reflection is essential for the learner to determine more accurately the nature of the problem presented in the learning situation, develop a broader range of possible alternatives, and interpret results of experimentation before deciding upon a solution.

Marsick and Watkins (1990) identify several aspects of workplace environments that relate to proactivity, critical reflection, and creativity. They suggest that proactivity and critical reflection are enhanced by participation in organizational decision making, shared authority and power, and opportunities for collective examination of individual and institutional expectations and beliefs. They suggest further that creativity is enhanced by open communication and group intellectual "play" (e.g., brainstorming, metaphor development). Communication and play are enhanced when participants hold equivalent status positions in the workplace. In this way, ideas are more likely to be considered on their merit rather than on the basis of their originator's status or position.

Argyris and Schön (1974) suggest that similar aspects of workplace environments are conducive to developing critical reflection. They contend that environments characterized by unilateral control, secrecy, and win–lose thinking stifle reflection. Environments with shared authority and power, open communication, and collaborative working relationships stimulate it.

Organizational Socialization Theory

Organizational socialization is the process by which an individual is taught and learns "the ropes" of a particular organization and his or her role in that organization. It is the process by which an individual acquires the social knowledge and skills necessary to assume and perform the role well (Van Maanen & Schein, 1979). This knowledge concerns behavior that is appropriate to work roles and the position of the individual vis-à-vis other individuals and groups (Hart, 1991; Katz & Kahn, 1978; Monane, 1967). It also concerns values, norms, rules, operating procedures, rewards, and sanctions that govern work-role performance and social interaction (Boyan, 1988; M. R. Louis, 1990; Miklos, 1988).

Organizational socialization differs from occupational or professional socialization in that it is related to a specific setting. Organizational socialization may have early and anticipatory elements (Katz & Kahn, 1978). Nevertheless, the greatest influence of socialization seems to occur once the individual enters the organization (Bucher & Stelling, 1977; Guy, 1985; Hart, 1991). Socialization may occur through formal, planned educational programs, through sponsorship (e.g., mentors and other institutionally designated models), and through self-guided, informal experiential, or incidental learning (Van Maanen & Schein, 1979; see also Marsick & Watkins, 1990). The influence of socialization may be greatest and most focused during the initial period of organizational membership. However, socialization continues throughout an individual's membership in the organization as he or she continuously negotiates work roles and social relationships (Hart, 1991; Miklos, 1988). The ongoing nature of organizational socialization makes this perspective meaningful for both beginning and experienced teachers.

A primary mechanism of organizational socialization is everyday experience. Individuals develop an understanding of organizational reality through work-role performance and interaction with co-workers (M. R. Louis, 1990). Like incidental learning, learning from socialization is thought to proceed from perceptions of discrepancy, to search and analysis of new information, to reconceptualization and development of new understanding and meaning. Learning is socially constructed (Bell & Staw, 1989; Berger & Luckmann, 1966; Festinger, 1954; Katz & Kahn, 1978; M. R. Louis, 1990). Peers, supervisors, and other superiors are important socialization agents (Mortimer & Simmons, 1978; see Hart, 1991). Peers control affiliation and sociability. Superiors control evaluation criteria and distribution of rewards. They may also control the nature and demands of an individual's work, which in turn defines specific tasks and task-related experiences, another source of learning.

Several theories of organizational socialization identify aspects of workplaces that are associated with learning. For example, Kohn and Schooler (1982, 1983) contend that certain features of work give rise to learned autonomy or conformity. The greater choice in work and freedom from close supervision an individual has on the job, the more reflective, self-directed, and intellectually flexible the individual will become. Reflection, intellectual flexibility, and self-direction are also enhanced by an individual's experiences with complex, nonroutine, and challenging tasks. On the other hand, the more routine and constraining the work, the more likely individuals are to learn conformity.

Van Maanen and Schein (1979) identify six variable dimensions of organizational socialization processes or experiences. First, persons may have collective learning experiences in groups of like others (e.g., inductees), or they may have individualistic experiences. Second, socialization experiences may be formal, planned, and segregated from everyday work, or they may be informal and integrated with work. Third, socialization experiences may be sequential or random; that is, the organization may denote a specific order of discrete learning experiences, or there may be no known or intended order of those experiences. Fourth, socialization experiences may be fixed in terms of preset time frame for learning to occur. On the other hand, those experiences may be open in that there is no specific time frame in which socialization outcomes can occur. Fifth, socialization may be serial or disjunctive. It may seek to groom individuals, particularly newcomers, to take the place of predecessors in established roles. It may help individuals to perform new work roles where there are no predecessors or models. Finally, socialization may seek individual investiture, to validate personal characteristics persons bring to the organization. Or these experiences may seek divestiture, to deny or strip away certain personal characteristics.

Van Maanen and Schein (1979) relate each of these dimensions to three different learning outcomes: (1) custodial responses, which include conformity to and perpetuation of present work roles; (2) innovation in the content and conduct of present work roles; and (3) change of work roles themselves (see also Jones, 1986). They argue that custodial learning—conformity and perpetuation—is likely to occur when individuals are exposed only to others like themselves. Custodial learning is also likely to occur when learning experiences follow a predetermined sequence of activity, have no specific time frame for completion, groom individuals to assume existing roles, and ask learners to deny certain personal characteristics. Innovation in role content and performance is likely to occur when learning experiences involve a variety of similar and dissimilar others, are separate from everyday work, have fixed time frames but no prescribed order, and relate to new roles or roles with no predecessors or models. Finally, role innovation is likely to occur when learning experiences are individualistic or when individuals learn with a variety of other people. Role innovation is also likely to occur when learning experiences are integrated with daily work, have no prescribed order, relate to new roles, and reaffirm the personal value of the individual in the organization.

Summary of Relationships

This review identifies several specific conditions that may promote learning in the workplace. One of the most salient conditions is opportunities for individuals to work with and learn from others on an ongoing basis. Learning may be enhanced through exposure to a variety of other individuals, particularly those with different knowledge and experiences. Collective learning experiences may provide individuals a greater variety of sources of information and ideas. They may also provide a greater variety of referents for assessing one's own ideas, performance, and needs for learning.

A second condition concerns the nature of collective learning opportunities. These theories emphasize the importance of collaboration in group work and learning. They stress the importance of open communication and examination of taken-for-granted beliefs and assumptions in work and learning. It is thought that open communication and examination of taken-for-granted beliefs and assumptions encourage the free exchange of ideas, which, in turn, promotes critical reflection, creativity and innovation, and self-directed, proactive thinking and learning.

A third related condition concerns the distribution of power and authority in the workplace. Virtually every theory reviewed here stresses the importance of opportunities to work with and learn from others of similar position or status. This condition is related to the presence of shared power and authority and participative decision making in the workplace. Egalitarianism presumably allows more freedom and flexibility for critical thinking and analysis. Ideas and information are more likely, then, to be considered according to their merit rather than according to their sources. This egalitarian view must be qualified with consideration of expertise. Acknowledged expertise and position or formal status are not necessarily equivalent. Individuals may find valuable opportunities to learn from experts, regardless of position or status. They may discount opportunities to learn from more experienced colleagues or those of superior position or status if those individuals do not possess acknowledged and valued expertise.

A final condition of the workplace concerns the nature of individuals' work. Varying aspects of work and creating autonomy and choice in work roles and tasks appear to promote learning. These conditions may increase prospects for dilemmas to arise during the course of daily work. They may also increase the opportunities individuals have for critical reflection, experimentation, and innovation. The presence of challenging but attainable goals and feedback mechanisms may promote self-efficacy and enhance subsequent learning and performance.

IMPLICATIONS FOR REDESIGNING SCHOOLS

These theoretical relationships suggest to me several implications for redesigning schools to promote teacher learning outcomes such as conceptual change, proactivity, critical reflection, experimentation, and innovation. These implications are outlined below as conditions of an optimal school learning environment. Several of the conditions I present are familiar. As I note in the conclusion to this chapter, similar arguments have been made from research on learning to teach and on the workplace conditions of schools. However, what is significant about this chapter is the strength it lends these arguments from the confluence of theories of adult learning and change in organizations with this previous research.

1. *Teacher collaboration.* An optimal school learning environment would provide teachers opportunities to work and learn together. It would provide ongoing, group-oriented activities with shared goals, responsibilities, and flexible agendas. It would promote sharing experiences and open exchange of opinions and ideas. This environment would encourage teachers to jointly identify and solve problems and develop new programs and practices. It would promote examination and critical analysis of current ideas, practices, and taken-

for-granted beliefs and assumptions. Collaboration would not only be encouraged in this environment; it would be publicly rewarded. In addition, opportunities for collaboration would not be confined to traditionally defined groups of teachers within a school (e.g., grade-level teams, subject-area departments, beginning teachers). These opportunities would be designed to cut across such groups when appropriate in order to provide teachers access to others with whom they might not have regular contact or working relationships.

2. *Shared power and authority.* An optimal environment for teacher learning would provide opportunities for teachers and administrators to share power and authority. One way these opportunities would be provided would be through shared leadership and participative decision making. Teachers' participation with administrators in decision making would be authentic, not symbolic. It would be available across decision domains (e.g., curriculum and instruction, staff development, personnel, general administration), even though teachers might not desire to share in decisions in all areas. Shared power and authority would define not only relationships between teachers and administrators but relationships among teachers themselves.

3. *Egalitarianism among teachers.* Egalitarianism in the workplace relates to issues of status as well as of power and authority. Taking a distributive approach to sharing power and authority may reduce positional status distinctions among teachers that may restrict development, exchange, and critical analysis of ideas and practices. However, status extends beyond power and authority to experience and recognized expertise. In an optimal school environment, status distinctions among teachers would be reduced by reciprocity in working and learning relationships. Individual talents and expertise would be identified and organized so everyone with expertise, regardless of position or status, at some time or another serves as a model for others. Hierarchical forms of teacher work redesign (e.g., career ladder, master teacher, and mentor teacher programs) would not serve as the basis of collaboration. These forms of work redesign may expand learning opportunities for some teachers but at the same time may create status distinctions that discourage collaboration and constrain open communication, critical thinking, and innovation among others (see Little, 1990).

4. *Variation, challenge, autonomy, and choice in teachers' work.* There are very few jobs more variant and challenging than classroom teaching. The demands and complexities of teachers' work have been well documented (Doyle, 1986; Lieberman & Miller, 1984; Lortie, 1975; Shulman, 1989). At the same time, routine and repetition exist in the organization of that work (Jackson, 1968; Lieberman & Miller, 1984). An optimal environment would provide variation and challenge in teachers' work through the types of collaborative working and learning relationships and opportunities for participation in decision making described above. Such an environment would cre-

ate additional opportunities for teachers to work outside the classroom. These opportunities might include developing school- and district-level programs and policies, working with parents and community agencies, developing and leading formal staff development activities, and conducting research. Each of these activities would relate in some way to the classroom.

One of the most enduring features of teachers' work is classroom autonomy (Feiman-Nemser & Floden, 1986). On one hand, autonomy may be considered a problematic by-product of the physical and social isolation of teachers and the absence of systematic evaluation and control mechanisms. On the other hand, autonomy may be viewed as an essential condition that permits teachers to meet the constantly changing needs of students through adaptation, experimentation, and innovation in classroom practice (see Lipsky, 1980). The autonomy that would be encouraged in an optimal learning environment would be guided by the joint responsibility and accountability teachers accept when they work collaboratively and share power and authority with others in the workplace.

5. *Organizational goals and feedback mechanisms.* Schools that are optimal learning environments would exhibit clear goals to give work, learning, and innovation direction and meaning. These goals would direct collective and individual activity and serve as referents for performance, outcomes, and learning needs. As suggested earlier, these school goals would be developed jointly. They would be subject to ongoing critical reflection and analysis in collaborative working and learning relationships. Feedback mechanisms would be more informal than formal and more formative and summative. Examination and assessment of practice would be an integral aspect of the collaborative working and learning relationships suggested above. They would also be a key aspect of participative decision making.

6. *Integration of work and learning.* Integration of teachers' learning and work is implicit in each of the conditions presented here. In an optimal workplace environment, learning experiences would arise from and feed back into work experiences. Indeed, learning would be considered part of teachers' work, not an ancillary activity bearing little relation to daily work with students and colleagues.

7. *Accessibility of external sources of learning.* This last condition relates to the concern that groups, like individuals, need access to multiple sources of information for learning and external referents to best assess their performance and accomplishments. The theories reviewed in this chapter suggest strongly that creativity and innovation may be constrained if individuals must rely primarily on enactive learning. Creativity and innovation may also be constrained if individuals have access only to others who share similar information, ideas, and experiences. As individual learning is likely to be enhanced by increased access to information and ideas from a group of colleagues within

a school, so, too, is group learning likely to be enhanced by increased access to information and ideas from resources outside the group. These resources include but are not limited to teachers and administrators from other schools and districts, professional workshops and conferences, university faculty and external consultants, and individuals and agencies in the school's community.

CONCLUSION

This review of adult learning theories reaches conclusions similar those from the learning-to-teach literature (Carter, 1990; Clift, Holland, & Veal, 1990; Richardson, 1990). Grossman (1992), for example, argues that teachers must be able to situate new knowledge and understanding within the specific contexts of their classrooms (see also Feiman-Nemser, 1983). They must also be able to see connections between their learning and their everyday work. Finally, they must be able to resolve tensions between abstract principles and the complexity of classroom practice (Cohen, 1990; Lampert, 1984). Grossman contends further that collegiality is a crucial element in learning to teach. To learn, teachers need feedback on what they are actually doing as they teach. They need to understand fully the rationales and consequences of their actions. Like Shulman (1989), Little (1990), and Feiman-Nemser (1983), she argues that learning with other teachers provides an important source of new ideas and feedback about practice.

The theories on adult learning also cross-validate what teachers tell us about their schools as places for work and learning (e.g., Clift et al., 1990; Smylie, 1989). They also validate empirical evidence of relationships between organizational contexts of schools and teacher learning and change (e.g., Fullan, 1991; Little, 1982, 1984; Rosenholtz, 1989; Smylie, 1988; see also K. S. Louis & Smith, 1990).

While confluence of theory, teachers' perceptions and opinions, and empirical evidence strengthens the case for developing these particular conditions of school environments, we must proceed cautiously. To simply identify workplace conditions conducive to teacher learning is not the same thing as understanding in greater depth the complex, potentially interactive functional relationships of those conditions to learning. It does not shed light on the interactions between the work environment and individual cognitive and psychological states in the learning process. Nor does identification help us understand or accomplish the complex and difficult task of redesigning schools to establish these workplace conditions. Efforts to establish these workplace conditions are likely to implicate prevailing patterns of belief, practice, and working relationships within a school. Both teachers and administrators may have to learn new skills, adopt new attitudes, and develop new working relationships. Thus the process of establishing conditions to promote learning is itself a process of learning.

Organizational theory reminds us of the persistence of organizational forms and processes. Inquiry into the complexities of persistence is at the heart of a growing body of literature now labeled "the new institutionalism" (e.g., March & Olsen, 1984; Powell & DiMaggio, 1991; Searing, 1991). This literature focuses on how the "order" of an organization is maintained through its symbolic systems, routines, habits or conventions, rules, environmental interactions, rewards, incentives, and sanctions. It suggests to us that systemic and persistent long-term efforts may be required to break and reform existing institutional orders in schools. It will not be easy. In the meantime, the theories presented here, in conjunction with teachers' opinions and available empirical evidence, show a direction in which we might work to redesign schools for teacher learning and classroom change.

Acknowledgments. This work was supported in part by the University of Illinois at Chicago's Center for Urban Educational Research and Development. I thank Karen Raino and Ute Tuermer for their assistance in identifying and reviewing much of the literature contained herein. Errors of omission and misinterpretations are mine alone.

REFERENCES

Argyris, C., & Schön, D. A. (1974). *Theory in practice: Increasing professional effectiveness.* San Francisco: Jossey-Bass.

Argyris, C., & Schön, D. A. (1978). *Organizational learning: A theory of action perspective.* San Francisco: Jossey-Bass.

Bandura, A. (1977). *Social learning theory.* Englewood Cliffs, NJ: Prentice-Hall.

Bandura, A. (1986). *Social foundations of thought and action: A social cognitive theory.* Englewood Cliffs, NJ: Prentice-Hall.

Bell, N. E., & Staw, B. M. (1989). People as sculptors versus sculpture: The roles of personality and personal control in organizations. In M. B. Arthur, D. T. Hall, & B. S. Lawrence (Eds.), *Handbook of career theory* (pp. 232–251). New York: Cambridge University Press.

Berger, P., & Luckmann, T. (1966). *The social construction of reality: A treatise in the sociology of knowledge.* Garden City, NY: Doubleday.

Bolger, N., Caspi, A., Downey, G., & Moorehouse, M. (1988). Development in context: Research perspectives. In N. Bolger, A. Caspi, G. Downey, & M. Moorehouse (Eds.), *Persons in context: Developmental processes* (pp. 1–24). New York: Cambridge University Press.

Boucouvalas, M., & Krupp, J. A. (1989). Adult development and learning. In S. B. Merriam & P. M. Cunningham (Eds.), *Handbook of adult and continuing education* (pp. 183–200). San Francisco: Jossey-Bass.

Boyan, N. J. (1988). Describing and explaining administrative behavior. In N. J. Boyan (Ed.), *Handbook of research on educational administration* (pp. 77–97). New York: Longman.

Bronfenbrenner, U. (1979). *The ecology of human development.* Cambridge, MA: Harvard University Press.

Brookfield, S. D. (1991). *Understanding and facilitating adult learning.* San Francisco: Jossey-Bass.

Brundage, D. H., & Mackeracher, D. (1980). *Adult learning principles and their application to program planning.* Toronto: Ministry of Education.

Bucher, R., & Stelling, J. G. (1977). *Becoming professional.* Beverly Hills, CA: Sage.

Buchmann, M., & Schwille, J. (1983). Education: The overcoming of experience. *American Journal of Education, 92,* 30–51.

Burden, P. R. (1990). Teacher development. In W. R. Houston (Ed.), *Handbook of research on teacher education* (pp. 311–328). New York: Macmillan.

Carnegie Forum on Education and the Economy (1986). *A nation prepared: Teachers for the 21st century.* New York: Author.

Carter, K. (1990). Teachers' knowledge and learning to teach. In R. W. Houston (Ed.), *Handbook of research on teacher education* (pp. 291–310). New York: Macmillan.

Cell, E. (1984). *Learning to learn from experience.* Albany: State University of New York Press.

Chapman, M. (1988). *Constructive evolution: Origins and development of Piaget's thought.* New York: Cambridge University Press.

Clark, D. L., & Meloy. J. M. (1990). Recanting bureaucracy: A democratic structure for leadership in schools. In A. Lieberman (Ed.), *Schools as collaborative cultures: Creating the future now* (pp. 3–23). New York: Falmer.

Clift, R. T., Holland, P. E., & Veal, M. L. (1990). School context dimensions that affect staff development. *Journal of Staff Development, 11*(1), 34–38.

Cochran-Smith, M. (1991). Learning to teach against the grain. *Harvard Educational Review, 61,* 279–310.

Cohen, D. K. (1990). A revolution in one classroom: The case of "Mrs. Oublier." *Educational Evaluation and Policy Analysis, 12,* 512–532.

Conley, S. (1991). Review of research on teacher participation in school decision making. *Review of Research in Education, 17,* 225–266.

Cytrynbaum, S., & Crites, J. O. (1989). The utility of adult development theory in understanding career adjustment process. In M. B. Arthur, D. T. Hall, & B. S. Lawrence (Eds.), *Handbook of career theory* (pp. 66–88). New York: Cambridge University Press.

Dalton, G. W. (1989). Developmental views of careers in organizations. In M. B. Arthur, D. T. Hall, & B. S. Lawrence (Eds.), *Handbook of career theory* (pp. 89–109). New York: Cambridge University Press.

Darkenwald, G. G., & Merriam, S. B. (1982). *Adult education: Foundations of practice.* New York: Harper & Row.

Darling-Hammond, L. (1988). Policy and professionalism. In A. Lieberman (Ed.), *Building a professional culture in schools* (pp. 55–77). New York: Teachers College Press.

Darling-Hammond, L., & Berry, B. (1988). *The evolution of teacher policy* (Report No. JRE-01). Santa Monica, CA: Rand.

Devaney, K., & Sykes, G. (1988). Making a case for professionalism. In A. Lieberman (Ed.), *Building a professional culture in schools* (pp. 3–22). New York: Teachers College Press.

Dewey, J. (1938). *Experience and education.* New York: Collier.

Doyle, W. (1986). Classroom organization and management. In M. C. Wittrock (Ed.), *Handbook of research on teaching* (3rd ed.; pp. 392–431). New York: Macmillan.

Elmore, R. F. (Ed.). (1990). *Restructuring schools: The next generation of educational reform.* San Francisco: Jossey-Bass.

Elmore, R. F., & Sykes, G. (1992). Curriculum policy. In P. W. Jackson (Ed.), *Handbook of research on curriculum* (pp. 185–215). New York: Macmillan.

Evertson, C. M., & Murphy, J. (1992). Beginning with classrooms: Implications for restructuring schools. In H. H. Marshall (Ed.), *Redefining student learning: Roots of educational change* (pp. 293–320). Norwood, NJ: Ablex.

Feiman-Nemser, S. (1983). Learning to teach. In L. S. Shulman & G. Sykes (Eds.), *Handbook of teaching and policy* (pp. 150–170). New York: Longman.

Feiman-Nemser, S., & Buchmann, M. (1985). Pitfalls of experience in teacher preparation. *Teachers College Record, 87,* 53–65.

Feiman-Nemser, S., & Floden, R. E. (1986). The cultures of teaching. In M. C. Wittrock (Ed.), *Handbook of research on teaching* (3rd ed.; pp. 505–526). New York: Macmillan.

Festinger, L. (1954). A theory of social comparison processes. *Human Relations, 7,* 114–140.

Fullan, M. (1991). *The new meaning of educational change* (2nd ed.). New York: Teachers College Press.

Gold, R. (1987). *The description of cognitive development.* Oxford: Clarendon Press.

Grossman, P. L. (1992). Teaching to learn. In A. Lieberman (Ed.), *The changing contexts of teaching* (91st Yearbook of the National Society for the Study of Education, Part I; pp. 179–196). Chicago: University of Chicago Press.

Guthrie, E. R. (1952). *The psychology of learning* (rev. ed.). New York: Harper & Row.

Guy, M. E. (1985). *Professional in organizations: Debunking a myth.* New York: Praeger.

Hannaway, J. (1992). Higher order skills, job design, and incentives: An analysis and proposal. *American Educational Research Journal, 29,* 3–21.

Hart, A. W. (1990). Work redesign: A review of literature for education reform. In S. B. Bacharach (Ed.), *Advances in research and theories of school management and educational policy* (Vol. I; pp. 31–69). New Haven, CT: JAI Press.

Hart, A. W. (1991). Leader succession and socialization. *Review of Educational Research, 61,* 451–474.

Hawley, W. D. (1988). Missing pieces of the educational reform agenda: Or, why the first and second waves may miss the boat. *Educational Administration Quarterly, 24,* 416–437.

Holmes Group. (1990). *Tomorrow's schools.* East Lansing, MI: Author.

Jackson, P. W. (1968). *Life in classrooms.* New York: Holt, Rinehart & Winston.

Jarvis, P. (1987). *Adult learning in social context.* London: Croom Helm.

Jones, G. R. (1986). Socialization tactics, self-efficacy, and newcomers' adjustments to organizations. *Academy of Management Journal, 29,* 262–279.

Katz, D., & Kahn, R. L. (1978). *The social psychology of organizations* (2nd ed.). New York: Wiley.

Knowles, M. S. (1984). *The adult learner: A neglected species* (3rd ed.). Houston: Gulf.

Knox, A. B. (1977). *Adult development and learning: A handbook on individual growth and competence in the adult years.* San Francisco: Jossey-Bass.

Kohn, M. L., & Schooler, C. (1982). Job conditions and personality: A longitudinal assessment of reciprocal effects. *American Journal of Sociology, 87,* 1257–1286.

Kohn, M. L., & Schooler, C. (1983). *Work and personality: An inquiry into social stratification.* Norwood, NJ: Ablex.

Lampert, M. (1984). Teaching about thinking and thinking about teaching. *Journal of Curriculum Studies, 16*(1), 1–18.

Lanier, J. E., & Little, J. W. (1986). Research on teacher education. In M. W. Wittrock (Ed.), *Handbook of research on teaching* (3rd ed.; pp. 527–569). New York: Macmillan.

Leinhardt, G., & Greeno, J. G. (1986). The cognitive skill of teaching. *Journal of Educational Psychology, 78*(2), 75–95.

Levine, S. L. (1989). *Promoting adult growth in schools.* Boston: Allyn & Bacon.

Lewin, K. (1935). *A dynamic theory of personality.* New York: McGraw-Hill.

Lieberman, A., & Miller, L. (1984). *Teachers, their world, and their work.* Alexandria, VA: Association for Supervision and Curriculum Development.

Lieberman, A., & Miller, L. (1991). Revisiting the social realities of teaching. In A. Lieberman & L. Miller (Eds.), *Staff development for education in the '90s* (2nd ed.; pp. 92–109). New York: Teachers College Press.

Lipsky, M. (1980). *Street-level bureaucracy.* New York: Russell Sage Foundation.

Little, J. W. (1982). Norms of collegiality and experimentation: Workplace conditions of school success. *American Educational Research Journal, 19,* 325–340.

Little, J. W. (1984). Seductive images and organizational realities in professional development. *Teachers College Record, 86,* 84–102.

Little, J. W. (1990). The mentor phenomenon and the social organization of teaching. *Review of Research in Education, 16,* 297–351.

Lortie, D. C. (1975). *Schoolteacher.* Chicago: University of Chicago Press.

Louis, K. S., & Smith, B. (1990). Teaching working conditions. In P. Reyes (Ed.), *Teachers and their workplace: Commitment, performance, and productivity* (pp. 23–47). Newbury Park, CA: Sage.

Louis, M. R. (1990). Acculturation in the workplace: Newcomers as lay ethnographers. In B. Schneider (Ed.), *Organizational climate and culture* (pp. 85–129). San Francisco: Jossey-Bass.

March, J. G., & Olsen, J. P. (1984). The new institutionalism: Organizational factors in political life. *American Political Science Review, 78,* 734–749.

March, J. G., & Simon, H. (1958). *Organizations.* New York: Wiley.

Marsick, V. J., & Watkins, K. (1990). *Informal and incidental learning in the workplace.* New York: Routledge.

Maslow, A. H. (1954). *Motivation and personality.* New York: Harper & Row.

Merriam, S. B., & Caffarella, R. S. (1991). *Learning in adulthood.* San Francisco: Jossey-Bass.

Miklos, E. (1988). Administrator selection, career patterns, succession, and socialization. In N. J. Boyan (Ed.), *Handbook of research on educational administration* (pp. 53–76). New York: Longman.

Moll, L. C. (Ed.). (1990). *Vygotsky and education: Instructional implications of sociohistorical psychology.* New York: Cambridge University Press.

Monane, J. H. (1967). *A sociology of human systems.* New York: Appleton-Century-Crofts.

Mortimer, J. T., & Simmons, R. G. (1978). Adult socialization. *Annual Review of Sociology, 4,* 421–454.

Murphy, J. (1991). *Restructuring schools: Capturing and assessing the phenomena.* New York: Teachers College Press.

Nadler, L. (1982). *The critical events training model.* San Francisco: Jossey-Bass.

Newmann, F. M. (1991). Linking restructuring to authentic student achievement. *Phi Delta Kappan, 72,* 458–463.

Oja, S. (1991). Adult development: Insights on staff development. In A. Lieberman & L. Miller (Eds.), *Staff development for education in the '90s* (2nd ed.; pp. 37–60). New York: Teachers College Press.

Powell, W. W., & DiMaggio, P. J. (Eds.). (1991). *The new institutionalism in organizational analysis.* Chicago: University of Chicago Press.

Richardson, V. (1990). Significant and worthwhile change in teaching practice. *Educational Researcher, 19*(7), 10–18.

Rogers, C. (1961). *On becoming a person.* Boston: Houghton Mifflin.

Rosenholtz, S. J. (1989). *Teachers' workplace: The social organization of schools.* New York: Longman.

Sarason, S. B. (1990). *The predictable failure of educational reform.* San Francisco: Jossey-Bass.

Schein, E. H. (1969). The mechanisms of change. In W. G. Bennis, K. D. Benne, & R. Chin (Eds.), *The planning of change* (2nd ed., pp. 98–107). New York: Holt, Rinehart & Winston.

Schein, E. H. (1988). *Organizational culture and leadership.* San Francisco: Jossey-Bass.

Schön, D. A. (1983). *The reflective practitioner.* New York: Basic Books.

Schunk, D. H. (1984). Self-efficacy perspective on achievement behavior. *Educational Psychologist, 19,* 48–58.

Schunk, D. H. (1991a). *Learning theories: An educational perspective.* New York: Merrill.

Schunk, D. H. (1991b). Self-efficacy and academic motivation. *Educational Psychologist, 26,* 207–231.

Searing, D. D. (1991). Roles, rules, and rationality in the new institutionalism. *American Political Science Review, 85,* 1239–1260.

Shulman, L. S. (1987). Knowledge and teaching: Foundations of the new reform. *Harvard Educational Review, 52,* 1–22.

Shulman, L. S. (1989). Teaching alone, learning together: Needed agendas for the new reforms. In T. J. Sergiovanni & J. H. Moore (Eds.), *School for tomorrow: Directing reforms to issues that count* (pp. 166–187). Boston: Allyn & Bacon.

Skinner, B. F. (1974). *About behaviorism.* New York: Knopf.

Smith, R. M. (1982). *Learning how to learn: Applied learning theory for adults.* New York: Cambridge Books.

Smylie, M. A. (1988). The enhancement function of staff development: Organizational and psychological antecedents to individual teacher change. *American Educational Research Journal, 25,* 1–30.

Smylie, M. A. (1989). Teachers' views of the effectiveness of sources of learning to teach. *Elementary School Journal, 89,* 543–558.

Smylie, M. A., & Conyers, J. G. (1991). Changing conceptions of teaching influence the future of staff development. *Journal of Staff Development, 12*(1), 12–16.

Sparks, D., & Loucks-Horsley, S. (1990). Models of staff development. In W. R. Houston (Ed.), *Handbook of research on teacher education* (pp. 234–250). New York: Macmillan.

Sprinthall, N. A., & Theis-Sprinthall, L. (1983). The teacher as an adult learner: A cognitive-developmental view. In G. A. Griffin (Ed.), *Staff development* (82nd Yearbook of the National Society for the Study of Education, Part II; pp. 13–35). Chicago: University of Chicago Press.

Tennant, M. (1988). *Psychology and adult learning.* New York: Routledge.

Thorndike, E. L., Bregman, E. O., Tilton, J. W., & Woodyard, E. (1928). *Adult learning.* New York: Macmillan.

Van Maanen, J., & Schein, E. H. (1979). Toward a theory of organizational socialization. In B. M. Staw (Ed.), *Research in organizational behavior* (Vol. 1; pp. 209–264). Greenwich, CT: JAI Press.

Wylie, R. C. (1979). *The self-concept* (Vol. 2). Lincoln: University of Nebraska Press.

Zeichner, K. M., & Liston, D. P. (1987). Teaching student teachers to reflect. *Harvard Educational Review, 57,* 23–48.

5

Professional Development in Education

In Search of the Optimal Mix

THOMAS R. GUSKEY

Although schooling can have a powerful impact on both students and teachers, that impact is not always positive. It has been noted, for example, that while 85% of kindergarten children are considered "creative," by second grade only 10% are considered so. Similarly, 80% of students entering first grade say they feel good about themselves, but by sixth grade only 20% say they do, and by high school that number has dropped to only 5% (Barth, 1991). Sobering figures such as these have led to loud calls for reform.

In the case of teachers, nearly all are confident and highly optimistic when they first enter the classroom. But within a relatively short time the unforeseen physical and emotional demands of teaching begin to take their toll (Jackson, 1968; Pajack & Blase, 1989). During their first two years of teaching, most beginning teachers experience a severe decline in their hopefulness and enthusiasm. They become increasingly pessimistic about their impact on students and more cynical about the effectiveness of the educational process (Harris & Associates, 1992). Oddly, these sobering figures go largely unnoticed.

Are consequences such as these for students and teachers inevitable, or can they be avoided? What factors cause these changes, and can they be altered? In the case of students, researchers seem to have clear ideas about what ought to be done to remedy the situation. Several have outlined specific guidelines on how learning experiences should be structured and classrooms organized to curb these negative effects (Floden, Porter, Schmidt, Freeman, & Schwille, 1981; Resnick, 1985, 1987; Rogers & Kimpston, 1992; Shuell, 1986). But in the case of teachers, few definitive plans have been forthcoming.

There is, of course, the suggestion that we must significantly alter the process by which teachers are prepared for classroom responsibilities. Recent investigations have helped to shed new light on what can be accomplished prior to classroom experience (Huberman, 1983, 1985) and how to better prepare teachers for the many uncertainties of teaching (Floden & Clark, 1988). But while improvements in teacher preparation are undoubtedly needed, that alone is unlikely to be sufficient. It may be that we expect too much from preservice training. Perhaps, as Ryan (1970) suggests, preservice education for teachers is too short and has too many built-in limitations to accomplish the awesome task of adequately preparing new teachers for the demands of the classroom.

To overcome these problems we need to look beyond the shortcomings of preservice teacher training and consider the structure of all forms of professional development in education. We need to address questions such as: What types of professional development experiences are most needed by modern educators? How are these experiences best planned, organized, and carried out? What impact can they, or should they, be expected to have? These questions are the focus of this chapter.

I begin with a description of the typical professional development experiences of beginning teachers. The inadequacies of these experiences are outlined, along with suggestions for improvement. Next, I turn to a series of guidelines for more effective professional development, drawn principally from the research on individual and organizational change. Finally, the potential impact of implementing these guidelines is explored.

EARLY PROFESSIONAL DEVELOPMENT EXPERIENCES

Although recently developed induction and internship programs have altered things somewhat (Burden, 1990), the professional development experiences of beginning teachers have remained much the same for the past three or four decades. The first postgraduate professional training in which most new teachers engage is a general orientation to the school or school district that has hired them. This training usually consists of a series of meetings in which new teachers are acquainted with district programs and policies, testing or assessment requirements, school schedules, payroll plans, and insurance policies. Issues related to curriculum, instruction, or classroom management are rarely discussed.

As the beginning of the school year approaches, they are required to attend a districtwide staff development meeting where the superintendent offers greetings, new staff members are introduced, and a motivational speaker entertains them for an hour or so. Later that day there are school-, department-, and grade-level meetings, followed by opportunities for them to organize their classrooms, prepare class lists, and decorate bulletin boards.

After two or three months of struggling with a multitude of management and organizational problems, they are asked to attend another staff development meeting at which a new, "research-based" instructional program is introduced (Guskey, 1992). A brief training session offers several ideas they try with their students in forthcoming weeks. But soon, unexpected problems are encountered, causing them to doubt the program's practical utility and effectiveness. Too embarrassed to admit they are having difficulties, and with no assistance readily available (Lortie, 1975), they abandon implementation efforts and continue their individual struggle to find a "better" way (Porter, 1986).

As the school year draws to a close, they reflect on what was accomplished, reassess the effectiveness of all that was tried, and generally lower their hopes and aspirations to match more closely what they now consider to be the realities of the classroom. Sadly, a large number will have serious doubts about the wisdom of their decision to enter the teaching profession and will begin to explore other career options (Harris & Associates, 1992).

Current efforts to restructure schools might alter this scenario somewhat. But if we are serious about wanting to prevent the negative consequences of these events, it is clear we must reconsider all that is done in the name of professional development in education. We need to reevaluate the way professional development experiences are structured, not only during teachers' early years in the classroom but also throughout their teaching careers. We must design professional development activities to help teachers maintain, or in some cases rediscover, the enthusiasm, hopefulness, and commitment they have for teaching. Moreover, we must find ways to help teachers build and refine their craft skills so that they can make better use of their powerful, and often untapped, influence on students.

FINDING THE OPTIMAL MIX

The problem in trying to identify the critical elements of successful professional development programs is that most efforts focus on a search for "one right answer." They begin by gathering evidence from a variety of studies and evaluations. This evidence is then synthesized to distinguish those characteristics that consistently relate to some measure of effectiveness. In most cases program effectiveness is judged by an index of participants' satisfaction with the program or some indication of change in their professional knowledge. Rarely is change in professional practice considered, and rarer still is any assessment of impact on student learning (Guskey & Sparks, 1991). What typically results are prescriptions of general practices that are described in broad and nebulous terms. Sadly, these prescriptions offer little guidance to practically minded re-formers who want to know precisely what to do and how to do it.

What is neglected in nearly all of these efforts is the powerful impact of *context.* In fact, synthesizing the evidence across studies is done specifically to decontextualize the data. Yet as Clark, Lotto, and Astuto (1984), Firestone and Corbett (1987), Fullan (1985), Huberman and Miles (1984), and others suggest, the uniqueness of the individual setting will always be a critical factor in education. What works in one situation may not work in another. Businesses and industries operating in different parts of the country or in different regions around the world may successfully utilize identical processes to produce the same quality product. But reforms based upon assumptions of uniformity in the educational system repeatedly fail (Elmore & McLaughlin, 1988). The teaching and learning process is a complex endeavor that is embedded in contexts that are highly diverse. This combination of complexity and diversity makes it difficult, if not impossible, for researchers to come up with universal truths (Guskey, 1993).

We know with certainty that reforms in education today succeed to the degree that they adapt to and capitalize on this variability. In other words, they must be shaped and integrated in ways that best suit regional, organizational, and individual contexts: the local values, norms, policies, structures, resources, and processes (Griffin & Barnes, 1984; McLaughlin, 1990; Talbert, McLaughlin, & Rowan, 1993).

Acknowledging the powerful influence of contextual differences shows the futility of the search for "one right answer." Because of the enormous variability in educational contexts, there will never be "one right answer." Instead, there will be a collection of answers, each specific to a context. Our search must focus, therefore, on finding the *optimal mix*—that assortment of professional development processes and technologies that work best in a particular setting.

It is also important to recognize that the optimal mix for a particular setting changes over time. Contexts, like the people who shape them, are dynamic. They change and adapt in response to a variety of influences. Some of these influences may be self-initiated, while others are environmentally imposed. Because of this dynamic nature, the optimal mix for a particular context evolves over time, changing as various aspects of the context change. What works today may be quite different from what worked five years ago, but it also is likely to be different from what will work five years hence.

GUIDELINES FOR SUCCESS

Because of the powerful and dynamic influence of context, it is impossible to make precise statements about the elements of an effective professional development program. Even programs that share a common vision and seek to attain comparable goals may need to follow very different pathways to succeed. The best that can be offered are *procedural guidelines* that appear to be critical to the professional development process. These guidelines are derived from research on professional development specifically and the change process generally (Crandall et al., 1982; Fullan, 1991; Guskey, 1986; Huberman & Miles, 1984; McLaughlin, 1990; Prochaska, DiClemente, & Norcross, 1992). Rather than representing strict requirements, however, these guidelines reflect a framework for developing that optimal mix of professional development processes and technologies that will work best in a specific context at a particular point in time.

In reviewing these guidelines it is important to keep in mind that presently we know far more about professional development processes that fail than we do about those that succeed (Gall & Renchler, 1985; Showers, Joyce, & Bennett, 1987). There is no guarantee, therefore, that following these guidelines will always bring success. Still, substantial evidence indicates that neglecting the issues described in these guidelines at best will limit success and at worst, will result in programs that fail to bring about significant or enduring change.

Recognize Change as Both an Individual *and* Organizational Process

An important lesson learned from the past is that we cannot improve schools without improving the skills and abilities of the teachers within them. In other words, we must see change as an *individual process* and be willing to invest in the intellectual capital of those individuals who staff our schools (Wise, 1991). Success in any improvement effort always hinges on the smallest unit of the organization and, in education, that is the classroom teacher (McLaughlin, 1991). Teachers are the ones chiefly responsible for implementing change. Therefore professional development processes, regardless of their form (D. Sparks & Loucks-Horsley, 1989), must be relevant to teachers and must directly address their specific needs and concerns (Hall & Loucks, 1978; Weatherley & Lipsky, 1977).

At the same time, to see change as *only* an individual process can make professional development an arduous and uncomfortable personal endeavor. Even changes that are empowering bring a certain amount of anxiety. And teachers, like professionals in many fields, are reluctant to adopt new practices or procedures unless they feel sure they can make them work (Lortie, 1975). To change or to try something new means to risk failure, and that is both highly embarrassing and threatening to one's sense of professional pride (Pejouhy, 1990).

Furthermore, it is important to keep in mind that organizations, like individuals, also adopt change (Sarason, 1982; Shroyer, 1990; Waugh & Punch, 1987). To focus exclusively on individuals in professional development efforts, while neglecting factors such as organizational features and system politics, severely limits the likelihood of success (Berman, 1978; Clift, Holland, & Veal, 1990; Deal, 1987; Fullan & Pomfret, 1977; Parker, 1980). A debilitating environment can squash any change effort, no matter how much we exhort individuals to persist (Beane, 1991).

To focus on change as *only* an organizational matter, however, is equally ineffective. Fiddling with the organizational structure is a favorite device of educational policy makers and administrators because it communicates to the public in a symbolic way that they are concerned with the performance of the system. But as Elmore (1992) argues, evidence is scant that such structural change leads in any reliable way to changes in how teachers teach, what they teach, or how students learn. McLaughlin (1990) describes this as the difference between macro-level concerns and micro-level realities. To facilitate change we must look beyond policy structures and consider the embedded structure that most directly affects the actions and choices of the individuals involved.

The key is to find the optimal mix of individual *and* organizational processes that will contribute to success in a particular context. In some situations, individual initiative and motivation might be quite high, but organizational structures stand in the way of significant improvement. In others, progressive and supportive organizational structures may be in place, but the lack of personal incentives for collaboration and experimentation inhibits any meaningful change in classroom practice. Viewing change as both an individual *and* organizational process that must be adapted to contextual characteristics will help clarify the steps necessary for success in professional development.

Think *Big*, but Start *Small*

There is no easier way to sabotage change efforts than to take on too much at one time. In fact, if there is one truism in the vast research literature on change, it is that the magnitude of change persons are asked to make is inversely related to their likelihood of making it (Guskey, 1991). Professionals at all levels generally oppose radical alterations to their present procedures. Hence the probability of their implementing a new program or innovation depends largely on their judgment of the magnitude of change required for implementation (Doyle & Ponder, 1977; Fullan, 1991; Mann, 1978).

Successful professional development programs are those that approach change in a gradual and incremental fashion. Efforts are made to illustrate how the new practices can be implemented in ways that are not too disruptive or require a great deal of extra work (G. M. Sparks, 1983). If a new program does require major changes be made, it is best to ease into its use rather than expect comprehensive implementation at once (Fullan, 1985).

But while the changes advocated in a professional development program must not be so ambitious that they require too much too soon from the implementation system, they need to be sufficient in scope to challenge professionals and kindle interest (McLaughlin, 1990). Crandall, Eiseman, and Louis (1986) argue that the greatest success is likely when the size of the change is not so massive that typical users find it necessary to adopt a coping strategy that seriously distorts the change, but is large enough to require noticeable, sustained effort. Modest, narrowly conceived projects seldom bring about significant improvement. This is what is meant by "think big."

The key, again, is to find the optimal mix. Professional development efforts should be designed with long-term goals based on a grand vision of what is possible. A program might seek to have *all* students become successful learners, for example. At the same time, that vision should be accompanied by a strategic plan that includes specific incremental goals for three to five years into the future, gradually expanding on what is successful in that context and offering support to those engaged in the change (Fullan, 1992; Louis & Miles, 1990).

Work in Teams to Maintain Support

The discomfort that accompanies change is greatly compounded if the individuals involved perceive that they have no say in the process or if they feel isolated and detached in their implementation efforts. For this reason it is imperative that all aspects of a professional development program be fashioned to involve teams of individuals working together. This means that planning, implementation, and follow-up activities should all be seen as joint efforts, providing opportunities for those with diverse interests and responsibilities to offer their input and advice (Massarella, 1980).

To insure that the teams function well and garner broad-based support for professional development efforts, it is important that they involve individuals from all levels of the organization. In school improvement programs, for example, the best professional development teams include teachers, noninstructional staff members, and building and central office administrators (Caldwell & Wood, 1988). In some contexts the involvement of parents and community members also can be helpful (Lezotte, 1989). Although the roles and responsibilities of these individuals in the professional development process will be different, all have valuable insights and expertise to offer.

Still, the notion of teamwork must be balanced. There is evidence to show, for instance, that large-scale participation during the early stages of a change effort is sometimes counterproductive (Huberman & Miles, 1984). Elaborate needs assessments, endless committee and task-force debates, and long and tedious planning sessions often create confusion and alienation in the absence of any action. Extensive planning can also exhaust the energy needed for implementation, so that by the time change is to be enacted, people are burned out (Fullan, 1991). Furthermore, broad-based participation in many decisions is not always essential or possible on a large scale (Dawson, 1981; Hood & Blackwell, 1980). As Little (1989) argues, there is nothing particularly virtuous about teamwork or collaboration per se. It can serve to block change or inhibit progress just as easily as it can serve to enhance the process.

To facilitate change, teamwork must be linked to established norms of continuous improvement and experimentation, and these norms then guide professional development efforts. In other words, there must be a balance of teamwork and collaboration with the expectation that all involved in the process—teachers, administrators, and noninstructional staff members—are constantly seeking and assessing potentially better practices (Little, 1989). Such a balance promotes collegial interaction and acknowledges the naturally occurring relationships among professionals.

The most successful professional development programs, for example, are those that provide regular opportunities for participants to share perspectives and seek solutions to common problems in an atmosphere of collegiality and professional respect (Fullan, Bennett, & Rolheiser-Bennett, 1989; Little, 1982). Working in teams also allows tasks and responsibilities to be shared. This not only reduces the workload of individual team members, it also enhances the quality of the work produced. Additionally, working in teams helps focus attention on the shared purposes and improvement goals that are the basis of the professional development process in that context (Leithwood & Montgomery, 1982; Rosenholtz, 1987; Stevenson, 1987).

Include Procedures for Feedback on Results

If the use of new practices is to be sustained and changes are to endure, the individuals involved need to receive regular feedback on the effects of their efforts. It is well known that successful actions are reinforcing and likely to be repeated while those that are unsuccessful tend to be diminished. Similarly, practices that are new and unfamiliar will be accepted and retained when they are perceived as increasing one's competence and effectiveness. This is especially true of teachers, whose primary psychic rewards come from feeling certain about their capacity to affect student growth and development (Bredeson, Fruth, & Kasten, 1983; Guskey, 1989; Huberman, 1992). New practices are likely to be abandoned, however, in the absence of any evidence of their positive effects. Hence specific procedures to provide feedback on results are essential to the success of any professional development effort.

Personal feedback on results can be provided in a variety of ways, depending on the context. In professional development programs involving the implementation of mastery learning (Bloom, 1968, 1971), for example, teachers receive this feedback through regular formative assessments (Bloom, Madaus, & Hastings, 1981). In mastery learning classrooms, formative assessments are used to provide students with detailed feedback on their learning progress and to diagnose learning problems. As such, they can take many forms, including writing samples, skill demonstrations, projects, reports, performance tasks, or other, more objective assessment devices such as quizzes or tests. These assessments are then paired with corrective activities designed to help students remedy any learning errors identified through the assessment.

But in addition to the feedback they offer students, formative assessments also offer teachers specific feedback on the effectiveness of their application of mastery learning. These regular checks on student learning provide teachers with direct evidence of the results of their teaching efforts. They illustrate what improvements have been made and where problems still exist. This information can then be used to guide revisions in the instructional process so that even greater gains are achieved (Guskey, 1985).

Of course, results from assessments of student learning are not the only type of personal feedback that teachers find meaningful. Brophy and Good (1974) discovered that providing feedback to teachers about their differential treatment of students resulted in significant change in their interactions with students. Information on increased rates of student engagement during class sessions and evidence of improvements in students' sense of confidence or self-worth have also been shown to be powerful in reinforcing the use of new instructional practices (Dolan, 1980; Stallings, 1980). Information from informal assessments of student learning and moment-to-moment responses during instruction can provide a basis for teachers to judge the effectiveness of alternative techniques as well (Fiedler, 1975; Green, 1983; Smylie, 1988).

Yet despite its importance, procedures for gathering feedback on results must be balanced with other concerns. The methods used to obtain feedback, for example, must not be disruptive of instructional procedures. Furthermore, they should not require inordinate amounts of time or extra work from those engaged in the difficult process of implementation. Timing issues are also critical, for it is unfair to expect too much too soon from those involved in implementation. As Loucks-Horsley and colleagues (1987) point out, this is analogous to pulling a plant out of the ground each day to check its roots for growth. In other words, there must be a balance, or optimal mix, in which the need for feedback is adapted to the characteristics of the program and the setting. Feedback procedures must focus on outcomes that are meaningful to the professionals involved, but they must also be timed to best suit program needs and the constraints of the context.

Provide Continued Follow-Up, Support, and Pressure

Few persons can move from a professional development experience directly into implementation with success. In fact, few will even venture into the uncertainty of implementation unless there is an appreciation of the difficulties that are a natural part of the process (Fullan & Miles, 1992). Fitting new practices and techniques to unique on-the-job conditions is an uneven process that requires time and extra effort, especially when beginning (Berman & McLaughlin, 1978; Joyce & Showers, 1980). Guidance, direction, and support with pressure are crucial when these adaptations are being made (Baldridge & Deal, 1975; Fullan, 1991; Parker, 1980; Waugh & Punch, 1987).

What makes the early stages of implementation so complicated is that the problems encountered at this time are often multiple, pervasive, and unanticipated. Miles and Louis (1990) point out that developing the capacity to deal with these problems promptly, actively, and in some depth may be "the single biggest determinant of program success" (p. 60). And regardless of how much advanced planning or preparation takes place, it is when professionals actually implement the new ideas or practices that they have the most specific problems and doubts (Berman, 1978; Fullan & Pomfret, 1977).

Support coupled with pressure at this time is vital for continuation. Support allows those engaged in the difficult process of implementation to tolerate the anxiety of occasional failures. Pressure is often necessary to initiate change among those whose self-impetus for change is not great (Airasian, 1987; Huberman & Crandall, 1983). In addition, it provides the encouragement, motivation, and occasional nudging that many practitioners require to persist in the challenging tasks that are intrinsic to all change efforts.

Of all aspects of professional development, this is perhaps the most neglected. It makes clear that to be successful, professional development must be seen as a *process*, not an event (Loucks-Horsley et al., 1987). Learning to be proficient at something new or finding meaning in a new way of doing things is difficult and sometimes painful. Furthermore, any change that holds great promise for increasing individuals' competence or enhancing an organization's effectiveness is likely to be slow and require extra work (Huberman & Miles, 1984). It is imperative, therefore, that improvement be seen as a continuous and ongoing endeavor (McLaughlin & Marsh, 1978).

If a new program or innovation is to be implemented well, it must become a natural part of practitioners' repertoire of professional skills and built into the normal structures and practices of the organization (Fullan & Miles, 1992; Miles & Louis, 1987). For advances to be made and professional improvements to continue, the new practices and techniques that were the focus of the professional development effort must become used almost out of habit. And for this to occur, continued support and encouragement, paired with subtle pressure to persist, are essential.

This crucial support with pressure can be offered in a variety of ways. McLaughlin and Marsh (1978) recommend that local resource personnel or consultants be available to provide on-line assistance when difficulties arise. They emphasize, however, that the quality of the assistance is critical and that it is better to offer no assistance than poor or inappropriate assistance. Joyce and Showers (1988) suggest that support for change take the form of coaching—providing practitioners with technical feedback, guiding them in adapting the new practices to their unique contextual conditions, helping them to analyze the effects of their efforts, and urging them to continue despite minor setbacks. In other words, coaching is personal, practical, on-the-job assistance that can be provided by consultants, administrators, directors, or professional colleagues. Simply offering opportunities for practitioners to interact and share ideas with one another also can be valuable (Massarella, 1980; McLaughlin & Marsh, 1978).

Here again, the notion of balance is critical. In some contexts a substantial amount of pressure may be necessary to overcome inertia, recalcitrance, or outright resistance (Mann, 1986). It is possible, for example, when making decisions about instructional practices, to overemphasize teachers' personal preferences and underemphasize concern about student learning (Buchmann, 1986). Yet in contexts where there is considerable individual initiative, such pressure may be seen as a strong-arm tactic and unprofessional (Leiter & Cooper, 1978). The key is to find the optimal mix for that context, understanding well the interpersonal dynamics of the individuals involved and the culture of the organization in which they work.

Integrate Programs

More so than any other profession, education seems fraught with innovation. Each year new programs are introduced in schools without any effort to show how they relate to the ones that came before or those that may come afterward. Furthermore, there is seldom any mention of how these various innovations contribute to a growing professional knowledge base. The result is an enormous overload of fragmented, uncoordinated, and ephemeral attempts at change (Fullan & Miles, 1992).

The steady stream of innovations in education causes many practitioners to view all new programs as isolated fads that will soon be gone, only to be replaced by yet another bandwagon (Latham, 1988). Having seen a multitude of innovations come into and go out of fashion, veteran teachers frequently calm the fears of their less experienced colleagues who express concern about implementing a new program with the advice, "Don't worry; this, too, shall pass."

If professional development efforts that focus on the implementation of innovations are to succeed, they must include precise descriptions of how these innovations can be integrated. That is, each innovation must be presented as part of a coherent framework for improvement. It is difficult enough for practitioners to learn the particular features of one innovation, let alone to figure out how it can be combined with others. And because no single innovation is totally comprehensive, implementing only one will leave many problems unresolved. It is only when several strategies are carefully and systematically integrated that substantial improvements become possible. Doyle (1992), Sarason (1990), and others also emphasize that coordinating programs and combining ideas releases great energy in the improvement process.

In recent years several insightful researchers have described how different combinations of innovations can yield impressive results (e.g., Arredondo & Block, 1990; Davidson & O'Leary, 1990; Guskey, 1988, 1990a; Mevarech, 1985; Weber, 1990). In addition, several frameworks for integrating a collection of programs or innovations have been developed that practitioners are finding especially useful. One example is a framework developed by Marzano, Pickering, and Brandt (1990) based on various dimensions of learning. I developed another that is built around five major components in the teaching and learning process (Guskey, 1990b). These frameworks allow skilled practitioners to see more clearly the linkages among various innovations. They also offer guidance to the efforts of seriously minded reformers seeking to pull together programs that collectively address the problems that are most pressing in a particular context.

A crucial point here is that the particular collection of programs or innovations that is best undoubtedly will vary from setting to setting. As a result, the way linkages are established and applications integrated will need to vary as well. Fullan (1992) stresses that, "schools are not in the business of managing single innovations; they are in the business of contending with multiple innovations simultaneously" (p. 19). By recognizing the dimensions of learning a particular innovation stresses or the components of the teaching and learning process it emphasizes, savvy educators can pull together innovations that collectively address what is most needed in that context at a particular point in time.

CONCLUSION

The ideas presented in these procedural guidelines are not new and certainly cannot be considered revolutionary. They may, in fact, appear obvious to those with extensive experience in professional development processes. Yet as self-evident as they may seem, it is rare to find a professional development program today that is designed and implemented with thorough attention to each of these guidelines or the factors that underlie them.

What is evident from these guidelines is that the key to greater success in professional development rests not so much in the discovery of new knowledge, but in our capacity to use deliberately and wisely the knowledge we have. This is true regardless of whether professional development is viewed as an integral part of one's career cycle, as a self-directed journey to find meaning and appreciation in one's work, or as a structured effort to keep professionals abreast of advances in their field. To develop this capacity requires a clear vision of our goals and a thorough understanding of the process by which those goals can be attained.

In the minds of many today there is a clear vision of what would be ideal in professional development. That ideal sees educators at all levels constantly in search of new and better ways to address the diverse learning needs of their students. It sees schools as learning communities where teachers and students are continually engaged in inquiry and stimulating discourse. It sees practitioners in education respected for their professional knowledge and pedagogic skill. The exact process by which that vision can be accomplished, however, is much more blurred and confused. The reason, as argued here, is that the process is so highly contextualized. There is no "one right answer" or "one best way." Rather, there are a multitude of ways, all adapted to the complex and dynamic characteristics of specific contexts. Success, therefore, rests in finding the optimal mix of process elements and technologies that then can be carefully, sensibly, and thoughtfully applied in a particular setting.

While it is true that the ideas presented here offer a very optimistic perspective on the potential of professional development in education, these ideas are not far-fetched. They illustrate that although the process of change is difficult and complex, we are beginning to understand how to facilitate that process through pragmatic adaptations to specific contexts so that ongoing professional growth and improved professional practice are ensured.

REFERENCES

Airasian, P. W. (1987). State mandated testing and educational reform: Context and consequences. *American Journal of Education, 95,* 393–412.

Arredondo, D. E., & Block, J. H. (1990). Recognizing the connections between thinking skills and mastery learning. *Educational Leadership, 47*(5), 4–10.

Baldridge, J. V., & Deal, T. (1975). *Managing change in educational organizations.* Berkeley, CA: McCutchan.

Barth, R. S. (1991). Restructuring schools: Some questions for teachers and principals. *Phi Delta Kappan, 73*(2), 123–128.

Beane, J. A. (1991). Sorting out the self-esteem controversy. *Educational Leadership, 49*(1), 25–30.

Berman, P. (1978). The study of macro- and micro-implementation. *Public Policy, 26*(2), 157–184.

Berman, P., & McLaughlin, M. W. (1978). *Federal programs supporting educational change: Vol. VIII. Implementing and sustaining innovations.* Santa Monica, CA: Rand Corporation.

Bloom, B. S. (1968). Learning for mastery. *Evaluation Comment, 1*(2), 1–12.

Bloom, B. S. (1971). Mastery learning. In J. H. Block (Ed.), *Mastery learning: Theory and practice* (pp. 47–63). New York: Holt, Rinehart & Winston.

Bloom, B. S., Madaus, G. F., & Hastings, J. T. (1981). *Evaluation to improve learning.* New York: McGraw-Hill.

Bredeson, P. V., Fruth, M. J., & Kasten, K. L. (1983). Organizational incentives and secondary school teaching. *Journal of Research and Development in Education, 16,* 24–42.

Brophy, J. E., & Good, T. L. (1974). *Teacher–student relationships: Causes and consequences.* New York: Holt, Rinehart & Winston.

Buchmann, M. (1986). Role over person: Morality and authenticity in teaching. *Teachers College Record, 87,* 529–543.

Burden, P. R. (Ed.). (1990). Teacher induction [entire issue]. *Journal of Staff Development, 11*(4).

Caldwell, S., & Wood, F. (1988). School-based improvement—Are we ready? *Educational Leadership, 46*(2), 50–53.

Clark, D., Lotto, S., & Astuto, T. (1984). Effective schools and school improvement: A comparative analysis of two lines of inquiry. *Educational Administration Quarterly, 20*(3), 41–68.

Clift, R. T., Holland, P. E., & Veal, M. L. (1990). School context dimensions that affect staff development. *Journal of Staff Development, 11*(1), 34–38.

Crandall, D., Eiseman, J., & Louis, K. (1986). Strategic planning issues that bear on the success of school improvement efforts. *Educational Administration Quarterly, 22*(3), 21–53.

Crandall, D. P., Loucks-Horsley, S., Bauchner, J. E., Schmidt, W. B., Eiseman, J. W., Cox, P. L., Miles, M. B., Huberman, A. M., Taylor, B. L., Goldberg, J. A., Shive, G., Thompson, C. L., & Taylor, J. A. (1982). *People, policies, and practices: Examining the chain of school improvement.* Andover, MA: The Network.

Davidson, N., & O'Leary, P. W. (1990). How cooperative learning can enhance mastery teaching. *Educational Leadership, 47*(5), 30–34.

Dawson, J. (1981). *Teacher participation in educational innovation: Some insights into its nature.* Philadelphia: Research for Better Schools.

Deal, T. (1987). The culture of schools. In L. Sheive & M. Schoeheit (Eds.), *Leader-*

ship: Examining the elusive (pp. 3–15). Alexandria, VA: Association for Supervision and Curriculum Development.

Dolan, L. J. (1980). *The affective correlates of home support, instructional quality, and achievement.* Unpublished doctoral dissertation, University of Chicago.

Doyle, D. P. (1992). The challenge, the opportunity. *Phi Delta Kappan, 73*(7), 512–520.

Doyle, W., & Ponder, G. (1977). The practical ethic and teacher decision-making. *Interchange, 8*(3), 1–12.

Elmore, R. F. (1992). Why restructuring alone won't improve teaching. *Educational Leadership, 49*(7), 44–48.

Elmore, R. F., & McLaughlin, M. W. (1988). *Steady work: Policy, practice, and reform in American education* (R-3574-NIE/RC). Santa Monica, CA: Rand Corporation.

Fiedler, M. (1975). Bidirectionality of influence in classroom interaction. *Journal of Educational Psychology, 67*, 735–744.

Firestone, W., & Corbett, H. D. (1987). Planned organizational change. In N. Boyand (Ed.), *Handbook of research on educational administration* (pp. 321–340). New York: Longman.

Floden, R. E., & Clark, C. M. (1988). Preparing teachers for uncertainty. *Teachers College Record, 89*, 505–524.

Floden, R. E., Porter, A. C., Schmidt, W. H., Freeman, D. J., & Schwille, J. R. (1981). Responses to curriculum pressures: A policy-capturing study of teacher decisions about content. *Journal of Educational Psychology, 73*, 129–141.

Fullan, M. G. (1985). Change processes and strategies at the local level. *Elementary School Journal, 85*, 391–421.

Fullan, M. G. (1991). *The new meaning of educational change.* New York: Teachers College Press.

Fullan, M. G. (1992). Visions that blind. *Educational Leadership, 49*(5), 19–20.

Fullan, M. G., Bennett, B., & Rolheiser-Bennett, C. (1989, April). *Linking classroom and school improvement.* Paper presented at the annual meeting of the American Educational Research Association, San Francisco.

Fullan, M. G., & Miles, M. B. (1992). Getting reform right: What works and what doesn't. *Phi Delta Kappan, 73*(10), 745–752.

Fullan, M., & Pomfret, A. (1977). Research on curriculum and instruction implementation. *Review of Educational Research, 27*(2), 355–397.

Gall, M. D., & Renchler, R. S. (1985). *Effective staff development for teachers: A research-based model.* Eugene, OR: ERIC Clearinghouse on Educational Management, University of Oregon.

Green, J. (1983). Research on teaching as a linguistic process: A state of the art. In E. Gordon (Ed.), *Review of research in education* (Vol. 10; pp. 151–252). Washington, DC: American Educational Research Association.

Griffin, G. A., & Barnes, S. (1984). School change: A craft-derived and research-based strategy. *Teachers College Record, 86*, 103–123.

Guskey, T. R. (1985). *Implementing mastery learning.* Belmont, CA: Wadsworth.

Guskey, T. R. (1986). Staff development and the process of teacher change. *Educational Researcher, 15*(5), 5–12.

Guskey, T. R. (1988). Mastery learning and mastery teaching: How they complement each other. *Principal, 68*(1), 6–8.

Guskey, T. R. (1989). Attitude and perceptual change in teachers. *International Journal of Educational Research, 13*(4), 439–453.

Guskey, T. R. (1990a). Cooperative mastery learning strategies. *Elementary School Journal, 91*(1), 33–42.

Guskey, T. R. (1990b). Integrating innovations. *Educational Leadership, 47*(5), 11–15.

Guskey, T. R. (1991). Enhancing the effectiveness of professional development programs. *Journal of Educational and Psychological Consultation, 2*(3), 239–247.

Guskey, T. R. (1992, November). What does it mean to be "research-based"? *The Developer,* p. 5.

Guskey, T. R. (1993, February). Why pay attention to research if researchers can't agree? *The Developer,* pp. 3–4.

Guskey, T. R., & Sparks, D. (1991). What to consider when evaluating staff development. *Educational Leadership, 49*(3), 73–76.

Hall, G. E., & Loucks, S. (1978). Teachers concerns as a basis for facilitating and personalizing staff development. *Teachers College Record, 80,* 36–53.

Harris, L., & Associates (1992). *The Metropolitan Life survey of the American teacher 1992. The second year: New teachers' expectations and ideals.* New York: Metropolitan Life Insurance Co.

Hood, P., & Blackwell, L. (1980). *The role of teachers and other school practitioners in decision making and innovations.* San Francisco: Far West Laboratory.

Huberman, M. (1983). Recipes for busy teachers. *Knowledge: Creation, diffusion, utilization, 4,* 478–510.

Huberman, M. (1985). What knowledge is of most worth to teachers? A knowledge-use perspective. *Teaching and Teacher Education, 1,* 251–262.

Huberman, M. (1992). Teacher development and instructional mastery. In A. Hargreaves & M. G. Fullan (Eds.), *Understanding teacher development* (pp. 122–142). New York: Teachers College Press.

Huberman, M., & Crandall, D. (1983). *People, policies and practice: Examining the chain of school improvement: Vol. 9. Implications for action: A study of dissemination efforts supporting school improvement.* Andover, MA: The Network.

Huberman, M., & Miles, M. B. (1984). *Innovation up close: How school improvement works.* New York: Plenum.

Jackson, P. W. (1968). *Life in classrooms.* New York: Holt, Rinehart & Winston.

Joyce, B., & Showers, B. (1980). Improving inservice training: The messages of research. *Educational Leadership, 37*(5), 379–385.

Joyce, B., & Showers, B. (1988). *Student achievement through staff development.* New York: Longman.

Latham, G. (1988). The birth and death cycles of educational innovations. *Principal, 68*(1), 41–43.

Leiter, M., & Cooper, M. (1978). How teacher unionists view inservice education. *Teachers College Record, 80,* 107–125.

Leithwood, K., & Montgomery, D. (1982). The role of the elementary school principal in program improvement. *Review of Educational Research, 52,* 309–339.

Lezotte, L. W. (1989). The open book. *Focus in Change, 1*(2), 3.

Little, J. W. (1982). Norms of collegiality and experimentation: Workplace conditions of school success. *American Educational Research Journal, 19,* 325–340.

Little, J. W. (1989, April). *The persistence of privacy: Autonomy and initiative in teachers' professional relations.* Paper presented at the annual meeting of the American Educational Research Association, San Francisco.

Lortie, D. C. (1975). *Schoolteacher: A sociological study.* Chicago: University of Chicago Press.

Loucks-Horsley, S., Harding, C. K., Arbuckle, M. A., Murray, L. B., Dubea, C., & Williams, M. K. (1987). *Continuing to learn: A guidebook for teacher development.* Andover, MA: Regional Laboratory for Educational Improvement of the Northeast & Islands.

Louis, K. S., & Miles, M. B. (1990). *Improving the urban high school: What works and why.* New York: Teachers College Press.

Mann, D. (1978). The politics of training teachers in schools. In D. Mann (Ed.), *Making change happen* (pp. 3–18). New York: Teachers College Press.

Mann, D. (1986). Authority and school improvement: An essay on "Little King" leadership. *Teachers College Record, 88*(1), 41–52.

Marzano, R. J., Pickering, D. J., & Brandt, R. S. (1990). Integrating instructional programs through dimensions of learning. *Educational Leadership, 47*(5), 17–24.

Massarella, J. A. (1980). Synthesis of research on staff development. *Educational Leadership, 38*(2), 182–185.

McLaughlin, M. W. (1990). The Rand change agent study revisited: Macro perspectives and micro realities. *Educational Researcher, 19*(9), 11–16.

McLaughlin, M. W. (1991). Test-based accountability as a reform strategy. *Phi Delta Kappan, 73*(3), 248–251.

McLaughlin, M. W., & Marsh, D. D. (1978). Staff development and school change. *Teachers College Record, 80*(1), 70–94.

Mevarech, Z. R. (1985). The effects of cooperative mastery learning strategies on mathematics achievement. *Journal of Educational Research, 78,* 372–377.

Miles, M. B., & Louis, K. S. (1987). Research on institutionalization: A reflective review. In M. B. Miles, M. Ekholm, & R. Vandenberghe (Eds.), *Lasting school improvement: Exploring the process of institutionalization* (pp. 24–44). Leuven, Belgium: Acco.

Miles, M. B., & Louis, K. S. (1990). Mustering the will and skill for change. *Educational Leadership, 47*(8), 57–61.

Parker, C. A. (1980). The literature on planned organizational change: A review and analysis. *Higher Education, 9,* 429–442.

Pejouhy, N. H. (1990). Teaching math for the 21st century. *Phi Delta Kappan, 72*(1), 76–78.

Porter, A. C. (1986). From research on teaching to staff development: A difficult step. *Elementary School Journal, 87,* 159–164.

Prochaska, J. O., DiClemente, C. C., & Norcross, J. C. (1992). In search of how people change. *American Psychologist, 47,* 1102–1114.

Resnick, L. B. (1985). Cognition and instruction: Recent theories of human competence. In B. L. Hammonds (Ed.), *Master lecture series: Vol. 4. Psychology and learning* (pp. 123–186). Washington, DC: American Psychological Association.

Resnick, L. B. (1987). Constructing knowledge in school. In L. S. Liben (Ed.), *Development and learning: Conflict or congruence?* (pp. 19–50). Hillsdale, NJ: Erlbaum.

Rogers, K. B., & Kimpston, R. D. (1992). Acceleration: What we do vs. what we know. *Educational Leadership, 50*(2), 58–61.

Rosenholtz, S. (1987). Education reform strategies: Will they increase teacher commitment? *American Journal of Education,* 95, 534–562.

Ryan, K. (Ed.). (1970). *Don't smile until Christmas.* Chicago: University of Chicago Press.

Sarason, S. (1982). *The culture of school and the problem of change.* Boston: Allyn & Bacon.

Sarason, S. (1990). *The predictable failure of educational reform.* San Francisco: Jossey-Bass.

Showers, B., Joyce, B., & Bennett, B. (1987). Synthesis of research on staff development: A framework for future study and a state-of-the-art analysis. *Educational Leadership, 45*(3), 77–87.

Shroyer, M. G. (1990). Effective staff development for effective organizational development. *Journal of Staff Development, 11*(1), 2–6.

Shuell, T. J. (1986). Cognitive conceptions of learning. *Review of Educational Research,* 56, 411–436.

Smylie, M. A. (1988). The enhancement function of staff development: Organizational and psychological antecedents to individual teacher change. *American Educational Research Journal, 25*(1), 1–30.

Sparks, D., & Loucks-Horsley, S. (1989). Five models of staff development for teachers. *Journal of Staff Development, 10*(4), 40–57.

Sparks, G. M. (1983). Synthesis of research on staff development for effective teaching. *Educational Leadership, 41*(3), 65–72.

Stallings, J. (1980). Allocated academic learning time revisited, or beyond time on task. *Educational Researcher, 9*(11), 11–16.

Stevenson, R. B. (1987). Staff development for effective secondary schools: A synthesis of research. *Teaching and Teacher Education, 3*(2), 233–248.

Talbert, J. E., McLaughlin, M. W., & Rowan, B. (1993). Understanding context effects on secondary school teaching. *Teachers College Record, 95*(1), 45–68.

Waugh, R. F., & Punch, K. F. (1987). Teacher receptivity to systemwide change in the implementation stage. *Review of Educational Research, 57*(3), 237–254.

Weatherley, R., & Lipsky, M. (1977). Street-level bureaucrats and institutional innovation: Implementing special education reform. *Harvard Educational Review, 47*(2), 171–197.

Weber, A. (1990). Linking ITIP and the writing process. *Educational Leadership, 47*(5), 35–39.

Wise, A. E. (1991). On teacher accountability. In *Voices from the field* (pp. 23–24). Washington, D.C.: William T. Grant Foundation Commission on Work, Family and Citizenship *and* Institute for Educational Leadership.

PART III

Phases, Models, and Requisite Supports

Professional development can also be viewed as a dynamic process that spans one's entire career in the profession, from preparation and induction to completion and retirement. The various phases of that career cycle are the focus of the authors in this part.

The formal and informal support mechanisms necessary to sustain any successful professional development effort are the emphasis of Chapter 6, by Harm H. Tillema and Jeroen G. M. Imants of the University of Leyden in The Netherlands. Beginning with a description of the internal factors of schools that can either stimulate or inhibit change, Tillema and Imants describe how professional development can be successful only if related to individuals' unique work environments and to their perceptions of their roles. They then outline how coaching, consultation, and supervision methods can be fashioned to support effective dissemination of ideas, knowledge utilization, and transfer.

Research literature relating to the developmental issues that characterize professional growth in teaching expertise is the basis of Chapter 7, by Zemira R. Mevarech of Bar Ilan University in Israel. Using information gathered from interviews with experienced classroom teachers involved in various forms of professional development, Mevarech shows how these activities have differential effects on the meaning teachers attribute to professional development and its influence on their instructional practices. The model she puts forth illustrates how these changes are affected by the social organization of the school and also fashion how teachers make sense of their role in the teaching and learning process.

In Chapter 8, Ralph Fessler of Johns Hopkins University illustrates how various philosophical and theoretical premises affect our views of the professional and career development of teachers. Using a social systems theory approach, he shows how personal and organizational factors dynamically interact to influence teacher growth and development. A teacher career cycle is then proposed to illustrate how development proceeds through the interplay and resolution of conflict between the growth needs of individual teachers and the demands of the organization.

In Chapter 9, Michael Huberman of Harvard University and the Network, Inc. describes a model for professional development that is both conceptually and empirically informed. Following a critical review of recent paradigms of teachers' life-span development, which Huberman contends are based on an artisan image of classroom instruction, a "contextually plausible" model for professional development is set forth. This model is construed in part from a social-constructivist perspective and calls for a group-based, problem-solving cycle of exchange, experimentation, and analysis of instructional practices that depends heavily on external expertise at critical junctures.

6

Training for the Professional Development of Teachers

HARM H. TILLEMA AND JEROEN G. M. IMANTS

Unlike in other professions, it appears that training and professional development in teaching bifurcate into different, even opposite, directions. In other, related professions—for instance, in the health professions, and even more in business and industry—training and development are interrelated to such a degree that growth in professional performance is regarded as virtually impossible without an accompanying training cycle (Prior, 1992).

In conceptualizations of professional development for the teaching profession (Burden, 1990; Dean, 1991; Stallings, 1982) there is a clear trend to separate the two facets. Training is hardly mentioned anymore in discussions of professional development (Grimmet & Mackinnon, 1992) and has even acquired a negative connotation with regard to development and professional growth (Sparks & Loucks-Horsley, 1990).

Obviously, our understanding of development and growth in teaching is dependent on our perspective of the profession (Kennedy, 1987; Liston & Zeichner, 1991). A reconsideration of the diminished role of training in the conceptualization of professional development must therefore take into account perspectives on the profession. In particular, a craft perspective on the teaching profession has recently received considerable attention both as a code for professional development (Greene, 1986) and as a concept for teacher education (Katz & Raths, 1991). Looking upon teaching as a craft calls for sensitivity to the practical aspects of teaching and to the nature of competence as "reflective practice" (Leinhardt, 1990; Schön, 1983). Growth in competence, from this perspective, can only be established within the cultural milieu of teaching itself through a (re)construction of knowledge in real-life situations (Clandinin & Connelly, 1986), where teachers learn from their own experience (by cumulative reflection) or from one another.

Training has become associated increasingly with a perspective on teaching as a technical skill (Cruickshank & Metcalf, 1990) and equated with the development of competence in specific behaviors (Macleod, 1987)—or at best with the application of general principles derived from a specific educational theory. Training research has been criticized for inventing competencies that are of little relevance to practice or are removed from the real problems of teaching (Clark, 1989).

The argument put forward in this chapter is that training can further the professional development of teachers, but only if it is compatible with and sensitive to the constructs and knowledge base of the teacher and only if it is related to the perceived task of the teacher.

Research on training in the context of educational change and staff development projects (Sparks & Loucks-Horsley, 1990) indicates that teachers can change their behavioral repertoires substantially (Joyce, Murphy, Showers, & Murphy, 1989). However, if there is to be lasting change (see Guskey, 1986), training programs must give credit to the teachers' available knowledge and experiences, whatever their level of professional development, since teachers will only "learn" from a training program inasfar as it is consistent with their own conceptions of their task environment (Fullan, Bennett, & Rolheiser-Bennett, 1990). Without evidence that new practices are personally congenial, teachers will not apply them in the classroom (Cousins & Leithwood, 1986). Training programs, however, are seldom explicitly related to teachers' existing beliefs and thinking (Griffin, 1990).

It also needs to be recognized that teachers' opportunities for professional learning in effect are largely confined to the situations they encounter in their immediate task environment (Doyle, 1990). This implies, on the one hand, that teachers produce and utilize knowledge in context; on the other hand, it calls for transforming teachers' task environments into opportunities for learning. The implication for training as a form of externally provided support for professional development is that it only becomes effective when it is closely connected with both the existing task environment and the knowledge base of the teacher. The professional context of the teacher circumscribes what can be achieved through training, and it also sets standards and goals for the individual development of teachers. Thus it is important that training models relate experientially to the task environment and that they foster the extension of the teaching repertoire in a stimulating way.

Training programs that successfully connect the existing professional milieu with professional development must take the following issues, presented here as dilemmas, into account:

1. The nature and structure of the teacher's available knowledge base. Training dilemma: The need to restructure that knowledge base through conceptual or experience-based learning.

2. The importance of providing opportunities for learning. Training dilemma: Providing instruction- or intervention-oriented practice.
3. The construction and communication of validated knowledge. Training dilemma: The utilization of research-based information or the production of information through active inquiry.

We first present four different training models. Then we discuss their position on the above-mentioned issues and examine the ways in which these models are directed at supporting teachers in their immediate professional development. The models, which have been selected to exemplify different solutions to the above-mentioned problems, could help in developing a structured view of training for professional development.

DEVELOPMENT-ORIENTED MODELS OF TRAINING

Training for Conceptual Change

Restructuring teacher cognitions (notably beliefs and knowledge) about instructional strategy is the focus of the training model of conceptual change developed by Smith and Neale (1989). In order to help teachers develop relevant subject-matter knowledge and pedagogical knowledge, Smith and Neale created a training program that focuses explicitly on the acquisition of conceptual knowledge necessary for applying a specific teaching strategy. Because of observations that pupils rely on their own preconceptions when attempting to comprehend new content in science instruction, and that these ideas are powerful determinants of new learning, teachers were trained to deal with the prior conceptions of pupils by matching these constructs to scientific concepts. Smith and Neale (also Neale, Smith, & Johnson, 1990) developed and trained teachers to apply a teaching strategy that includes the following characteristics:

1. Teaching is directed toward a confrontation between the existing ideas of pupils and valid scientific concepts.
2. Instruction aims at eliciting pupils' informal experiences.
3. Activities are provided to test and diagnose pupils' predictions under the careful control and guidance of the teacher.
4. Simple exercises and questions are provided that furnish immediate results.

The training of teachers is conceptual in nature in that it focuses on altering the teacher's own knowledge base and instructional strategies. Prior to the training, the teachers' classroom lessons were videotaped so that training could be more directly related to the ongoing task environment. Teachers were also interviewed to establish their levels of scientific knowledge—including their beliefs about scientific concepts and the teaching of science—and their knowledge of both children's conceptions and instructional strategies in relation to the mastery of scientific concepts.

During an initial training phase, teachers read and discussed research on children's misconceptions, then interviewed pupils about their conceptions. Activities were designed to model procedures of teaching for conceptual change. After the initial phase, teachers themselves taught topics to small groups, following the lesson segments that were indicated by the teaching strategy and using an instructional sequence that followed a conceptual change model of teaching. Teachers' lessons were videotaped and discussed.

In a final training phase, teachers designed lessons for a larger unit and made preliminary lesson plans. These lessons were analyzed, using a checklist to record the use of elements that addressed conceptual change. The results indicated that teachers were generally successful in implementing a conceptual change lesson unit of their own.

This training model begins with the already existing beliefs and conceptions of the teacher about the subject matter, the learner, and the appropriate instructional sequences. It builds on this available knowledge base by gradually introducing new concepts and strategies. Learning by teachers is seen as a result of their involvement in relevant training activities; it is a model that emphasizes a learning-to-learn mentality and a willingness to apply the new strategy. Training is focused on the acquisition of essential conceptual knowledge and the gradual building of new knowledge structures that will guide future classroom activity. As such, teachers are engaged in contextually meaningful activities during the training.

Cognitively Guided Training and Instruction

Another conceptual approach to teacher training is the cognitively guided instruction model developed by Carpenter, Fennema, Peterson, Chiang, and Loef (1989; see also Chapter 2 of this volume). These researchers conducted a study that provided teachers with access to explicit knowledge derived from research.

The training consisted of a workshop to familiarize teachers with information and knowledge within the subject-matter domain, that is, by presenting research on learning and development in addition and subtraction by young children. Teachers read relevant research literature and learned to classify problems and identify children's problem-solving processes. The training also involved discussion of more general principles of instructional design reported in the professional literature. Teachers subsequently designed their own programs of instruction on the basis of these principles. The teachers were encouraged, for instance, to apply a particular strategy of asking appropriate questions and listening to children's responses. Specific design suggestions were directed at the planning of instruction; for instance, the teachers were asked to consider how instruction should build on children's informal counting strategies. During the training—which lasted five hours a day, four days a week, for four weeks—the teachers read research papers, watched videotapes of children solving problems, and had the opportunity to interview some children.

The teachers were observed afterwards to see whether they had adopted the appropriate teaching procedures. Teachers' knowledge of students' cognitive levels was tested by having them predict how particular students would solve specific problems. It was also found that these teachers encouraged their students to use a greater variety of problem-solving strategies and were more attentive to processes of student learning than teachers who had not participated in the training. They also knew more about their students' problem-solving approaches. The study showed that providing teachers with access to explicit knowledge derived from research literature *did* influence their instruction and *did* raise levels of student achievement.

Study Groups of Teachers

Within the larger framework of a school-improvement project, Joyce, Murphy, Showers, and Murphy (1989) developed a training program that implements research-based strategies of teaching. The model is of interest because it combines an experiential approach to teacher knowledge with explicit attention to use of externally produced knowledge. The training program, which instructs the teacher in a series of teaching skills, is aimed at restructuring the workplace by organizing teachers into study groups. The training model stresses collegial work as a way of reaching specific and clearly stated goals regarding teaching performance. This program takes into account teacher beliefs and encourages clear understanding of the principles and practices they are expected to apply. The content of the training is focused on learning to use established teaching strategies that increase student learning.

Central to the model is that teachers learn to work with one another in study groups, collegially generating knowledge about the use of particular teaching strategies. The program consists of two weeks of intensive training in the teaching strategies, followed by six weeks of practice. The effectiveness of the study groups and subsequent peer coaching depends greatly on the leadership of a relatively small number of teachers.

The strategies to be learned were clearly stated and documented, and teachers were provided with illustrative materials. The primary task of the teacher study groups was to develop ways of using the models in their own classrooms. Teachers had a sufficient amount of time to become acquainted with the information and techniques and to achieve a high level of proficiency. The success of the training program depended greatly on both organizational factors, such as administrative support and availability time and resources, and conceptual factors, such as quality of discussion in the study groups. A favorable combination of factors led to transfer to and sustained implementation in classrooms. The training program also relied heavily on the amount of practice in the teacher's own school environment; the teaching strategies were practiced at least 30 times by the teachers.

The program, as conceived by Joyce and his colleagues, makes use of research-based models of teaching in which achievement of a high level of proficiency in executing the models by the teachers is essential. This calls for a considerable amount of practice and study, explicit training, and conceptual clarity in the training. The collegial setting provides an incentive to learn new teaching strategies, leading to an understanding of the teaching models that is shared among the teachers at the school. In particular, the training model sets a premium on linking teachers' experiences and fostering acquaintance with new information through discussion, exchange, and practice.

Promoting Change in Teaching

Richardson (1990) describes a model that heavily stresses the available experiental knowledge of teachers as well as school organization as important considerations in professional development. This training model evolved in the context of a teacher change program developed by the University of Arizona to foster curriculum change in reading. The training program focused on the existing experiences and cognitions of teachers with respect to teaching reading, taking into account the situational conditions within the school. Borrowing from Fenstermacher (1986), it was assumed that explicating their own deliberations and arguments would help teachers to examine their beliefs and possibly alter certain invalid conceptions about the intended change.

The model used both individual and group sessions for discussions of the experiences and beliefs of teachers. Videotaped lessons were presented, and teachers were asked individually to comment on their own lessons and to provide a rationale for the ongoing action. In the course of the discussion, alternate views, based on either research or the intended curriculum, were introduced into the discussion to see whether the teachers' beliefs would make them receptive to alternative practices. Apparently, the teachers' work experiences and belief systems acted as filters through which research-based practice had to pass if it was to alter existing teaching practices.

This was the beginning of a process in which teachers were provided with supplementary information, lesson materials, and models to try out in their classrooms. The teachers had considerable control over the process; in particular, they had control over the direction and focus of the information to be presented. The trainer provided the materials and gave the teachers support that was appropriate to their level of professional development; the trainer also worked to encourage the teachers to take control of the process and address issues important to them. The program was evaluated positively by the teachers, and it showed that they could change their practices over time. It was noteworthy that the teachers' deliberations about whether or not to use a given curriculum element were quite broad and contextual rather than in strict correspondence with the theoretical and conceptual notions provided.

Finally, the amount of change was clearly related to school culture and climate (i.e., collegiality). A shared language appeared to promote collegiality and give rise to a sharing of ideas and to follow-up in the field.

These four training models present different solutions to the central issues articulated earlier with respect to the nature and design of training that will promote professional development. Table 6.1 shows the type of solution reflected in each model with respect to the restructuring of teachers' knowledge, to teachers' practice, and to the production of validated knowledge.

TABLE 6.1 Four models of training aimed at professional development

Models of Training	Teachers' Knowledge Restructuring		Teachers' Practice		Production of Validated Knowledge	
	Conceptually Based	*Experience Based*	*Instruction Oriented*	*Intervention Oriented*	*Research Based*	*Inquiry Based*
Training for conceptual change (Smith & Neale, 1989)	X			X	X	
Cognitively guided training (Carpenter et al., 1989)	X		X		X	
Study groups (Joyce et al., 1989)		X	X		X	
Promoting change in teaching practice (Richardson, 1990)		X		X		X

RESTRUCTURING TEACHER KNOWLEDGE
AS A FOCAL POINT IN TRAINING

Two questions are central to effective training design. On the one hand, under what conditions do teachers accept and eventually use new information that is presented to them? On the other hand, how far is the training equipped to deal with the available knowledge base of the teacher? Is it possible to change preexisting structures and achieve new learning by merely presenting new information (Bereiter, 1990)? These questions are by no means shallow; they relate to the nature of professional knowledge. This knowledge base is coherent and elaborate (Schön, 1983), has proven valuable in practice, and acts as a frame for action (Mannes & Kintsch, 1988). The restructuring of knowledge is not simply a matter of replacing old concepts with new ones (Iran-Nejad, 1990; Vosniadou & Brewer, 1987); through the lens of preexisting conceptions, teachers decide which new knowledge elements to accept and integrate. The question remains: When precisely do teachers integrate new knowledge and restructure their existing knowledge?

Training provides a setting for the acquisition and restructuring of teachers' knowledge that is meant to be integrated into subsequent action. It is only with the help of an adequate diagnosis of existing conceptions and beliefs that a training program can successfully connect with the existing knowledge structures or schemata of teachers.

In each of the four training models described earlier, the existing knowledge of teachers is taken as the focal point. At the same time, however, the four models reflect different orientations with respect to the nature of the knowledge-restructuring process; as a consequence they differ in the kinds of learning opportunities provided, which are either conceptually-based or experience-based (Tillema, De Jong, & Mathijssen, 1990). Also, the models differ with respect to the position of (explicit) diagnosis of teacher knowledge as a recognizable element of the training model. By diagnosis we mean the availability of information about the present knowledge and beliefs of teachers to the trainer for use during training. Diagnostic information can be valuable in all the training models mentioned, although in different ways.

Conceptual or Experience-Based Models of Training

Training somehow has to take place in a situation in which teachers have developed coherence (stability) in their own knowledge and experiential structures (Buchmann & Floden, 1992), at the same time being able to incorporate new concepts to arrive at a new and coherent structure. In training design, this calls for connection with and restructuring of existing knowledge as well as subsequent presentation of new concepts (Carter, 1990; Prawat, 1989).

Two solutions to this problem have been adopted. One, from a conceptual perspective, states that the key role of training lies in the clear presentation of core information, leaving it to the teacher to assimilate it into his or her own knowledge structure. Training, thus conceived, must exert control over the process of knowledge acquisition. The other, experience-based perspective states that the training design must ensure that a sufficient amount of the teacher's experience is communicated during the training, thus providing a natural immersion context for the introduction of new concepts.

In general, conceptual models of training have the following characteristics:

1. They give high priority to clear delivery of essential concepts, because the acquisition of central and basic concepts and the understanding of their characteristics are seen as prerequisites for actual application.
2. The task of training is primarily one of presenting the concepts and subject matter and giving enough opportunities for teachers to acquaint themselves with the correct meaning of these concepts.
3. By establishing a relation between conceptual information presented in training and the teachers' own understanding and use of concepts, a foundation can be laid for the correct use and integration of new knowledge about classroom practices.
4. It is important to provide a thorough diagnosis, or "mapping," of the concepts teachers use, as a representation to be focused on during training. Although this last position is not necessarily akin to the conceptual orientation to training, it shows the primacy on clear conceptual understanding.

Both the conceptual change model and the cognitively guided training model adopt a position in which clarification of existing knowledge leads to the subsequent presentation of new concepts. Both pay attention to the preconceptions and beliefs of teachers that have to be incorporated, either by instruction or by trail, in the teacher's repertoire.

Experience-based models use a different approach to diagnose and incorporate teacher knowledge in training:

1. The trainer is primarily a facilitator of (group) learning processes in which teachers are invited to exchange and discuss ideas and solutions they have encountered in practice.
2. The focus of training is on sharing experiences and ideas derived from practice; learning is regarded as reflection upon one's own or another's behavior.

3. Sessions are directed for the most part by the teachers themselves. Knowledge is acquired through discussions and self-evaluation of one's own learning (Tillema et al., 1990).

This model thus relies on the input of teachers' knowledge and expertise, which are used as anchor points in the subsequent introduction of new information. The study group model is a more structured learning opportunity than the more discovery-oriented approach in the Arizona model, but both provide concrete settings for the application of conceptual learning in teachers' task environments.

THE FUNCTION OF PRACTICE IN TEACHER LEARNING: INSTRUCTION OR INTERVENTION?

The position of training in the professional development of teachers cannot be ascertained without a clarification of the function of practice as a supplement to the expertise that teachers already possess. A training rationale that highlights the use of practice in the acquisition of teaching competence is defended in the work of Gliesman and Pugh (1987). According to these authors, competence can be acquired only through instruction. The development of teaching skills follows from the comprehension of clear instances of relevant concepts about a given competency. Gliesman argues that performance, if it is to be enacted, must be conceptualized. For a conceptual understanding of performance, it is necessary that a teacher first acquire a clear definition of the relevant concepts, defining their characteristics and identifying their instances. Instruction is typically the method used first in concept acquisition. Clear instances can be provided and misconceptions eventually can be corrected. It involves labeling, defining, providing a variety of examples, highlighting essential characteristics, and contrasting information with other concepts. The goal of instruction is to establish a knowledge base about performance for the teacher (e.g., the cognitively guided instruction model).

An alternative model stresses concept formation instead of concept acquisition (e.g., the conceptual change training model). In concept formation, integration of concepts into the existing knowledge structure is central; clustering and integration of concepts leads to an active restructuring of the training content by the teacher, and a reformulation of the teacher's own teaching repertoires may be achieved. A training environment stressing concept formation uses specific interventions (such as assignments, questions, tasks) aimed at a clear conceptualization of the information to be learned and provides explicit description of performance.

Instruction and intervention are complementary methods in training.

Instruction focuses on definition and explanation by the trainer; intervention, on exchange between trainer and trainee in the form of questions, clarifications, and so forth aimed at a clear understanding on the part of the trainee.

The studies of Gliesman and his colleagues show that clarification of concepts as a means of facilitating mastery can be a highly reliable way of achieving change in performance. The direct implication of the studies is that concept mastery should be the primary goal of training: "If concepts about skills are mastered, skills are highly likely to follow" (Gliesman & Pugh, 1987, p. 562). Particularly effective training variables are those related to direct instruction and concept mastery. Successful intervention techniques include feedback and reinforcement. Through intervention and instruction, teachers can acquire complex interactive teaching skills that will produce significant changes in their teaching performance.

Common to most of the conceptual models of training is the idea that practice in itself will not result in significant and lasting changes in performance. Practice may lead to changes in perception and attitude, but there is little evidence that practice alone can influence or produce changes in performance. Gliesman, Pugh, and Plowden (1989) contend that practice in itself is not a significant contributor to the acquisition of competence. It is, however, possible that supervised practice could promote competency, although Gliesman and colleagues (1989) did not find such an effect in their review of programs. Nevertheless, attempts have been made to extend practice- and rehearsal-oriented training models, such as micro-teaching, by including procedures that aim at conceptual clarification and take into account pre-existing knowledge (Cornford, 1991). It could be stated that the success of conceptual models in achieving competent performance derives from their clear presentation of concepts *in relation* to the existing knowledge structures of the teacher (Macleod, 1987).

Another matter of debate is how much concept attainment should be under the control of the trainer, an issue of special relevance to the professional development of teachers within schools. Several training programs use instruction and intervention techniques that are more or less under the control of the teacher: self-reports, peer groups, experience exchange, and study groups. All these methods have in common a reliance on the prior work experience of the teacher. Available research (Cruickshank & Metcalf, 1990; Tillema & Veenman, 1987) suggests that with respect to achieving high levels of knowledge attainment, trainer-controlled learning is preferable to teacher-controlled learning; the latter is more time-consuming and does not ensure that relevant and explicit concepts are clarified. The more precise the focus of training (e.g., through modeling, cueing, and shaping) with regard to the intervention component, and the more precise the training in clarification, definition, and discrimination with respect to the instruction component, the more effective concept acquisition will be.

THE CONSTRUCTION OF VALIDATED KNOWLEDGE;
TEACHER LEARNING THROUGH INFORMATION OR INQUIRY

Training is a vehicle for communicating knowledge and is therefore dependent upon the acquisition of validated knowledge that can be disseminated. Research is the most important supplier of validated knowledge. There remains the question, however, of how validated knowledge is construed (Cochran-Smith & Lytle, 1990; Yarger & Smith, 1990): Is research viewed as an activity or as content to be utilized?

There has been a growing interest in teacher research as a means for teachers themselves to become systematically and actively involved in collecting validated knowledge about their daily activity (Katz & Raths, 1991). Teacher research is systematic and intentional inquiry carried out by teachers. In a growing number of places (e.g., Pittsburgh, Pennsylvania), experience-based information is being collected in this way. As with most action-oriented research, teachers have developed and worked out methods of data collection and data analysis through study of their own work environment. Partly an outgrowth of the teachers' own interest in self-development and autonomy, teacher research is a way of organizing professional development in such a way that it remains closely related to what teachers acknowledge as their domain of professional autonomy (Rosenholtz, 1989) and what they see as fundamental to their work within the school organization. Research in this sense is closely related to meaningful school development in which there is a close connection among development, reflection, professionalization, and school renewal. Favorable results have been reported in studies in which teachers have been involved in inquiry-oriented activities (Cochran-Smith & Lytle, 1990).

Another approach to the construction of validated knowledge, which seems to have been more widely enacted (Huberman, 1991), consists of informing teachers about research of relevance to their work. In this approach research does not provide prescriptions for practice but furnishes practical arguments for reconsidering practice (Fenstermacher, 1986).

In both cases, at issue is what teachers perceive as relevant information. Does it address the problems the teacher directly experiences in the classroom (e.g., dropping reading scores after Easter or lack of motivation) or does it concern the teacher's meaningful understanding of his or her practice?

A few models emphasize the construction of validated knowledge as input for training. They differ in the emphasis placed upon either existing research or independent inquiry:

- The most well-known model is no doubt the dissemination model in which external, research-based information is given to teachers for them to study and to learn about. Teachers may come to use this information because they find it interesting or because there is some type of administrative coercion to use it. The roles are most often clearly divided: The trainer provides the information, the teacher adopts it. The teacher, in fortunate cases, gets a chance to tailor the information to the work environment.

- The interactive model involves a more equal communication about research-based information between trainer and teacher. Innovative programs often use this model, in which teachers are invited to comment on and react to information presented to them because of their instructional expertise. In this type of training, teachers act as information seekers, critical judges of results, and eventually agents who try out products under the control and evaluation of trainers. In this model, teachers are still not the producers of knowledge.

- The teacher-as-a-researcher, or inquiry, model distinguishes itself from the interactive model by explicitly viewing teachers as construing knowledge of their own for the purpose of studying classroom phenomena. The problem identification, as well as the connection between development and renewal or change in practice, is in the hands of teachers.

The major advantage of information- over inquiry-oriented models is their explicitness and focus; the teacher can rely on a sometimes extensive knowledge base. On the other hand, inquiry-oriented models help to set standards for being systematic and active over a prolonged period; they are also more motivating when embedded in a school-based program of development, in which case they benefit the school organization as well. As such, both contribute to the professional development of teachers, but in different ways. An inquiry-oriented model lends itself very well to some form of external support or program development, in the sense that teachers become more serious partners in the construction of validated knowledge.

CONCLUSION

The prime focus of this chapter was to relate training to professional development and to demonstrate that cognitive factors exert considerable influence on professional development. Although teacher knowledge can be "handled" quite differently in various training models, it undoubtedly affects the design and delivery of training; as such it must be recognized that training for professional development implies a position on such issues as the restructuring of knowledge, the use of practice, and the production of knowledge. Conceptual training methods in particular seem to promise results with respect to lasting conceptual change in teacher action and thinking. Experience-based models seem to yield greater acceptance of presented knowledge and an active production of knowledge under the control of teachers. We have argued that there is a dynamic relation between the teacher's responsibility for his or her own learning and the training models that can be adopted. This calls for an active search and construction of relevant training models.

Training has been called a cornerstone of the professional development of teachers. However, most training models to date have had little connection to the teacher's knowledge and task perception, which makes them obsolete. A new orientation in training is emerging (Wilson & Cole, 1992). The models discussed in this chapter stress that available teacher knowledge has to be accounted for in delivering new knowledge to teachers. As such, they can be used to acquaint teachers with central concepts or new teaching perspectives, as well as to provide means for thinking and trying out new practices. In this view, training serves crucial functions in the process of teacher development. The "confrontation" of a teacher's existing, internalized concepts and beliefs with "conflicting" externally provided training concepts stimulates and challenges the teacher to change routines and to experiment with new insights and skills. This "cognitive dissonance" is crucial to the process of perceiving, interpreting, evaluating, and understanding new teaching practices, and thus also making the teacher's task environment a place for learning.

REFERENCES

Bereiter, C. (1990). Aspects of an educational learning theory. *Review of Educational Research, 60*, 603–624.

Buchmann, M., & Floden, R. E. (1992). Coherence, the rebel angel. *Educational Researcher, 21*(9), 4–9.

Burden, B. R. (1990). Teacher development. In W. R. Houston (Ed.), *Handbook of research on teacher education* (pp. 311–328). New York: Macmillan.

Carpenter, T. P., Fennema, E., Peterson, P. L., Chiang, C. P., & Loef, M. (1989). Using knowledge of children's mathematics thinking in classroom teaching: An experimental study. *American Educational Research Journal, 26*(4), 499–531.

Carter, K. (1990). Teachers' knowledge and learning to teach. In W. R. Houston (Ed.), *Handbook of research on teacher education* (pp. 291–310). New York: Macmillan.

Clandinin, D. J., & Connelly, F. M. (1986). Rhythms in teaching. *Teaching and Teacher Education, 2*, 377–387.

Clark, C. M. (1989). Asking the right questions about teacher preparation. In J. Lowyck & C. M. Clark (Ed.), *Teacher thinking and professional action* (pp. 7–20). Leuven, Belgium: University Press.

Cochran-Smith, M., & Lytle, S. L. (1990). Research on teaching and teacher research, the issues that divide. *Educational Researcher, 19*(2), 2–11.

Cornford, I. R. (1991). Macroteaching skill, generalisation and transfer. *Teaching and Teacher Education, 7*(1), 25–56.

Cousins, J. B., & Leithwood, N. A. (1986). Current empirical research on evaluation utilization. *Review of Educational Research, 56*(5), 331–364.

Cruickshank, D. R., & Metcalf, K. N. (1990). Training within teacher preparation. In W. R. Houston (Ed.), *Handbook of research on teacher education* (pp. 469–497). New York: Macmillan.

Dean, J. (1991). *Professional development in schools.* Milton Keynes, UK: Open University Press.

Doyle, W. (1990). Themes in teacher education research. In W. R. Houston (Ed.), *Handbook of research on teacher education* (pp. 3–24). New York: Macmillan.

Fenstermacher, G. D. (1986). Philosophy of research on teaching. In M. C. Wittrock (Ed.), *Handbook of research on teaching* (3rd ed.; pp. 37–49). New York: Macmillan.

Fenstermacher G. D., & Berliner, D. C. (1986). Determining the value of staff development. *The Elementrary School Journal, 85*(3), 281–314.

Fullan, M., Bennett, B., & Rolheiser-Bennett, C. (1990). Linking classroom and school improvement. *Educational Leadership, 48,* 13–19.

Gliesman, D. H., & Pugh, R. (1987). Conceptual instruction and intervention as methods of acquiring teaching skills. *International Journal of Educational Research, 11*(5), 555–563.

Gliesman, D. H., Pugh, R., & Plowden, D. E. (1989). Variables influencing the acquisition of a generic teaching skill. *Review of Educational Research, 58*(1), 25–46.

Greene, M. (1986). How do we think about our craft. In A. Lieberman (Ed.), *Rethinking school improvement* (pp. 13–25). New York: Teachers College Press.

Griffin, G. A. (1990). The knowledge driven school. In M. C. Reynolds (Ed.), *Knowledge base for beginning teaching.* New York: Pergamon.

Grimmet, P. P., & Mackinnon, A. M. (1992). Craft knowledge and the education of teachers. In G. Grant (Ed.), *Review of research in education* (Vol. 18; pp. 385–456). Washington, DC: American Educational Research Association.

Guskey, T. R. (1986). Staff development and the process of teacher change. *Educational Researcher, 15*(5), 5–12.

Huberman, M. (1991, June). *Changing minds: The dissemination of research and its effects on practice and theory.* Paper presented to the International Study Association on Teacher Thinking, Surrey, UK.

Iran-Nejad, A. (1990). Active and dynamic self regulation of learning processes. *Review of Educational Research, 60,* 573–602.

Joyce, B. R., Murphy, C., Showers, B., & Murphy, J. (1989). School renewal as cultural change. *Educational Leadership, 47*(3), 70–77.

Katz, L. G., & Raths, J. D. (1991). *Advances in teacher education* (Vol. 4). Norwood, NJ: Ablex.

Kennedy, M. M. (1987). Inexact sciences, professional education and the development of expertise. In E. Z. Rothkopf (Ed.), *Review of research in education* (Vol. 14; pp. 133–167). Washington, DC: American Educational Research Association.

Leinhardt, G. (1990). Capturing craft knowledge in teaching. *Educational Researcher, 19*(2), 18–26

Liston, D. P., & Zeichner, K. M. (1991). *Teacher education and the social conditions of schooling.* New York: Routledge.

Macleod, G. (1987). Microteaching: End of a research era. *International Journal of Educational Research, 11,* 531–542.

Mannes, S. M., & Kintsch, W. (1988). Action planning, routine tasks. In *Program of the 10th annual meeting of the Cognitive Science Society* (pp. 97–103). Hillsdale, NJ: Lawrence Earlbaum.

Neale, D. C., Smith, D., & Johnson, V. G. (1990). Implementing conceptual change teaching in primary science. *The Elementary School Journal, 91*(2), 109–131.

Pajares, M. F. (1992). Teacher beliefs and educational research, cleaning up a messy construct. *Review of Educational Research, 62,* 307–332.

Posner, G. J., Strike, K. A., Hewson, P. W., & Gertzog, W. A. (1982). Accommodation of a scientific concept; toward a theory of conceptual change. *Science Education, 66*(2), 211–227.

Prior, J. (1992). *Gower handbook of training and development.* London: Gower Publishing Company.

Prawat, R. S. (1989). Promoting access to knowledge strategy and disposition in students: A research synthesis. *Review of Educational Research, 59*(1), 1–41.

Richardson, V. (1990). Significant and worthwhile change in teaching practice. *Educational Researcher, 19*(7), 10–18.

Rosenholz, S. (1989). *Teachers' workplace: The social organization of schools.* New York: Longman.

Schön, D. A. (1983). *The reflective practitioner. How professionals think in action.* New York: Basic Books.

Shulman, L. S. (1986). Those who understand, knowledge growth in teaching. *Educational Researcher, 15*(2), 4–14.

Smith, D. C., & Neale, D. C. (1989). The construction of subject matter knowledge in primary science teaching. *Teaching & Teacher Education, 5*(1), 1–20.

Sparks, D., & Loucks-Horsley, S. (1990). Models of staff development. In W. R. Houston (Ed.), *Handbook of research on teacher education* (pp. 234–250). New York: Macmillan.

Stallings, J. (1982). Effective strategies for teaching basic skills. In D. Wallace (Ed.), *Developing basic skills programs in secondary schools* (pp. 1–19). Alexandria: ASCD.

Sykes, G., & Bird, T. (1992). Teacher education and the case idea. In G. Grant (Ed.), *Review of research in education* (18). Washington, DC: American Educational Research Association.

Tillema, H. H., De Jong, R., & Mathijssen, C. (1990). Conceptual or experience based learning of teachers. *Teaching & Teacher Education, 6*(2), 165–172.

Tillema, H. H., & Veenman, S. (1987). Conceptualizing training methods in teacher education. *International Journal of Educational Research, 11,* 519–530.

Vosniadou, S., & Brewer, W. F. (1987). Theories of knowledge restructuring in development. *Review of Educational Research, 57,* 51–72.

Wilson, B., & Cole, P. (1992). A review of cognitive models of teaching. *Educational Training & Development, 39*(4), 47–64.

Yarger, S., & Smith, P. L. (1990). Issues on research in teacher education. In W. R. Houston (Ed.), *Handbook of research on teacher education* (pp. 329–348). New York: Macmillan.

7

Teachers' Paths on the Way to and from the Professional Development Forum

ZEMIRA R. MEVARECH

Professional development programs, whether they are intended for the individual, for discipline-based groups of teachers, or for all school personnel, are assumed to be important stimuli for teachers' professional growth. Typically, designers of such programs anticipate that the main outcome will be the improvement of teachers' classroom practice and pedagogical-content knowledge. Is it possible, however, that unfavorable outcomes may also occur? Under what conditions could professional development programs have the effect of temporarily stripping away teachers' self-perceptions of expertise and efficacy, giving rise to ways of thinking and acting that are common to novices? Are such negative changes indeed unavoidable? And if they are, can the social organization of school facilitate the way teachers cope with the negative changes?

 This chapter addresses these issues. It describes the stages experienced teachers pass through when they attempt to implement innovations introduced in staff development programs. In particular, it focuses on innovations related to instruction methods and learning environments based on advanced technology. Drawing on literature related to knowledge acquisition (e.g., Pintrich, Marx, & Boyle, 1993), career development (e.g., Huberman, 1989), and teachers' beliefs regarding the adoption and maintenance of instructional innovations (Guskey, 1989; Hall, 1976; Rich, 1993), it questions the widely accepted assumption described in the novice–expert literature that gaining expertise is a linear, developmental process (e.g., Dreyfus & Dreyfus, 1986). Instead, it represents professional development in education as a U-curve process that involves a negative side of decline in performance and attitudes followed by a positive side of overcoming the difficulty and reconstructing teachers' pedagogical-content knowledge.

The core of this investigation is information obtained from a series of observations and interviews with experienced and novice teachers who were participating in two kinds of staff development projects: One focuses on using cooperative computer learning environments (e.g., Mevarech, 1993, 1994b, in press; Mevarech & Kramarski, 1993; Mevarech & Light, 1992; Mevarech, Silber, & Fein, 1991), and the other relates to implementing cooperative–mastery learning in heterogeneous classrooms (e.g., Mevarech, 1985, 1991, 1994a; Mevarech & Susak, 1993). These two projects were selected for three reasons. First, many teachers who are experts in a specific discipline start to use computer environments and/or cooperative–mastery learning programs to enrich their instructional activities. Second, implementing each project involves both technical and nontechnical implications. Finally, the investigation of two kinds of staff development programs, one based on domain-specific knowledge in a certain subject matter (cooperative–mastery learning strategies) and the other based on general strategies (computer learning environments) may allow the generalization of our observations to a larger sample of teachers. Insights from these interviews may enable us to suggest tentative answers to the above questions and to enhance our ability to design more satisfying and beneficial professional development programs.

STAGES IN PROFESSIONAL DEVELOPMENT

Professional growth in education is considered as a process of change in teachers' mental models, beliefs, and perceptions regarding children's minds and learning. Research on the effects of staff development programs on teachers' pedagogical mental models and attitudes has been inconsistent. Most studies indicate that teachers' perceptions are rather stable and that staff development programs do not bring significant change to these perceptions and/or classroom practices (e.g., Guskey, 1989; Harris, Bessent, & McIntyre, 1969; McLaughlin & Marsh, 1978; Mevarech & Netz, 1991; Wood & Thompson, 1980).

In contrast, a number of studies report positive change in teachers' perceptions. Guskey (1989), for example, showed that teachers involved in mastery learning (Bloom, 1976) programs

> seemed to like teaching more, to feel more effective as teachers, and to be more confident of their abilities to handle challenging instructional problems. Some even described their experience as a rebirth, a rekindling of the flame which years of heartache and frustration in the classroom had nearly extinguished. (p. 443)

Crandall (1983) and Huberman and Miles (1984) reported similar findings: Teachers who implemented innovative methods and experienced positive changes in their students' learning developed more positive changes in attitudes, beliefs, and understandings.

Our own experience has not been different. Teachers who implemented an application-based cooperative (ABC) computer course that is deliberately designed to enhance creative problem solving (Mevarech, in press), and who succeeded in changing their students' way of thinking to be more fluent, flexible, and original, expressed both a higher level of self-efficacy and a more elaborated pedagogical schema, a term used by Berliner (1987) to indicate networks of knowledge for understanding practice.

In another study we observed similar changes in teachers' performance and attitudes. In this study, we designed an instructional method, called IMPROVE, for teaching mathematics in heterogeneous classrooms (Mevarech, 1994a). The method is based on metacognitive activities, student interactions on academic tasks, and the provision of systematic feedback–corrective–enrichment. IMPROVE is the acronym that describes the instructional steps of the method:

*I*ntroducing the new material
*M*etacognitive questioning
*P*racticing
*R*eviewing
*O*btaining mastery
*V*erification
*E*nrichment.

Empirical research has indicated that students exposed to IMPROVE showed significant improvement in their mathematical thinking, problem-solving ability, and use of mathematical language (Mevarech, 1994a). Parallel to the change in student learning, teachers experienced a tremendous change in their own pedagogical schemata, beliefs, and attitudes toward teaching and learning. The change, however, was not linearly structured. The entry stage was characterized by anxiety, confusion, and hesitation regarding the possibility of teaching *all* students higher-thinking processes. Then came a stage in which anxiety was reduced and the method was explored and adapted to the needs of the teachers and their particular classes. Only after teachers mastered the elements of the method and implemented it successfully in their classes did they reach a stage of positive change in their pedagogical schemata, skills, and beliefs. It is interesting to note that some teachers internalized the method so deeply that a year later, when asked to participate in a research project that required them to teach in a traditional way, they had difficulty moving back to what they did before they were trained to use IMPROVE.

These findings and the current research on the processes of conceptual change (Pintrich et al., 1993) and career development (Huberman, 1989) led us to describe a U-curve model of professional growth that explains both the positive and negative change in teachers' pedagogical schemata, beliefs, and perceptions. The model is based on the studies of Dwyer, Ringstaff, and Sandholtz (1991), who focused on teachers in technology-rich classrooms; on Guskey (1989), who explored changes in teachers' attitudes and perceptions; on Hall and his colleagues (Hall, Loucks, Rutherford, & Newlove, 1975; Hall, 1976), who suggested the LoU chart to describe the levels of use and concerns about an innovation; on Huberman (1989), who described a sequence of stages in teacher career development; and on Rich (1993), who observed expert teachers implementing a cooperative learning method for the first time. The model includes five stages: survival, exploration and bridging, adaptation, conceptual change, and invention. This progression can be viewed as a continuous, evolutionary process, gradually developed over time, from the initial stage of entering the classroom after being exposed to an inservice program, to actual adoption of the method and reconstruction of teachers' pedagogical schemata (Shulman, 1987). The model does not, however, include preimplementation stages described by Hall and colleagues (1975) as involving: (1) nonuse—a state in which teachers have little or no knowledge of the innovation and do nothing toward becoming involved; (2) orientation—a state in which teachers take action to get information about the innovation but do not actually use it; and (3) preparation—a state in which teachers are preparing for first use of the innovation and establishing time to begin. It should be noted that although the process as a whole is continuous, the articulation of a sequence of stages was introduced to clarify the progression.

Survival—Experienced Teachers Become (Temporary) Novices

Coming out of the inservice forum, teachers begin to implement a new method or a new learning environment with which they have little or no experience. This creates two problems. First, how do teachers go about applying the new knowledge in the classroom? Second, what effects do the new method have on teachers' mental models, beliefs, and perceptions? These two problems are elaborated below.

Instructional Activities. Generally speaking, at the entry stage teachers' activities can be characterized as "survival." Teachers are concerned that the new technique will not fulfill its promises, and thus they show little inclination to significantly change their traditional manner of instruction. When speaking about the new method or learning environment, they typically describe implementation in terms of "technical" changes.

In the first weeks of using a new method, many teachers, including experienced ones, face typical first-year-teacher problems such as discipline, resource management, and personal frustration (Dwyer et al., 1991). Others act in a rigid way, as if following a recipe from a cookbook. Still others change the physical organization of the classroom but continue to teach as they did before. Hall and colleagues (1975) termed this stage "mechanical use of the innovation—[a] state in which the user focuses most effort on the short-term, day-to-day use of the innovation with little time for reflection. . . . [At this stage] teachers solicit management information about such things as logistics, scheduling techniques, and ideas for reducing amount of time and work required of [the] user" (p. 8). For example, teachers employing computer-assisted instruction (CAI) argued that they "cannot interfere with the computer work" or that "the computer is yet another seven-day wonder, which, if ignored, will go away" (Riding, 1984, p. 1). Cooperative–mastery learning teachers (e.g., Mevarech, 1985, 1991, 1994a) often changed the physical environment of the classroom to fit small-group learning but continued to teach the core material in traditional ways, arguing that the new and difficult material should be explained by the teacher to the whole class; otherwise the children would not understand. A common excuse for continuing to use traditional methods was: "I have to adapt the new method to the needs of my students." Ironically, acting under the hat of "adapting teaching," these teachers did not introduce any changes into their ongoing instructional activities.

Interestingly, although most of the teachers we observed and interviewed had more than five years of experience, at the survival stage they acted like novices. It seems that in implementing the new method they forgot their rich pedagogical knowledge base. Rather than basing their decisions on that knowledge, they developed extensive dependence on the inservice designers and mentors assigned to help them in applying the new knowledge in classroom practice. For example, teachers using computers often asked the mentors: "What should I do if a student asks me a question for which I have no answer?" This concern is never raised with regard to traditional classrooms, even though such events also occur there. Expert teachers probably can solve problems related to traditional classrooms more efficiently than those related to innovations because their advanced pedagogical schemata enable them to process classroom events in ways that are more elaborated as compared to novices (e.g., Borko & Livingston, 1989; Rich, 1993; Shulman, 1987).

These observations are in accord with those of Rich (1993):

Prior to the investigation, six of the nine participating teachers could be characterized as experts according to a variety of criteria (see Bents & Bents, 1990). They were experienced, were highly regarded by their principals and colleagues, expressed confidence in their teaching ability, and generally facilitated good progress in student achievement. Nevertheless, all six teachers acted very much like novices during the initial two or three weeks of implementing STAD [a cooperative learning method]. They were more teacher-centered than before and expressed anxiety about what and how to teach. They rarely used their usual routines in instruction even when they were easily transferable to the new situation. The teachers used the jargon and tactics of cooperative learning but did not seem to "own" them. Recommended lesson units were implemented in an inflexible manner so that the unique interests, abilities, and quirks of individual teachers were not apparent during instruction. They had difficulties in identifying critical elements in classroom situations, in defining priorities, and in choosing feasible alternative, when lessons did not proceed as planned. (p. 139)

The application of innovations creates a new situation in which experienced teachers shift from being experienced to being a novice. For experienced teachers, this is not an easy situation. It may involve frustration, which may in turn evolve into skepticism and even withdrawal from the innovative method. Some teachers have psychological problems admitting their difficulties; others may deny their problems altogether. This may explain why so many innovations in education do not survive the first year of implementation (Cuban, 1990).

Theoretical Framework. Since professional development in education involves teacher learning (Rosenholtz, 1989), cognitive theories may explain the negative changes observed at the survival stage.

Cognitive theories assume that learners' prior knowledge influences all aspects of information processing, including perceptions of cues in the environment, encoding of these cues, levels of information processing, retrieval of the information, comprehension, thinking, and problem solving (Pintrich et al., 1993). Intensive research has shown that new knowledge is acquired via an interaction with existing knowledge (e.g., Alexander & Judy, 1988). When the new knowledge is in accord with the existing mental models, it may be easily assimilated within the cognitive schemata. However, when the appropriate schemata do not exist or when the new and preexisting knowledge contradict each other, the learner may face considerable difficulty in acquiring the new knowledge. The old knowledge often interferes with the new knowledge and causes a decline in performance. This is the case, for example, when one learns to use a new keyboard or when one learns a new language. In both cases, the existing knowledge interferes with the acquisition of the new knowledge and causes repetitive mistakes. It is quite possible, therefore, that a similar negative transfer may occur when a teacher is exposed to new knowledge regarding the innovation: The rich pedagogical knowledge base and the mental model the teacher possesses about the nature of children's minds and learning may interfere with the acquisition of the new information introduced in the inservice training forum. This, in turn, may be associated with a decline in performance.

Cognitive theories may also explain the stability or negative change in teachers' beliefs observed at the survival stage (Mevarech & Netz, 1991). Current theories on self-concept in general and teacher self-concept (TSC) in particular are based primarily on an information-processing model. According to this model, TSC is conceived to be a function of information encoded and transformed into a set of beliefs (Byrne, 1984). Mevarech and Netz (1991) explains that "in school, feedback that teachers receive from students, both formal evaluation of academic learning and moment to moment responses during instruction, provides a major source of information for self assessment of teaching abilities" (p. 233). If indeed the entry stage is associated with survival activities, there would be either no change or a temporary decline in teachers' beliefs and perceptions.

Mevarech and Netz (1991) tested this hypothesis in an empirical study that focused on 145 elementary teachers—90 of them implemented a CAI program for the first year, and 50 others served as a nontreatment control group. All participants were female, with a mean of 10.8 years of teaching experience. Among the teachers, 22% taught first or second grade, 30% taught third or fourth grade, 30% taught fifth or sixth grade, and 19% taught seventh or eighth grade. Results showed that although the major purpose of the CAI program was to carry out the practicing activities and diagnosis processes, no significant differences were found between the CAI and control teachers on their professional self-concept, sense of responsibility for student learning, or allocations of time to various instructional activities, including practicing and testing. Furthermore, within the CAI group, no significant differences were found between novice and experienced teachers on any variable. Similar findings were reported by Guskey (1984) regarding teachers implementing mastery learning programs for the first year.

Other evidence on teachers' behavior at the survival stage was provided by Sandholtz, Ringstaff, and Dwyer (1991). In this study, teachers using application-based computer systems were engaged with technical problems relating to the advanced technology. They replicated traditional instructional and learning activities, and they almost never interacted with other teachers sharing the same problems, even though supports for interaction, such as professional release time, training workshops, and a telecommunications network between sites, were available. As the year progressed, the frequency of interaction among teachers increased. Yet exchanges remained informal, providing only emotional support.

Fortunately, survival is not the only theme that characterizes the entry stage. Survival is usually intertwined with what Huberman (1989) calls "discovery." The implementation of something new elicits motivation and excitement. Experienced teachers may rediscover the initial enthusiasm of teaching, the pride of using innovations, and the satisfaction of continuing to learn.

Quite often, as Huberman (1989) indicates, "empirical studies show that these two aspects occur in parallel, and that the excitement and challenge of 'discovery' is what brings many teachers through the attrition of day-to-day 'survival'" (p. 349).

To sum up, the initial stage of implementing something new is characterized by survival activities. Experienced teachers temporarily feel like novices. They swing from permissiveness to excessive strictness, are concerned with discipline and management problems, focus on physical changes in classroom organization, and show mechanical use of the innovation. Sometimes they become so frustrated that they withdraw from the innovation. In other cases, they experience "discovery" moments, which facilitate coping with the innovation. This stage resembles the career entry stage described by Huberman (1989).

Exploration and Bridging

Teachers who survive the entry stage move into a stage of exploration and bridging. At this stage, teachers approach the new method more positively. In particular, they ask themselves how the new method differs from what they did before in terms of both instructional activities and pedagogical theories. However, their questions remain basically "technical." For example, computer teachers were interested in locating relevant software and managing the equipment (Dwyer et al., 1991). IMPROVE teachers were concerned with how to weight the formative and corrective tests in calculating the total grade for the report cards. It is as if they start to believe there are some alternatives to "traditional instruction," but they are still hesitant and probing.

Another characteristic of the exploration and bridging stage is teachers' preoccupation with themselves (Hall, 1976). Often teachers express their concerns by asking: How can *I* cope with the innovation? How will the implementation of the new method affect *my* sense of adequacy? How will *I* utilize the innovative learning environment? Thus, rather than asking how the innovation facilitates student learning, they ask how it affects them.

Exploring and bridging often result in a routine use of the innovation (Hall et al., 1975). Knowing the requirements, teachers apply those requirements smoothly, with less stress and minimal management problems. When speaking about the innovation, teachers report that "implementation is going along satisfactorily with few if any problems" (p. 8).

Yet stabilizing the use of the innovation does not guarantee reflective implementation. On the contrary, the routine use is characterized by monotonous implementation, with little thought given to improving the innovation

(Hall et al., 1975). Teachers pay little attention to ways of adapting the innovation to the special needs of the classroom. They make no special effort to seek additional information about the innovation, and they do not use formative evaluation to modify any aspect of the new method or learning environment.

Given that the transition from the survival to the exploration stage is a crucial phase in professional growth, we must consider how that transition can be smoother. Dembo and Gibson (1985), Ashton and Webb (1986), and Smylie (1988) have emphasized the role of being involved in school decision making as an important factor in facilitating teachers' attitudes and perceptions. It is possible, as Calderhead (1987) argued, that when the innovation is self-selected rather than imposed on teachers, or when teachers are involved in making decisions regarding the adoption of the innovation, teachers are more motivated to try out the innovation and willing to take more responsibility for the outcomes.

Support for this assumption comes from the study of Mevarech and Netz (1991) described above. This study found that CAI teachers involved in school-level decision making developed more positive teacher self-concept and a greater sense of responsibility for student achievement than their counterparts who were not involved in such processes. In addition, compared to the non–decision makers, the decision makers reported allocation of more time for teaching new materials. These differences were all statistically significant.

Adaptation: From Technical Application to Reflective Implementation

The adaptation stage is characterized by reflective use of the innovation. Teachers apply their pedagogical-content knowledge to examine the innovation and adapt it to the needs of their students. They use their expertise in making decisions and do not hesitate to introduce changes in the learning environment. At this stage the new technology becomes thoroughly integrated into teachers' ongoing classroom practice.

The adaptation process is observed in many different ways. CAI teachers, for example, started to use the diagnostic information provided by the computer in assessing and planning their instructional activities. IMPROVE teachers designed their own feedback–corrective materials, changed the order of instruction according to the knowledge of their students, and were more flexible in allocating time to various instructional activities. ABC teachers applied different kinds of software in introducing and teaching new topics. They were concerned with how to balance the cognitive, social, and technological aspects of the program in order to maximize its effectiveness.

At this stage teachers are confident enough to discuss problems with their colleagues. Their discussions are based on their expertise: How can the innovation fit the needs of the poor/good students? What can be done to further enhance the effectiveness of the innovation? How can the innovation be used by a particular student who has a special problem (e.g., cannot study in a small group, suffers from computerphobia, or is a computer whiz who does not let other students use the software). In planning a lesson, for example, IMPROVE teachers activated their pedagogical schemata about children's cognitive developmental stage, preexisting knowledge, and memory capacity. They knew what children at this age were like, what kinds of difficulties to expect, and what it is important to teach. They can integrate that knowledge with new knowledge about the innovation. Thus, while at the survival stage teachers are helpless and at the exploration stage they are preoccupied with themselves, at the adaptation stage they have moved to a more student-centered approach showing reflective implementation of the new method. Rather than asking "How am *I* going to use the computer in teaching graphs?" they are concerned with the problem "How can Johnny be motivated to use the computer more mindfully in interpreting the graphs?"

Another change in teacher behavior relates to planning and problem solving. While in the previous stages teachers were concerned mainly with planning and solving moment-to-moment problems, at the adaptation stage they can look at the entire unit and plan instruction by considering children's existing knowledge, developmental stage, and motivational variables as well as the unit objectives. At this stage planning is often oriented toward long-term objectives. Teachers are concerned, for example, with summative testing and evaluation. They look for alternative procedures of evaluation and are willing to examine these procedures.

The reflective, adaptive implementation of the innovation may result in positive changes in schooling outcomes. IMPROVE teachers, for example, expressed the feeling that even low achievers showed learning capabilities that they had never shown before. ABC teachers claimed that pupils could process information much better than they did without using the computer. These changes in students' performance were commonly followed by changes in teachers' beliefs and perceptions (Fullan, 1985; Guskey, 1989). As Guskey (1989) indicates:

> When teachers see that an innovation enhances the learning of students in their classes—when, for example they see students attaining higher level of achievement, becoming more involved in instruction, or expressing greater confidence in themselves or in their abilities to learn—then, and perhaps only then, a significant change in teachers' attitudes and perception is likely to occur. (p. 446)

Conceptual Change

The progression from survival, through exploration and bridging, to adaptation builds a readiness for conceptual change in teachers' pedagogical mental model. The basic mental model many experienced teachers hold is the information-processing model (Strauss, 1993). That is, teachers believe: (1) Knowledge is possessed by the teachers and thus external to children's minds; (2) children's minds operate like a filter, having openings of a certain size that allow information to enter; (3) teachers have to pass the knowledge into the children's mind by serving up knowledge in chunks of a size that can "get through" the openings (Strauss, 1993). However, as teachers apply the innovation in a reflective, dynamic way, they realize that learning can be the result of several processes, not only the "transmission of knowledge." ABC teachers, for example, developed a constructivist approach to learning, which is based on the assumption that students have to construct knowledge. They talked about learning in terms of hypothesis formulation and testing, rule assessment, and general skill acquisition. Many teachers started to talk about "creative learning" as a team synonym for "constructivism." ABC teachers felt that teaching in a creative learning environment, such as that provided by the ABC program, enhanced not only their students' creativity but also their own. The following are typical examples of ABC teachers' responses that express conceptual changes:

> Although I always believed that students could be creative, I did not know how to enhance it. The ABC course gave the means to do it.

> Before I was exposed to the ABC course I thought that school depressed students' creativity. I thought that only high-achieving students could be creative. Now I think that there is still some hope and school can enhance creativity, including that of "weak" students.

Another interesting change in teachers' pedagogical mental models relates to their emphasis of the sociocognitive aspects of learning. Teachers who used the advanced technology in small groups realized the crucial role of student–student interaction as a powerful means for enhancing cognitive development. As one of the district technology supervisors reported:

> "The student really enjoy these group activities and, as we all know, learn more since they are actively rather than passively participating in the learning experience. Our teachers are learning to be facilitators rather than the total dispensers of knowledge. Everyone benefits." (In Dwyer et al., 1991, p. 50)

Instructional activities at this stage are quite different from those used before. Here, teachers focus on the cognitive and psychosocial objectives of the unit. They ask themselves: What are the main objectives of the program? Are these objectives legitimate? If they are, what is the best way to attain them? Long-term planning is based on a deep understanding of classroom events and elaborated pedagogical-content knowledge, such as usually characterized expert teachers (Shulman, 1987). Teachers at this stage are able to meet the needs of diverse students by activating highly abstract knowledge structures that involve information about many aspects of learning (Rich, 1993).

Once teachers assimilate the new method in their existing schemata, they develop advanced needs to learn more about the program. Their questions are not limited to ones of technical assistance but are extended to other areas, such as how to avoid misconceptions and bugs in children's learning. Conversely, because they begin to accept the innovation, they have questions and concerns that compel them to seek assistance from their colleagues, observe other teachers using the innovation, share instructional strategies with others, and look for more theoretical background related to the new program. As Dwyer and colleagues (1991) indicate: "The most important change in this phase was an increasing tendency of teachers to reflect on teaching, to question old patterns, and to speculate about the causes behind changes they were seeing in their students" (p. 50).

Theoretical Background. In the psychological literature, two main approaches explain the processes of conceptual changes: conflict resolution and mutual reasoning. Neo-Piagetian approaches emphasize the value of sociocognitive conflict (e.g., Perret-Clermont, 1980). Guided by the principle of equilibration, these researchers argue that learners seek a relatively stable homeostasis between the preexisting schema and the new knowledge. Thus, when learners, be they children or adults, are confronted with an alternative point of view, opportunities for cognitive contradictions (conflicts) are created that push individuals to change their conceptualizations.

Vygotskian approaches, by contrast, focus on what is cooperatively produced and shared in interactions with others (Vygotsky, 1978). According to this approach, mutual reasoning is the key element that leads to conceptual change. Vygotsky assumed that common engagement in cooperative problem solving and the opportunity to discussions with a partner make learners more aware of the relevant dimensions of a problem. This allows individuals to take advantage of aspects of the solution that the partner may offer. This mechanism may also create the zone of proximal development and thus produce a higher level of understanding. Thus, for Vygotsky, conceptual change is a gradual process based on mutual refinement of knowledge.

Both the neo-Piagetian and Vygotskian approaches may explain teachers' conceptual change at this stage. According to Piaget, the contradiction between teachers' preexisting knowledge (e.g., that learning is mainly a matter of knowledge transmission) and the new conceptualization (e.g., that learning can occur through many other ways, including knowledge construction) sets the opportunity for conceptual change. On the other hand, according to Vygotskian sociocognitive approaches, interactions between teachers, as well as between them and the environment (e.g., mentors, principals, and students), are crucial for attaining conceptual changes in pedagogical schemata.

Although these two approaches represent different conceptualizations of knowledge acquisition, recent studies have shown that neither conflict resolution nor mutual reasoning are sufficient for conceptual change to occur (e.g., Pintrich et al., 1993). Other special conditions are necessary. Posner, Strike, Hewson, and Gertzog (1982) posited four conditions. The first is *dissatisfaction* with current conceptions. This suggests that teachers who are more dissatisfied with current classroom events are likely to consider a radical change in their mental models regarding children's learning and the roles of instruction. The second condition is that a new concept be *intelligible*. Teachers must understand the innovation and consider it to be a better means for improving learning. The third condition is that the new concept be *plausible*. While the teachers may be able to understand the new concept, they may not be convinced that it can be applied in the real life of the classroom or "may deem the new concept too inconsistent with other understandings to merit further consideration" (Pintrich et al., 1993, p. 172). Finally, the new concept must appear *fruitful*. That is, it must show teachers that it indeed solves the problems or enables the learners to achieve higher standards and better psychosocial outcomes.

The four conditions for conceptual change (Posner et al., 1982) provide further support for the model of the process of teacher change suggested by Guskey (1986, 1989). As mentioned above, Guskey (1989) argued that

> significant change in teachers' attitudes and perceptions is likely to take place only *after* changes in student learning outcomes are evident. The changes in student learning result, of course, from specific changes in classroom practice; for example, a new instructional approach, the use of new materials or curricula, or simply some modification in teaching procedures or classroom format. Whatever the case, significant change in the attitudes and perceptions of teachers is seen as contingent on their gaining evidence of change in the student learning outcomes. (p. 445)

In other words, only *after* teachers realize the innovation is plausible and fruitful can change in their attitudes, perceptions, and/or pedagogical mental models be expected.

Invention

The stage of conceptual changes may be followed by a stage of renewal and invention in which teachers use their reconstructed pedagogical knowledge to experiment with new materials, new assignments, or different ways of teaching (Hall et al., 1975). Few teachers, however, move into this stage. To do so requires teachers to question the very foundations of their craft. Probably, as Huberman (1989) indicates, "these attempts compensate for the uncertainties of the entry stage, which translated into a rigid, rudimentary, no-risk set of lesson plans and activity formats" (p. 351).

The teachers we interviewed at this point spoke, for example, of greater pleasure, satisfaction, and certainty about the potential of education to improve schooling outcomes. The following quotation from one teacher's interview illustrates this point:

> I was a high-level programmer in the army. I thought that I would never be a teacher, not to speak of being a counselor or a homeroom teacher. I moved into education because I felt that education is a profession for women. Teachers do not have to work long hours and they get vacation with their kids. Before I experienced ABC, I thought that I would only teach programming languages, because it is a subject-oriented job not based on "talking and listening." Now I changed my mind. I may become a homeroom teacher because only through talking with children may one understand their minds and help them learn. [Indeed, a year later, she became a homeroom teacher].

Similar conceptual change was experienced by a literature teacher who started to teach the ABC course. At the end of the first year, this teacher expressed her feelings as follows:

> I had a second degree in humanities and education. I considered "talking" to be the main theme of the teaching profession. I like to talk with children and listen to them. I never thought that I would become a computer teacher because I perceived the work with computers to be inflexible and uncreative. Now my perception is completely different. I know that learning with computers can be creative. Learning does not involve only recall of information, but also generating new ideas, formulating hypotheses, and testing them. Computers can be utilized for enhancing creativity, which for me is the most important goal of education.

Today, this teacher is involved in developing new programs and learning activities based on the ABC approach. She, together with other teachers who also had reached the invention stage, designed an interdisciplinary course for junior high school students based on application-based computer software. The purpose of such a course is threefold: (1) improving students' ability to solve complex, ill-defined problems; (2) enhancing students' competency to work in teams; and (3) increasing students' familiarity with various kinds of application-based computer software. To achieve these goals, students were faced with an ill-defined problem that could be approached from different perspectives, using various computerized tools. In one school, the interdisciplinary course focused on Jerusalem. Some students chose to look at Jerusalem from an archaeological point of view; others focused on the vegetation unique to this city. Several student–teams investigated the sources of the historical-political conflicts related to Jerusalem, whereas others examined the economic problems of a city so reliant on tourism. Teaching children to attempt to solve these problems required close collaboration among teachers from different disciplines, including history, social sciences, natural sciences, economics, and so forth. Furthermore, teachers had to use the appropriate software and adopt cooperative learning methods, since the ABC course is based on a social-cognitive approach to learning. In this particular case, it seemed the teacher who reached the invention stage convinced other teachers to take a new path in their professional growth.

CREATING CONDITIONS FOR PROFESSIONAL GROWTH

The U-curve model of professional growth outlined here, based on a sequence of stages, raises a series of legitimate, classical critiques. First, we have posited a universal model, as if inservice conditions and school constraints are unimportant. Obviously, the kind of inservice training, the amount and quality of support given to teachers after the training, and school conditions (e.g., involving teachers in school-level decision making) play a crucial role in professional growth.

Second, describing a sequence of changes raises questions about individual differences in moving along the stages:

- Who are the teachers who are likely to remain at the first stage, and who are those who will reach the highest stage?
- Are the stages hierarchically organized?
- Can teachers, at a given time, alternate between different stages or be at one stage with regard to one aspect of the innovation (e.g., teaching the content knowledge) and at another stage with regard to another aspect (e.g., implementing the cooperative activities)?
- Is the rate of progress along the stages equal for different types of teachers?

Rich (1993) argues that teachers can be novices and experts at the same time, depending on the classroom context and the instructional method they use. Berliner (1987) believes the development of expertise in teaching is normally a time-consuming process, but within each stage of development, stability is assumed. Undoubtedly, the process of gaining expertise merits further research.

Finally, the model suggested here is based on interviews and observations of two groups of experienced teachers: computer teachers and IMPROVE teachers. The question regarding the extent to which this model can be generalized to other groups of teachers and/or to other kinds of staff development programs having different goals and different techniques is still open.

In spite of these limitations, the model may have important implications for teachers, practitioners, and educational psychologists. One implication is that staff developers as well as teachers should be aware of the U-curve changes in professional growth. In most cases, experienced teachers and practitioners expect a linear growth of professional development. They do not expect temporary negative outcomes, nor do they know that the process is slow, gradual, and difficult to achieve. Having inappropriate expectations may create additional difficulties in the process.

Another implication is that staff development programs must be combined with intensive support provided at all stages of professional growth. Yet the kind of support should fit the stage in which the teacher is functioning. At the survival stage, affective support and precise, step-by-step guidance are most important. During this period, teachers have to be motivated to continue implementing the innovation in spite of the difficulties encountered. As Guskey (1989) indicates: "Support is necessary so that teachers can tolerate the anxiety of occasional failures and persist in their implementation efforts" (p. 447). At the exploration stage, teacher need ongoing guidance and direction to help them bridge their own experience and the innovation. At the stage of adaptation, teachers need to know how to make changes in the program while maintaining fidelity to it. When they ask, for example, how to divide their time among various instructional activities, the mentor may guide them to reflect on their instructional goals, decide their priorities, and allocate time according to these priorities. Finally, at the stages of conceptual change and invention, teachers should be guided in discovering their espoused and in-use pedagogical schemata and how to make connections between new and old pedagogical knowledge (Strauss, 1993).

Support can be provided by mentors, colleagues, heads of departments, or principals. However, a more effective way of inducing change is by conducting staff development programs at the school level rather than with individual teachers. Our experience shows that training the entire school faculty has several advantages: (1) It enables teachers to discuss difficulties with other teachers; (2) it informs the principal about the innovation and what difficulties teachers may expect; and (3) it increases the effectiveness of the mentors' work, since they are able to provide support to all school personnel, or to groups of teachers teaching the same subject matter or the same grade level. Implementing such support in small groups may further enhance understanding of social-cognitive theories and how to apply them in classroom practice. Thus the support shows the teachers not only their implicit models of learning and instruction but also how to make connections between existing and new knowledge.

Systematic feedback to teachers is another crucial factor in the provision of guidance and support. Teachers in learning situations, like other learners, need regular feedback on their performance. Since conditions for conceptual changes involve successful application of the innovation, teachers need to observe changes in their students' learning and psychosocial development. Formative tests, diagnostic information, or mentors' observations can provide such feedback.

The model described here may be used by educational psychology instructors who wish to build upon and expand teachers' existing mental models via mutual reasoning. As Strauss (1993) suggests, such a course should include the following units: (1) helping teachers discover their espoused mental models about instruction and children's learning by beginning the course with semi-instructional interviews; (2) providing opportunities to discuss espoused pedagogical knowledge; (3) introducing the new model of learning and instruction by making connections between the old and the new knowledge; and (4) informing the teachers of the expected process of gaining expertise. Thus the course would show teachers not only their implicit models of learning and instruction, but also how to make connections between existing knowledge and new knowledge. Furthermore, since cognitive-only models of learning do not explain the entire process of knowledge acquisition, noncognitive factors should also be taken into account. In particular, Pintrich and colleagues (1993) emphasized the crucial roles of contextual factors and of four motivational constructs (goals, values, self-efficacy, and control beliefs) as potential mediators of conceptual change. Although studies have shown a relationship between teachers' self-efficacy and schooling outcomes, much research is needed to clarify the ways in which teachers' motivational beliefs about themselves as teachers, and their students' minds and learning processes, can facilitate or hinder professional growth.

In summary, a U-curve model of professional growth was used to explain both the positive and negative outcomes of staff development programs. In particular, it was shown how experienced teachers become temporary novices, but then get over their difficulties and gain a higher level of expertise than they possessed prior to entering the staff development program. Being aware of these negative processes associated with professional growth may ease the process and lessen the payoffs associated with the U-curve. Furthermore, talking with the teachers about the expected difficulties while reflecting upon their technical and pedagogical knowledge may be a powerful means in helping teachers to implement the innovation. Of course, many issues related to professional growth in education remain open. Some relate to the model itself. Others regard the influence of other variables, such as self-efficacy, on teachers' professional growth. These issues may be addressed in future research.

Acknowledgments. Many thanks to Professor Yisrael Rich for his overall contribution to this work, including his suggestion for the title of the chapter. Thanks also are due to Ms. Ahuva Budai at the Institute for the Advancement of Social Integration in the Schools at Bar-Ilan University and the teachers, mentors, and principals who participated in this research.

REFERENCES

Alexander, P. A., & Judy, J. (1988). The interaction of domain specific and strategic knowledge in academic performance. *Review of Educational Research, 58*, 375–404.

Ashton, P., & Webb, R. (1986). *Making a difference: Teachers' sense of efficacy and student achievement.* New York: Longman.

Bents, M., & Bents, R. (1990, April). *Development of expertise in teaching prototypes: Novice, advanced beginner, expert.* Paper presented at the annual meeting of the American Educational Research Association, Boston.

Berliner, D. (1987). Ways of thinking about students and classrooms by more and less experienced teachers. In J. Calderhead (Ed.), *Exploring teachers' thinking* (pp. 60–83). London: Cassell.

Bloom, B. S. (1976). *Human characteristics and school learning.* New York: McGraw-Hill.

Borko, H., & Livingston, C. (1989). Cognition and improvisation: Differences in mathematics instructed by expert and novice teachers. *American Educational Research Journal, 26*, 473–498.

Byrne, B. M. (1984). General academic self concept nomological network: A review of construct validation research. *Review of Educational Research, 54*, 427–460.

Calderhead, J. (1987). *Exploring teachers' thinking.* London: Cassell.

Crandall, D. P. (1983). The teachers' role in school improvement. *Educational Leadership, 41*(3), 6–9.

Cuban, L. (1990). Reforming again, again, and again. *Educational Researcher, 19*(1), 3–14.

Dembo, M. H., & Gibson, S. (1985). Teachers' sense of efficacy: An important factor in school improvement. *Elementary School Journal, 86*, 173–184.

Dreyfus, H., & Dreyfus, S. (1986). *Mind over machine.* New York: Free Press.

Dwyer, D. C., Ringstaff, C., & Sandholtz, J. H. (1991). Changes in teachers' beliefs and practices in technology-rich classrooms. *Educational Leadership, 48*(8), 45–52.

Fullan, M. (1985). Change processes and strategies at the local level. *Elementary School Journal, 85,* 391–421.

Guskey, T. R. (1984). The influence of change in instructional effectiveness upon the affective characteristics of teachers. *American Educational Research Journal, 21,* 245–259.

Guskey, T. R. (1986). Staff development and the process of teacher change. *Educational Researcher, 15*(5), 5–12.

Guskey, T. R. (1989). Attitude and perceptual change in teachers. *International Journal of Educational Research, 13,* 439–454.

Hall, G. E. (1976). The study of individual teacher and professor concerns about innovations. *Journal of Teacher Education, 27,* 22–23.

Hall, G. E., Loucks, S. F., Rutherford, W. L., & Newlove, B. W. (1975). Levels of use of the innovation: A framework for analyzing innovation adoption. *Journal of Teacher Education, 26,* 52–56.

Harris, B. M., Bessent, W., & McIntyre, K. E. (1969). *Inservice education: A guide to better practice.* Englewood Cliffs, NJ: Prentice-Hall.

Huberman, M. (1989). On teachers' careers: Once over lightly, with a broad brush. *International Journal of Educational Research, 13,* 347–362.

Huberman, M., & Miles, M. (1984). *Innovation up close: How school improvement works.* New York: Plenum.

McLaughlin, M. W., & March, D. D. (1978). Staff development and school change. *Teachers College Record, 80,* 69–93.

Mevarech, Z. R. (1985). The effects of cooperative mastery learning strategies on mathematics achievement. *Journal of Educational Research, 78,* 372–377.

Mevarech, Z. R. (1991). Learning mathematics in different mastery environments. *Journal of Educational Research, 84,* 225–231.

Mevarech, Z. R. (1993). Who benefits from computer assisted cooperative learning? *Journal of Educational Computing Research, 9,* 451–464.

Mevarech, Z. R. (1994a, April). *Cognition, metacognition, and mathematical thinking: Teaching mathematics in heterogeneous classrooms.* Paper presented at the annual meeting of the American Educational Research Association, New Orleans.

Mevarech, Z. R. (1994b). The effectiveness of individualized versus cooperative computer-based integrated learning systems. *The International Journal of Educational Research, 21,* 39–52.

Mevarech, Z. R. (in press). Information processing technologies: What do students learn and how?

Mevarech, Z. R., & Kramarski, B. (1993). Vygotsky and Papert: Social-cognitive interactions within Logo environments. *The British Journal of Educational Psychology, 63,* 96–109.

Mevarech, Z. R., & Light, P. (Ed.). (1992). Cooperative learning with computers [special issue]. *Learning and Instruction, 2*(3).

Mevarech, Z. R., & Netz, N. (1991). Stability and change in affective characteristics of teachers: Can computer environment make a difference? *British Journal of Educational Psychology, 61,* 233–239.

Mevarech, Z. R., Silber, O., & Fein, D. (1991). Learning with computers in small groups: Cognitive and affective outcomes. *Journal of Educational Computing Research, 7,* 233–243.

Mevarech, Z. R., & Susak, Z. (1993). Effects of learning with cooperative–mastery method on elementary students. *Journal of Educational Research, 86,* 197–205.

Perret-Clermont, A. N. (1980). *Social interaction and cognitive development in children.* New York: Academic Press.

Pintrich, P. R., Marx, R. W., & Boyle, R. A. (1993). Beyond cold conceptual change: The role of motivational beliefs and classroom contextual factors in the process of conceptual change. *Review of Educational Research, 63,* 167–200.

Posner, G., Strike, K., Hewson, P., & Gertzog, W. (1982). Accommodation of a scientific conception: Toward a theory of conceptual change. *Science Education, 66,* 211–227.

Rich, Y. (1993). Stability and change in teacher expertise. *Teachers and Teacher Education, 9,* 137–146.

Riding, J. R. (1984). *Computers in the primary school: A practical guide for teachers.* London: Open Books.

Rosenholtz, D. (1989). *Teachers' workplace.* London: Longman.

Sandholtz, J. H., Ringstaff, C., & Dwyer, D. C. (1991, April). *The relationship between technological innovation and collegial interaction.* Paper presented at the annual meeting of the American Educational Research Association, Chicago.

Shulman, L. (1987). Those who understand: Knowledge growth in teaching. *Educational Researcher, 15*(2), 4–14.

Smylie, M. A. (1988). The enhancement function of staff development: Organizational and psychological antecedents to individual teacher change. *American Educational Research Journal, 25,* 1–30.

Strauss, S. (1993). Teachers' pedagogical content knowledge about children's minds and learning: Implications for teacher education. *Educational Psychologist, 28,* 279–290.

Vygotsky, L. S. (1978). *Mind in society: The development of higher psychological processes.* Cambridge, MA: Harvard University Press.

Waugh, R. F., & Punch, K. F. (1987). Teacher receptivity to system wide change in the implementing stage. *Review of Educational Research, 57,* 237–254.

Wood, F. H., & Thompson, S. R. (1980). Guidelines for better staff development. *Educational Leadership, 37,* 374–378.

8

Dynamics of Teacher Career Stages

RALPH FESSLER

The following is a series of quotes recorded in conversations with teachers:

> I am overwhelmed with all of the decisions I have to make every day. I can't keep track of everything I have to do—and nobody ever told me the kids wouldn't behave!!

> I just attended a workshop on cooperative learning. I can't wait to try it with my kids. I know they will love it.

> My greatest satisfaction is seeing the "light" go on when I have helped a youngster learn, understand, and appreciate something that was difficult for him.

> Teaching used to be fun—but not any longer. With all of the regulations and rules in our school, I no longer have the freedom to teach. And—I am getting tired of reading in the paper every day what a rotten job we teachers are doing.

> Ten more years until retirement. I've paid my dues—and I'll continue to do my job. But—don't expect me to be a cheerleader for change. I'll leave that up to the youngsters teaching in our school.

These statements carry messages regarding how the teachers quoted view their jobs. The variations in confidence, enthusiasm, and commitment reflect different phases or stages they are experiencing in their careers. For some, teaching is filled with excitement and enthusiasm, with each day bringing new opportunities to positively influence the lives of children. For others, the complexity of the job is overwhelming, with details and pressures that seem impossible to master. For still others, teaching is just a job to get through. Teachers experience many shifts in stages throughout their careers, often meandering back and forth between periods of growth and frustration in response to factors in their personal and organizational lives. Understanding the dynamics of what these teachers are experiencing can serve as a foundation for planning appropriate actions to support their changing personal and professional growth needs.

This chapter presents the Teacher Career Cycle Model as a framework for analyzing and understanding the stages teachers experience in their careers. In the following sections, previous work that influenced model development is reviewed, the process used for model building is presented, model components are described, and implications for teacher growth and development and research are considered.

PREVIOUS VIEWS OF THE TEACHER CAREER CYCLE

A number of individual studies and previous attempts at model building have influenced the development of the model presented in this chapter. Much of the research available on the stages of teachers' career development has its roots in the work of Frances Fuller (1969), who was interested in planning meaningful preservice programs for education students at the University of Texas–Austin. Her Teacher Concerns Questionnaire, which was a product of extensive interviews, literature reviews, and refined checklists, has yielded the following categories or clusters of concerns of individuals at various stages in the process of becoming a teacher (Fuller & Bown, 1975):

- *Preteaching concerns* cluster around education students' deep involvement in the pupil role and their criticism or even hostility toward classroom teachers they observe.
- *Early concerns about survival* arise when preservice teachers first come into contact with actual teaching. Now their concerns are with their own survival in teaching as well as control, mastery of content, and supervisor evaluations. Stress in this period is great.
- *Teaching situations concerns* incorporate both the survival concerns and concerns about the demands and limitations of teaching and trying to transfer their learning to a teaching situation.
- *Concerns about pupils* are expressed by preservice teachers, but they are often unable to respond to pupils' needs until they learn to cope with their own survival needs.

Fuller noted that, through these stages, the focus of those who are becoming teachers seemed to progress from concerns for *self*, to concerns for teaching *tasks*, to, finally, concerns for the *impact* they were having on students.

During the 1970s several authors presented views of teacher development that were based primarily on their own observations and anecdotal reflections. Although these contributions did not have much hard substantiating data, they did provide the beginning of a framework for further analysis.

Unruh and Turner (1970) were among the first to propose the notion of career stages. Their periods included:

1. *Initial teaching period* (approximately 1 to 5 years). This period is characterized by problems with management, organization, new curriculum developments, and being accepted by the rest of the staff.
2. *Period of building security* (approximately 6 to 15 years). Teachers here find satisfaction in a career and "know what they are doing." They seek ways to improve their background and knowledge and take additional courses and advanced degrees both to qualify for salary increases and to improve their teaching.
3. *Maturing period* (approximately 15 years and more). This period is characterized by security in professional life and involvement in outside interests (politics, art, literature, music, etc.). The secure attitude of teachers at this stage allows them to see change as a process, not a threat. They look for verification of new ideas and thrive on new concepts.

Gregorc (1973) reported on observations of teachers at University High School in Urbana, Illinois, and described the following four stages of teacher development:

1. *Becoming stage.* The individual demonstrates an ambivalent commitment to teaching and is beginning to develop initial concepts about the purposes of education, the nature of teaching, the role expectations in the educational process, and the role of the school as a social organization.
2. *Growing stage.* The individual's level of commitment is based on his or her minimal expectations of the school and those that the school has of the individual. The basic concepts and stereotypes of the educational process and of personal discipline and responsibilities are forming.
3. *Maturing stage.* The individual has made a strong commitment to education, functions beyond the minimum expectations, and draws upon and contributes to the varied resources of the school. In this stage, the individual tests concepts about education, self, others, subject matter, and the environment.
4. *Fully functioning stage.* The individual has made a definite commitment to the education profession. Immersed in the process of education, the person is trying to realize full potential as an individual teacher and as a contributing member of the profession. Concepts and beliefs are constantly undergoing testing and restructuring.

Katz (1972) described the following four developmental stages of pre-school teachers and the training needs necessary at each of the stages.

1. *Survival* lasts about one to two years and requires technical, on-site support.
2. *Consolidation* lasts into the third year and requires on-site assistance, access to specialists, and the advice of colleagues and consultants.
3. *Renewal* lasts through the fourth year. Strategies prescribed to meet professional training needs include conferences, professional organizations, demonstration projects, teacher centers, and professional journals.
4. *Maturity* extends through the fifth year and beyond. Appropriate professional development activities here include seminars, institutes, courses, degree programs, books, conferences, and journals.

The views posited by Unruh and Turner, Gregorc, and Katz provided valuable insight into the notion of differentiated stages of teacher development. A major limitation of these early attempts at model building is that they tended to "lump" all mature teachers together without further differentiation. The view that experienced, mature teachers continue to grow and change was not emphasized in the works of these early theorists.

Kevin Ryan (Ryan et al., 1979) directed a series of qualitative studies on teacher career development at Ohio State University. These studies were based on structured interviews of teachers at various phases of their careers. Included were teachers at the following levels of experience:

First-year teachers
Teachers with minimal through intermediate—4 to 20 years
Experienced teachers—20 to 30 years
Retired teachers

The Ohio State studies are significant in the literature about teachers' career stages because they were based on structured interviews and provided the beginning of a research-driven database that yielded empirical data about teacher needs and concerns at various stages of their careers. Much of the previous work had been based primarily on perceptions, personal observations, and some anecdotal references. Other studies of the same genre include Hange (1982), Ingvarson and Greenway (1981), and Newman, Burden, and Applegate (1980a, b). A limitation of these studies lies in the small number of people interviewed and the limited geographic areas represented.

Several researchers have synthesized the work of others to present frameworks of teacher career cycles. Of particular note here is Burden's (1982) synthesis, which provided refinement in the labeling and characteristics of teacher careers. Burden's three stages are:

1. *Survival stage* (first year). Teachers were concerned about their adequacy in maintaining classroom control, teaching the subject, improving their teaching skills, and knowing what to teach (lesson and unit planning, organizing materials, etc.).
2. *Adjustment stage* (second through fourth year). Teachers were more knowledgeable about teaching and were more relaxed. They started to see the complexities of children and sought new training techniques to meet the wider range of perceived needs. Teachers became more open and genuine with children and felt they were meeting children's needs more capably.
3. *Mature stage* (fifth year and beyond). When teachers were comfortable with teaching activities and understood the teaching environment, they felt secure and that they could handle anything that happened in their teaching. They were continually trying new techniques and were concerned with their relationships to the children and with meeting the needs of the children.

Burden's model helped to sharpen the view of career stages through a synthesis of interview data. While an important contribution, this view of teacher career stages continued to consolidate all "mature" teachers into one homogeneous group. Further differentiation among "mature" teachers was not explored.

Feiman and Floden (1981), in their review of research findings, identified three approaches to teacher development. The first approach described stages in teachers' careers. These include survival, consolidation, renewal, and maturity. They also described approaches concerned with the personal development of teachers (ego, moral, and cognitive development) and approaches to supporting teacher development through programs of professional inservice.

The first version of the Teacher Career Cycle Model, which is the focus of this chapter, appeared in 1984 (Burke, Fessler, & Christensen, 1984), and subsequent versions followed shortly thereafter (Burke et al., 1987; Fessler, 1985; Fessler & Christensen, 1992). The basic notion underlying this model was that the teacher career cycle is influenced by external environmental factors, some from the teacher's personal environment, others from the organizational environment. The model, rather than positing a linear progression from one step to the next, presented the view that environmental influences create a dynamic ebb and flow, and teachers respond by moving up, down, and through various stages. The model also presented differentiation among "mature" teachers. Specific stages of the cycle included:

Preservice
Induction
Competency building
Enthusiastic and growing
Career frustration
Career stability
Career wind-down
Career exit

A more detailed presentation of the model is found later in this chapter.

Two models of teacher career development have recently been presented by Hans Vonk (1989) and Michael Huberman (1993). These views provide schemata that differentiate among career teachers and, further, introduce the notion of alternative career options experienced by teachers at various stages.

Vonk's model of teachers' professional development is based on a review of the literature and on his studies of teachers' professional development. His framework provides for the following stages:

- *Preprofessional phase*, reflecting the period of initial education and training during which time the perspective teacher is preparing for the role of teacher and exploring various role options.
- *Threshold phase*, describing the first year of teaching, when much activity is centered around attempting to get a handle on the job and gaining acceptance by students, peers, and administrators.
- *The phase of growing into the profession*, usually between the second and seventh years of teaching, during which time attention is focused on improving teaching skills and competencies.
- *The first professional phase*, when the teacher demonstrates the accomplishments, skills, and mastery of an accomplished professional.
- *Phase of reorientation to oneself and the profession*, during which the teacher may question and doubt his or her commitment to teaching. This is sometimes associated with midlife crises. Some teachers may drop out of teaching at this point; others may continue but with less energy and enthusiasm than before.
- *The second professional phase*, a time when some teachers reenergize themselves and continue on to further professional accomplishments.
- *The phase of running down*, which is the period before retirement.

As described in Chapter 9 of this volume, Huberman has offered several models that describe a series of optional paths or trajectories that occur during teachers' careers. Both Vonk and Huberman present sophisticated, multifaceted views of the teacher career cycle. Their notion of alternative career paths is more complex than those of earlier theorists, who presented more linear, unidimensional views. Comparisons between these models and the Teacher Career Cycle Model will be addressed later in this chapter.

The literature reviewed above yielded many "first attempts" at analyzing the career cycles of teachers and uncovered some suggestions, trends, and weaknesses. Many of the studies that have been conducted have had limited samples; therefore their results have limited generalizability. Others have been based on observations and "feelings," with little empirical verification. Some extensive research studies have been conducted in specific areas, such as stages of concern about innovations, and a qualitative database on teachers' careers is beginning to emerge. The works of Vonk and Huberman provide some fresh insights into a career-long approach to teacher development and the notion of alternative paths or options.

THE PROCESS OF MODEL BUILDING

The process of model building that was used in the development of the Teacher Career Cycle Model is described in Figure 8.1. The first step in the process is to gather data that present a view of the "real world." For this project, this refers to an observation of the world of teachers' careers. Data sources used to develop this view included observing common practice, interviewing 160 teachers, conducting case studies, and conducting a comprehensive literature review (Christensen, Burke, & Fessler, 1983; Christensen, Burke, Fessler, & Hagstram, 1983).

Based on a synthesis of data collected, an explanation of the "real world" of teacher careers was hypothesized into a "working model." As mentioned previously, early iterations of this model and data sources for its development have been presented elsewhere (Burke et al., 1984, 1987; Fessler, 1985) and are described in greater detail in a book co-authored by members of the Collegial Research Consortium that conducted the research that contributed to the model-building process (Fessler & Christensen, 1992).

This model-building phase of theory development requires the synthesis and expansion of prior knowledge into a framework that adds new insights and structures for analysis. The working model developed at this stage should not be viewed as fixed, but rather as a tentative paradigm that offers the current best explanation of existing data. Subsequent data gathered should be cycled back into the model to make modifications and refinements. The Teacher Career Cycle Model presented in the next section of this chapter is the latest version of a model that has evolved and been modified as new data and analyses have emerged.

FIGURE 8.1 Model Building

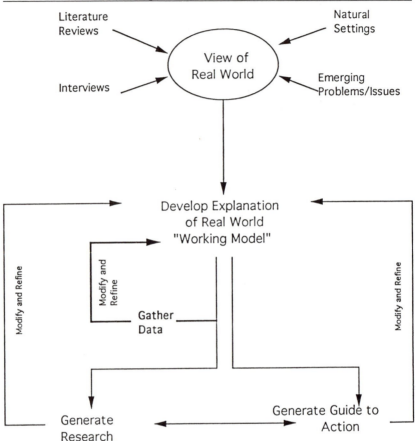

Given the dynamic nature of model building described above, the working model should serve the dual purpose of providing guidelines for action and a structure for future research. This "guide to action" function provides a framework whereby practitioners can use the model constructs as a guide in decision making, planning, and policy formation. A number of such practical implications and applications exist for the Teacher Career Cycle Model, and these will be presented later in this chapter.

For the researcher, the working model offers a framework for research and further analysis. Model constructs suggest interrelationships among complex phenomena and hypotheses about additional relationships. This provides a schema to systematically drive research and add to the knowledge base and body of theory in a systematic and interactive way. The model has served as the framework for the design of instrumentation, the generation of research questions, and the formation of research designs (Burke et al., 1983, 1987; Price, 1986).

As indicated in Figure 8.1, both the "guide to action" and the "research-generation" components of a model should be fed back into the model constructs to provide necessary refinements and modifications. It is through this constant feedback that the knowledge base supporting a model can be expanded and the model itself can be maintained as an evolving framework that is responsive to new data.

THE TEACHER CAREER CYCLE: A WORKING MODEL

The process of model building described above and outlined in Figure 8.1 was applied to the development of the Teacher Career Cycle Model. Extensive interviews of teachers and a comprehensive literature review provided the "picture" of the real world that was then synthesized into a working model. The literature in teachers' career stages reviewed earlier in this chapter influenced the building of the model.

The model presented here builds on and synthesizes the existing literature and incorporates data from interviews. Further refinement occurred on the basis of a national survey of teachers' perceptions of career stages, influences upon their careers, and preferred incentives and professional development activities (Burke et al., 1987). The model builds on previous work by offering a comprehensive and expanded picture of the career cycle and by placing the career cycle concept into the context of influences from personal and organizational factors (see Figure 8.2). This approach, which borrows heavily from social systems theory (Getzels, Lipham, & Campbell, 1968; Hoy & Miskel, 1991), presents a view of teacher career cycles that is dynamic and flexible, rather than static and fixed. The components of the model are described in the following sections.

The teacher career cycle responds to environmental conditions. A supportive, nurturing, reinforcing environment can assist a teacher in the pursuit of a rewarding, positive career progression. Environmental interference and pressures, on the other hand, can impact negatively on the career cycle. The environmental factors are often interactive, making it difficult to sort out specific influences that affect the cycle. In an attempt to sort out the variables, however, the influences may be separated into the broad categories of *personal environment* and *organizational environment.*

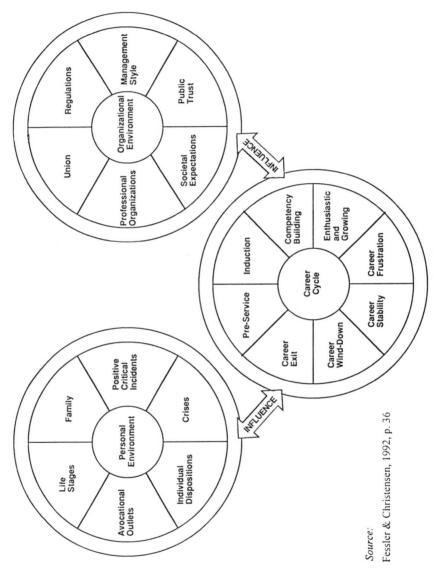

Source:
Fessler & Christensen, 1992, p. 36

FIGURE 8.2 Dynamics of the Teacher Career Cycle

Personal Environment

The personal environment of the teacher includes a number of interactive facets. Among the variables from the individual personal environment that impact upon the career cycle are family support structures, positive critical incidents, life crises, individual dispositions, avocational outlets, and the developmental life stages experienced by teachers. These facets may impact alone or in combination, and during some periods they may become the driving force in influencing job behavior and the career cycle. Positive, nurturing, and reinforcing support from the personal environment that does not foster conflict with career-related responsibilities will likely have favorable impact upon the career cycle. Conversely, a negative crisis–ridden, conflict-oriented personal environment will likely impact negatively upon the teacher's world of work. The following outline illustrates potential concerns in each of the above facets.

Family. The family life of a teacher is a key environmental component. The internal support systems can be supportive or negative. Parents who encourage and support the decision of a young adult to become a teacher will likely have a positive impact during preservice and early career experiences. Displeasure with this career choice will likely make it more difficult to meet the challenges of becoming a teacher. These internal support systems also carry over into the teacher's own primary family unit, as choice of mate, having children, and related family events may have a great impact on career activities.

The various family roles that a teacher is expected to assume may also impact on the career cycle. If the spouse of a female teacher expects her to perform all traditional homemaking and parenting roles in addition to the demanding activities of teaching, there may be great strain on the career. Alternatively, a spouse who shares in homemaking and parenting responsibilities will facilitate career enrichment.

Other family factors that may impact on the teacher's career include birth of children, financial conditions, and the health and welfare of other family members. These may take the form of positive critical incidents and crises.

Positive Critical Incidents. Positive critical incidents may take many forms, including marriage, birth of children, and religious experiences. Such positive events in one's life may provide the foundation for security and support that will carry over into career activities. Significant others may also include mentors or others who have had positive impacts on choices and life decisions.

Crises. Personal or family crises may have a dramatic impact on job-related activities. The illness of a loved one, death of a close relative, personal illness, financial loss, marital difficulties, and legal problems are all examples of crises that may turn a teacher's priorities away from teaching. Chemical-abuse problems of a family member, a particularly difficult problem to cope with, have been increasing greatly in recent years.

Teachers presented with crises of these kinds frequently find it difficult to cope with career expectations and pressures. Many teachers experience job-related difficulties during periods of crises. Some, however, are able to rechannel their energies into their jobs as a way of escaping from their problems.

Individual Dispositions. Each person is unique, with behavioral traits, cumulative experiences, aspirations and goals, and personal values that combine to define the individual's personality. These factors influence career decisions and directions. Personal aspirations and goals may have influenced a decision made in young adulthood about selecting teaching as a career. Through experience and changing needs, priorities are sometimes reassessed in later years, perhaps resulting in career changes or career frustration. In other cases, maturity may help one be a more reflective, professional teacher, primed for continued growth and development.

Avocational Interests. Opportunities for continued growth may be provided by avocational interests that may be channeled back into teaching activities. In addition, they may provide outlets for fulfillment, achievement, and recognition that may supplement rewards received from teaching. For some teachers, these are outlets for needs not met in their teaching. Examples of avocational interests frequently available to teachers include hobbies, volunteerism, religious activities, travel, and sports and exercise.

Life Stages. The literature on life stages, popularized by Sheehy (1976) and Levinson, Darrow, Klein, Levinson, and McKee (1978), identifies personal factors that may have an important impact on the career cycle. During various adult life stages, there is often questioning and reflection about career, family, life goals, and personal priorities. This is particularly true during the period of midlife crises, when individuals are sometimes preoccupied with questions about what they want to do with the rest of their lives. Periods of intense questioning and reassessment may have considerable impact on job performance and career options.

IT SHOULD BE NOTED that the list of facets of the personal environment is not all-inclusive. What is presented here is a description of some key components in the personal environment that impact upon the career cycle.

Organizational Environment

The organizational environment of schools and school systems comprises a second major category of influences on the career cycle. Among the variables impacting here are school regulations, the management style of administrators and supervisors, the presence or absence of public trust in a community, the expectations a community places on its educational system, the activities of professional organizations and associations, and the union atmosphere in the system. A supportive posture from these organizational components will reinforce, reward, and encourage teachers as they progress through their career cycles. Alternatively, an atmosphere of mistrust and suspicion will likely have a negative impact. The following outline illustrates some of the concerns in these organizational facets.

School Regulations. Teachers are subject to numerous regulations from school, district, state, and national sources. These regulations often provide order and structure to the school and reflect the goals and values of the system, community, and nation. At other times, however, regulations may result in bureaucratic layering that could have negative impacts on teachers. Examples of school regulations include curriculum requirements, development of individual education plans for special education students, and mandates about student testing or evaluation. Each of these may be perceived by teachers as positive or negative, depending on how they affect their classrooms and careers.

Management Style. The management style of the school principal may have a dramatic impact on individual teachers' career cycles. If a principal has established an atmosphere of trust and support, with opportunities for teacher empowerment and leadership, the response of teachers is likely to be positive. A less trusting, more inspection-oriented approach to management and supervision will likely yield less enthusiasm from teachers.

New leadership may result in changes in management styles and in teacher responses. It is not uncommon for frustrated teachers to be recharged by new leadership that gives them a fresh start and opportunities for renewed growth. Conversely, a new principal with a more controlling orientation may result in problems for teachers accustomed to greater autonomy.

Public Trust. The atmosphere of public trust may have a profound impact on teachers' careers and job performance. A positive atmosphere, where confidence is expressed in teachers and schools, will result in high teacher self-esteem and a positive outlook on teaching as a career. Conversely, a steady bombardment or criticism of schools and teachers is bound to have a negative impact on the way teachers see themselves. These external elements also are reflected in the financial support provided to schools.

The recent intense criticism of schools and teachers, especially those in urban settings, has resulted in low morale and frustration among many teachers. Daily press coverage of the woes of the schools, with teachers' competencies and commitment often the central theme, has left some teachers wondering about the future of education and their future as teachers.

Alternative approaches to the problems of large city schools, such as school–business partnerships and plans to move toward school-based management, provide a more positive, proactive environment for teachers. Opportunities for renewal and growth allow teachers to view their careers in more positive terms.

Societal Expectations. In addition to issues of trust, societal expectations for schools take many forms that impact on teachers and their career cycles. Community goals, ethics, values, expectations, and aspirations play an important role, as do the views of special-interest groups and national and regional reports about schools and teachers. All these factors help to define the external climate that teachers and schools find themselves in, and the dynamics of a given community may have a dramatic impact on the way teachers see themselves and on the expectations for their roles.

One aspect of these external expectations takes the form of financial support for school activities. This may be reflected in the level of budgetary support for school operations and needed reforms, the extent of support for school construction needs, and the support reflected in funds given by the private sector through school partnerships and volunteerism.

Professional Organizations. Teachers often receive opportunities for leadership and growth from professional organizations, such as the National Reading Association, the National Science Teachers Association, the National Council of Teachers of Mathematics, the National Council of Teachers of English, the National Council for the Social Studies, the Association of Teacher Educators, and the Association of Supervision and Curriculum Development. These national groups, along with their state affiliates, offer opportunities for teacher renewal, growth, and leadership.

Unions. Teacher empowerment in the United States has been enhanced by the two major teacher unions—the National Education Association and the American Federation of Teachers. Mutual concern for the professional growth of teachers has evolved in recent years from an earlier period of confrontation and mistrust between the unions and management. The specific climate still varies greatly from community to community, and teachers' views of their jobs and careers are influenced by the atmosphere and agenda of teachers' unions. A positive climate promoting teacher growth and empowerment can lead to feelings of pride and accomplishment, while an atmosphere of mistrust between the union and management can lead to negative feelings.

AGAIN, IT SHOULD BE NOTED that the above list is not all-inclusive but rather illustrates key organizational factors that impact upon the career cycle.

Career Cycle

The components of the career cycle are described below.

Preservice. The preservice phase is the period of preparation for a specific professional role. Typically, this would be the period of initial preparation in a college or university. It might also include retraining for a new role or assignment, either by attending an institution of higher education or as part of staff development within the work setting.

Induction. The induction stage is generally defined as the first few years of employment when the teacher is socialized into the system. It is a period when a new teacher strives for acceptance by students, peers, and supervisors and attempts to achieve a comfort and security level in dealing with everyday problems and issues. Teachers may also experience induction when shifting to another grade level or another building, or when changing districts completely.

Competency Building. During this phase of the career cycle, the teacher is striving to improve teaching skills and abilities, seeking new materials, methods, and strategies. Teachers at this stage are receptive to new ideas, attend workshops and conferences willingly, and enroll in graduate programs on their own initiative. They see their job as challenging, and they are eager to improve their repertoire of skills. This is a pivotal period for teachers in the early stages of their careers. Those who are successful in "grabbing the handles" of teaching go on to periods of positive growth and development. Those who flounder during this period (either through lack of ability or lack of support) often experience career frustration or instability, as described below.

Enthusiastic and Growing. At this stage teachers have reached a high level of competence in their jobs but continue to progress as professionals. Teachers in this stage love their jobs, look forward to going to school and to the interaction with their students, and are constantly seeking new ways to enrich their teaching. Key ingredients here are enthusiasm and a high level of job satisfaction. These teachers are often supportive and helpful in identifying appropriate inservice education activities for their schools. The ideal climate reinforces teachers in this stage with opportunities to learn and apply new ideas.

Career Frustration. This period is characterized by frustration and disillusionment with teaching. Job satisfaction is waning, and teachers begin to question why they are doing this work. Much of what is described in the literature as teacher burnout occurs in this stage. While this sense of frustration tends to occur most often during a midpoint in one's career, there is an increasing incidence of such feelings among teachers in relatively early years of their careers. This is particularly true for those new staff who face the continual threat of "last hired/first fired," for those who find their school climate stifling, and for those who never developed the skills to succeed.

Career Stability. Stable teachers have plateaued in their careers. Some have become stagnant and have resigned themselves to putting in "a fair day's work for a fair day's pay." These teachers are doing what is expected of them, but little more. They may be doing an acceptable job, but they are not committed to the pursuit of excellence and growth. Teachers at this stable stage are in the process of disengaging from their commitment to teaching.

Career Wind-Down. This is the stage when a teacher is preparing to leave the profession. For some, it may be a pleasant period during which they reflect on the many positive experiences they have had and look forward to a career change or retirement. For others, it may be a bitter period, one in which they resent a forced job termination or cannot wait to get out of an unrewarding job. A person may spend several years in this stage, or it may occur only during a matter of weeks or months.

Career Exit. The exiting stage of a teacher's career represents the period of time after the teacher leaves the job, but it includes circumstances other than simply retirement after many years of service. It could be a period of unemployment after involuntary or elective job termination or a temporary career exit for child rearing. It could also be a time of alternative career exploration or of moving to a nonteaching position in education, such as administration.

As described earlier, the process of model building in the social sciences should be reviewed as tentative and dynamic. New data and fresh insights into existing data may change model components and interpretations. The Teacher Career Cycle Model as described above is the developers' best current interpretation of available data (Fessler & Christensen, 1992). Readers are encouraged not to view model components as fixed, but rather as useful constructs that enhance our understanding of the dynamics of the changing nature of teachers' careers.

THE DYNAMIC NATURE OF THE CAREER CYCLE

At first glance there is a tendency to view the career cycle as a linear process, with an individual entering at the preservice level and progressing through the various stages. While there is a certain logic to this view, it is hypothesized here that this is not necessarily an accurate picture of the process. Rather, a dynamic ebb and flow is postulated, with teachers moving in and out of stages in response to environmental influences from both the personal and organizational dimensions. The following scenarios are presented to demonstrate this view.

First, consider the teacher who exhibits classic characteristics of "enthusiastic and growing." She loves her job and is constantly seeking new ways to make her classroom an exciting and lively learning environment. At the height of this climate of enthusiasm, however, she is informed that her job is about to be terminated (organizational influence—budgetary cutbacks). After perhaps moving through a period of "career frustration," this once-enthusiastic teacher will be entering career wind-down and career exit. It is possible she will find herself in a new preservice stage as she prepares for a career change.

A second "enthusiastic and growing" teacher learns that his son has a severe chemical-abuse problem (personal environment—family crisis). The trauma of this experience may drain his resources and cause him to reorder his priorities. Such a teacher may settle into a "career stability" stage in order to devote more attention to his family problem.

A third case might be one in which a teacher has resigned himself to a "fair day's work for a fair day's pay." This "stable" individual may have great talent, but he views teaching as a job, not a commitment to excellence. Enter on this scene a very sensitive and supportive supervisor (organizational environment—management style) who accurately assesses this situation and works with the teacher to rekindle enthusiasm for teaching. Strategies might include giving the teacher greater input into decisions affecting him, modifying assignments to maximize his strengths, and reinforcing positive actions through verbal praise and positive evaluations. Many teachers will respond to such actions with renewed enthusiasm and growth.

Finally, consider the "career wind-down" teacher who is about to leave the profession. Very unexpectedly, her husband dies (personal environment—crisis). This dramatic change in her personal life may result in a reassessment of this career wind-down decision. Depending on the nature of additional personal and organizational environmental conditions, this teacher may renew a commitment to teaching and enter an "enthusiastic and growing" phase or may fall back into a period of "stability."

IMPLICATIONS OF THE MODEL

Teacher Growth and Development

If the notion of individual career stages is to go beyond the "interesting-to-know" level, there is a need to identify personalized support systems for teachers at various stages of their careers. In recent years there have been numerous attempts to develop supervision and staff development models that emphasize personalized approaches to teacher development. Particular attention might be given to the works of Burke (1987), Christensen, McDonnell, and Price (1988), Fessler and Burke (1988), Glatthorn (1984), Glickman (1990), Krey and Burke (1989), and Levine (1989). Each of these authors presents models and approaches to individualizing professional development that are very supportive of the constructs presented in this chapter.

Schools and school systems may want to examine their current practices and policies in light of the concepts set forth in the Teacher Career Cycle Model. There is much here to reinforce the traditional use of inservice or staff development activities that emphasize improving teacher skills, especially during the skill-building periods associated with the induction and competency-building stages and, to some extent, during the enthusiastic-and-growing stage. The ideas presented here also suggest a broadening of the notion of staff development and professional growth to include concern for personal needs and problems of teachers. This might include support systems to assist teachers in dealing with family problems, chemical abuse, financial planning, and crisis resolution. Larger school districts may want to consider internal employee assistance programs for this purpose, while smaller districts could explore linkages with existing social service agencies.

In addition, organizational policies should be examined to find new and creative ways of supporting teachers at various stages of their careers. Examples could include more liberal sabbatical and leave-of-absence policies, modifications of job assignments, job sharing, internal transfers, and other procedures that would give teachers the opportunity to explore career alternatives or pursue solutions to personal problems.

Finally, school systems must attempt to understand the linkages between teacher career stages and the organizational environment. The leadership and management style of the principal may be the single most important factor in that environment. The recent movement toward school-based management and shared decision making may have a major impact in providing outlets for teacher growth needs. Other organizational environmental factors that must be examined in the context of the concepts set forth in this chapter include the amount of teachers' time consumed by rules, regulations, and "administrivia," and the atmosphere of trust and professional respect for teachers present in the school system and community. All these factors relate to the tone and climate set by the administration and have a major impact upon teachers' progression through the career stages.

Research

As indicated earlier, this model was developed through a process of model building that emphasizes the need to continually feed new data back into the process to confirm, refine, and, when needed, dramatically alter model components. For the researcher, the working model offers a framework for further analysis. Model constructs suggest interrelationships among complex phenomena and hypotheses about additional relationships. For example, by examining the model, research questions are raised concerning the relationship between specific personal and organizational environmental factors and specific teacher career stages. Questions regarding appropriate incentives and support systems can be tested using model components, as can specific strategies aimed at moving (for example) a "stable" or "frustrated" teacher into a more productive mode.

COMPARISON TO VONK AND HUBERMAN MODELS

Although developed independently, the models offered by Vonk, Huberman, and Fessler and colleagues have similar orientations. While some of the language and emphases vary, each addresses the unique characteristics and needs of early career teachers, teachers who are building skills, teachers who are experiencing frustration, and, eventually, teachers who leave or "disengage" from their positions.

There are parallels as well regarding the dynamic, nonlinear approaches to career stages presented in each model. The Huberman model (and to a lesser extent the Vonk model) emphasizes pathways along which teachers branch off from previous stages to one of several options (some more positive than others—see Chapter 9 of this volume). While this branching is not immediately evident in the Teacher Career Cycle Model, it is present in the form of the emphasis placed on its nonlinear nature and on the ebb and flow among stages that results from personal and organizational environmental influences.

The importance of environmental factors on career paths is noted in all three models but seems to have a higher profile in the Teacher Career Cycle Model because of its roots in social systems theory.

While some differences in structure and emphasis among the three models are evident, they seem to complement one another quite well and, when viewed in combination, provide a comprehensive picture of current thinking regarding the teacher career cycle process.

SUMMARY

The Teacher Career Cycle Model highlighted in this chapter reflects a synthesis and integration of the existing available data into an explanation of the "real world" of teacher careers. It presents a series of structures that can be further studied and developed. As suggested in the model-building process described earlier (see Figure 8.1), it should not be viewed as fixed, but rather as a dynamic working explanation of the "real world" that must be subjected to refinement and modification as new data are fed back into the process. Along with the Vonk and Huberman models, the Teacher Career Cycle Model offers a framework for viewing the complex process of teachers' careers and provides implications for teacher growth and development.

REFERENCES

Burden, P. R. (1982, February). *Developmental supervision: Reducing teacher stress at different career stages.* Paper presented at the annual conference of the Association of Teacher Educators, Phoenix, AZ.

Burke, P. J. (1987). *Teacher development, induction, renewal, and redirection.* Cherry Hill, PA: Falmer.

Burke, P., Christensen, J., Fessler, R., McDonnell, & Price, J. (1987, April). *The teacher career cycle: Model development and research report.* Paper presented at the annual meeting of the American Educational Research Association, Washington, DC.

Burke, P., Fessler, R., & Christensen, J. (1983, April). *Teacher life-span development: An instrument to identify stages of teacher growth.* Paper presented at the annual meeting of the American Educational Research Association, Montreal, Quebec.

Burke, P., Fessler, R., & Christensen, J. (1984). *Teacher career stages: Implications for staff development.* Bloomington, IN: Phi Delta Kappa.

Christensen, J., Burke, P., & Fessler, R. (1983, April). *Teacher life-span development: A summary and synthesis of the literature.* Paper presented at the annual meeting of the American Educational Research Association, Montreal, Quebec.

Christensen, J., Burke, P., Fessler, R., & Hagstram, D. (1983). *Teachers' career development.* Washington, DC: ERIC Clearinghouse.

Christensen, J., McDonnell, J., & Price, J. (1988). *Personalizing staff development: The career lattice model.* Bloomington, IN: Phi Delta Kappa.

Feiman, S., & Floden, R. E. (1981). *A consumer's guide to teacher development.* East Lansing: Institute for Research on Teaching, Michigan State University. (ERIC Document Reproduction No. ED 207970).

Fessler, R. (1985). Teacher career cycle. In P. Burke & R. Heideman (Eds.), *Career-long teacher education* (pp. 181–193). Springfield, IL: Thomas.

Fessler, R., & Burke, P. (1988, Winter). Teacher assessment and staff development: Links in the same chain. *Journal of Staff Development, 9*(1), 14–18.

Fessler, R., Burke, P., & Christensen, J. (1983, April). *Teacher career cycle model: A framework for viewing teacher growth needs.* Paper presented at the annual meeting of the American Educational Research Association, Montreal, Quebec.

Fessler, R., & Christensen, J. (1992). *The teacher career cycle: Understanding and guiding the professional development of teachers.* Boston: Allyn & Bacon.

Fuller, F. (1969). Concerns of teachers: A developmental conceptualization. *American Educational Research Journal, 6,* 207–226.

Fuller, F., & Bown, O. (1975). Becoming a teacher. In *Teacher education* (74th Yearbook of the National Society for the Study of Education, Part 2). Chicago: University of Chicago Press.

Getzels, J., Lipham, J., & Campbell, R. (1968). *Administration as a social process: Theory, research, and practice.* New York: Harper & Row.

Glatthorn, A. A. (1984). *Differentiated supervision.* Alexandria, VA: Association for Supervision and Curriculum Development.

Glickman, C. D. (1990). *Supervision of instruction: A developmental approach.* Boston: Allyn & Bacon.

Gregorc, A. F. (1973). Developing plans for professional growth. *NASSP Bulletin, 57,* 1–8.

Hange, J. (1982, March). *Teachers in their fifth year: An analysis of teaching concerns from the perspectives of adult and career development.* Paper presented at the annual meeting of the American Educational Research Association, New York.

Hoy, W., & Miskel, C. G. (1991). *Educational administration: Theory, research and practice.* New York: Random House.

Huberman, M. (1993). *The lives of teachers.* New York: Teachers College Press.

Ingvarson, L., & Greenway, P. (1981). *Portrayals of teacher development.* Washington, DC: ERIC Document Reproduction Service No. ED 200 600.

Katz, L. G. (1972). Development stages of preschool teachers. *Elementary School Journal, 3,* 50–54. (ERIC No. EJ 064 759).

Krey, R., & Burke, P. (1989). *A design for instructional supervision.* Springfield, IL: Thomas.

Levine, S. L. (1989). *Promoting adult growth in schools.* Boston: Allyn & Bacon.

Levinson, D. J., Darrow, C. N., Klein, E. B., Levinson, M. H., & McKee, B. (1978). *The seasons of a man's life.* New York: Knopf.

Newman, K. K., Burden, P. R., & Applegate, J. H. (1980a, October). Adult development is implicit in staff development. *Journal of Staff Development, 1*(2), 7–56.

Newman, K. K., Burden, P. R., & Applegate, J. (1980b). *Helping teachers examine their long-range development.* Paper presented at the Association of Teacher

Educators annual conference, Washington, DC. (ERIC Document Reproduction Service No. ED 204 321).

Price, J. R. (1986, April). *The teacher career cycle: Development and validation of research instruments.* Paper presented at the annual meeting of the American Educational Research Association, San Francisco.

Ryan, K., Flora, R., Newman, K., Peterson, A., Burden, P., & Mager, J. (1979). *The stages in teaching: New perspectives on staff development for teachers' needs* (ASCD audiotape). Presentation to the Association for Supervision and Curriculum Development, Anaheim, CA.

Sheehy, G. (1976). *Passages: Predictable crises of adult life.* New York: Dutton.

Unruh, A., & Turner, H. E. (1970). *Supervision for change and innovation.* Boston: Houghton Mifflin.

Vonk, J. H. C. (1989). *Becoming a teacher, brace yourself.* Unpublished paper. Vrije University, Amsterdam.

9

Professional Careers and Professional Development
Some Intersections

MICHAEL HUBERMAN

This chapter is a modest attempt to grasp a vast topic: teachers' professional lives and the relationship between that trajectory and the domain of professional development. The hypothesis is fairly obvious: Teachers have different aims and different dilemmas at various moments in their professional cycle, and their desires to reach out for more information, knowledge, expertise and technical competence will vary accordingly. Which moments are these? Which external sources are sought out? Is there a generic mode of professional development that cuts across phases of the teaching career?

A core assumption here is that there will be commonalities among teachers in the sequencing of their professional lives and that one particular form of professional development may be appropriate to these shared sequences. We shall be looping back to that issue throughout this chapter.

The text itself will be divided roughly into three parts. First, I shall review very briefly some of the recent paradigms of teachers' life-span development. Then I shall extract from each some of the guideposts around which professional development activities could be tied. Finally, I shall devise a more generic model of professional collaboration among teachers, however many years of experience they have compiled.

THE PROFESSIONAL LIFE CYCLE OF TEACHERS AS A FIELD OF STUDY

Life-cycle research has been around since philosophers, historians, and theologians have been studying lives. The more "scientific" study of lives, however, has followed disciplinary tracks. For example, there is a clear psychodynamic track running from Freud through Henry Murray and Gordon Allport and culminating in Erikson's "life crises" and Robert White's *Lives in Progress* (1952). Another, more sociological track began in the 1920s with the Chicago School and the revival of the oral history tradition, coupled with the development of symbolic interactionism. The pioneering studies of adult socialization and career patterning come from here. Finally, we have been blessed with the transdisciplinary, multivolume studies of life-span developmental psychology (e.g., Featherman, Lerner, & Perlmutter, 1994; Schaie & Schooler, 1989).

"Phase" and "Stage" Models of Teaching: A Caveat

In much of the classic work, the life course is construed as a progressive series of cycles or sequences, that is, a normative path along which most—or many—individuals pass on their way through life. To imagine such a developmental sequence in the teaching career more particularly is to open a line of inquiry that is both appealing and problematic. The appeal is an obvious one: If large numbers of teachers traverse similar phases, we can begin to identify modal profiles of the teaching career and, from there, see what determines more and less "successful" or "satisfactory" careers. We can also identify the conditions under which a particular phase in the career cycle is lived out happily or miserably and, from there, put together an appropriate support structure. In both cases, we are assembling the rudiments of a personnel policy in education that goes well beyond conventional practices, with their purely administrative or ad hoc character.

To find out, for example, that teachers make the most energetic attempts to revise their instructional practices during the first six to eight years of the career cycle, as some empirical work suggests (Burden, 1986; Huberman, 1989, 1993a), is useful information for planning inservice training and organizing release time for staff. More ambitiously, to identify the predictors of perceived career satisfaction, as several studies have tried to do, is important knowledge for revising some of the features of the school as workplace.

On the other hand, studies of the teaching career that look for a discernible sequence of phases are vulnerable to many of the criticisms leveled at stage theorists working with ontogenetic models of development, where chronological age is the key variable. First, most of this work is resolutely biological or psychological; when transferred to teaching, it tends to underestimate the importance of social and historical factors (cf. Neugarten & Datan, 1973). Teachers do not "mature" in the course of their profession in the same ways as do ducklings; teachers active in 1890 classrooms are facing radically different circumstances from those in 1990 settings (cf. Warren, 1989); teachers playing out their careers in periods of social turbulence or during wartime or in moments of structural reform within their school system are likely to have different trajectories from peers working in different social environments. Most of the available data show, in fact, that teachers who traverse together the same cultural and historical periods are more alike than any other set (e.g., Woodruff & Birren, 1972). Finally, as Aristotle had it, some people resemble no others and some resemble some parts of some others. The closer we look, the more distinct each career profile appears, or, put another way, the more the same parameters of a teaching career are put together in wondrously different ways.

Second, stage theory tends to view individuals passively, somewhat like marionettes whose developmental strings are being pulled at critical ages, or in response to a social "time clock" (more on this later), or as a function of an intrapsychic "crisis" that characterizes particular ages and circumstances. As it happens, much of individual development is "teleological," that is, individuals observe and plan out the sequences through which they pass, and can thereby influence or even determine the nature or the succession of stages in their career.

For that matter, a large part of development is neither externally programmed nor personally engineered but rather discontinuous, that is, lacking in continuity and order, and sometimes downright random. As it happens, such discontinuity is fairly obvious when analysts review the flow of events in individual biographies (cf. Elder, 1977) and see that the next step in a developmental sequence was unexpected or was one of several equally plausible outcomes. But discontinuity is typically underestimated by individuals who recount their own lives and who tend to use the lens of their present life to make sense of their past—and to do it in a coherent, internally consistent way, as if today were the almost inevitable product of the chain of events of one's yesterdays (cf. Cohler, 1982; Handel, 1987). This, in fact, is one of the main perils of life-history interviewing. In other words, some career sequences may be artifacts that we researchers, with the tacit help of our informants, create from a succession of disjointed events in order to give shape and meaning to them.

What do we know in particular about the careers of teachers? Until the late 1970s precious little, aside from Becker's (1970) seminal study and a perceptive chapter by Peterson (1964) on secondary school teachers. Since then, the picture has brightened, both in number and in the international nature of empirical research in this field—in the United States (Adams, 1982; Burden, 1981, 1986; M. Cooper, 1982; McLaughlin & Yee, 1988; Newman, 1979,), in England (Ball & Goodson, 1985; MacDonald & Walker, 1974; Sikes, Measor, & Woods, 1985), in the Netherlands (Prick, 1986), in Australia (Ingvarson & Greenway, 1984), in France (Hamon & Rotman, 1984), in Canada (Butt, Raymond, McCue, & Yamagishi, 1986; Connelly &

Clandinin, 1988), in Spain (Coloma, 1988), in Switzerland (Hirsch & Ganguillet, 1988; Huberman, 1989, 1993a), and in Belgium (Kelchtermans & Vandenberghe, 1993).

Most of these studies have conceptualized the passages of teachers in terms of a progression through a "career" (Super, 1992). This is fine, so long as we bear in mind that some school personnel may not have a staged, continuous sequence of life experiences (e.g., teacher substitutes) and that we are talking about a process filled with plateaus, discontinuities, regressions, spurts, and dead ends.

Career Entry and Socialization

In the sociological literature, the initial career typically begins with an "exploration" phase, followed by a "stabilization" phase. (For a full treatment of the possible "stages" in a teaching career, see Huberman, 1989, 1993a.) Exploration has to do with making a provisional choice, feeling out the contours of the profession, and trying out one or several roles within it. If this phase is globally positive, the individual then moves to a "stabilization" or "engagement" phase, in which he or she tries to master core aspects of the job, defines an area of focus, tries for better working conditions, and, in many cases, seeks out greater rewards or responsibilities.

Empirical studies show that such a sequence is faithful to a great number, even the majority, of career profiles, but not to all of them (cf. Phillips, 1982). For example, Super (1985) has noted aptly that some people "stabilize" early, others later, others never, and still others stabilize and then destabilize later on.

As it happens, the thematic sequence "exploration → stabilization" corresponds to several studies of induction into teaching. In this work, the leitmotif of the "exploration" phase is one of "*survival and discovery.*" The "survival" aspect involves what is commonly called the "reality shock" of the initial year—the initial confrontation with the same complexity of professional work that the most experienced members of the profession contend with—and its attendant dilemmas.

On the other hand, the "discovery" theme involves the initial enthusiasm of teaching, the sharp learning curve, the headiness of at last having one's own pupils, classroom, and program; the pride of collegiality and of "place" within a profession. In fact, empirical studies show that these two aspects often occur in parallel and that the excitement and challenge of "discovery" are what bring many teachers through the attrition of day-to-day "survival." But there are also induction phases stressing one or the other aspect and accounts that highlight other themes.

In the classic life-cycle literature, the phase defined as "exploring" or as "making a provisional choice" typically gives way to career concerns having to do with "commitment" or "stabilization" or with "becoming responsible." In the psychoanalytic tradition (Erikson, 1950; White, 1952), the choice of a professional identity is an important step in the consolidation of ego identity; postponing such a choice is seen as leading to role dispersion and, thereby, to a more diffuse sense of self. In more recent work (e.g., Levinson, 1978), this passage is seen as a critical transition. Similarly, sociological studies of the life cycle (e.g., Becker, 1964) have delineated a "commitment" phase in occupational socialization, which, often for the first time, forces a young person to follow a consistent pattern of behavior.

What does "stabilization" consist of in the teaching career? Generally speaking, there is the juncture of a personal commitment (the decision to make a career of teaching) and an administrative act (the granting of tenure). One is now a teacher, both in one's own eyes and in the eyes of others—not necessarily forever, but for a good block of time. Some autobiographical accounts (e.g., Ball & Goodson, 1985; Sikes et al., 1985) suggest that this decision is often difficult, especially for teachers in upper-secondary streams, whose credentials can lead to other jobs, or for teachers in artistic or athletic areas who dream of a professional career. But there is also the more general difficulty, highlighted in the psychoanalytic literature, of choosing a professional identity that excludes others—of giving up, at least for now, other desirable lives.

Stabilization in teaching has other meanings. For example, there is the informal induction into a professional guild and the functional independence from close supervision. There is, finally, the pedagogical dimension of "stabilization." Virtually all empirical studies associate the period of three to five years into the career with a growing sense of instructional "mastery." Studies have spoken of a sense of assurance or "comfort" (e.g., Burden, 1986; Fuller, 1969; Lightfoot, 1985; Sikes, 1985), along with a greater "decentering" in the sense of a lessened concern with self and a greater concern with instructional goals. In Adams's (1982) sample, "mastery" is also the modal theme after three to five years of teaching and is associated with a more "systematic, effective and stimulating style of teaching" (p. 43). With greater ease in more complex or unexpected classroom situations, teachers describe themselves as consolidating, then refining, a basic set of instructional repertoires on which they can, finally, rely.

Diversification and Change

If both the career literature and the research bearing on stages in teaching can make strong claims for a sequence leading from an "exploration" to a "stabilization" phase, the evidence is more equivocal beyond that point. In effect, beyond socialization into the profession, it would appear that trajectories in the middle phases of the career cycle are more diverse than earlier or later ones.

There are, however, some common streams in the research literature that identify subsets of teachers. One of the common ones involves a phase characterized by experimentation and diversification. For some analysts (e.g., M. Cooper, 1982; Feiman-Nemser, 1985), the consolidation of an instructional repertoire leads naturally to attempts to increase one's effectiveness within the classroom. There then follows a series of modest, largely private experiments with new materials, different pupil groupings, new assignments, different combinations of lessons and exercises. In a sense, these attempts compensate for the uncertainties of the first years of teaching and are often characterized by a more rigid, rudimentary, low-risk set of lesson plans and activity formats.

In other work, especially in the European context, this phase has a more "activist" flavor (cf. Sikes, 1985). The desire to increase one's impact on pupils brings a sharper awareness of the institutional constraints limiting that impact. Having "stabilized" one's classroom, one then takes aim at the aberrant practices or inadequate resources within the system by joining or mobilizing groups of peers, signing on for reforms, lobbying or joining key commissions. Coloma (1988) discerns strong involvement in school and community affairs, with levels of "idealism" and "dedication" that will not reappear in the career cycle.

Finally, most studies that identify a "diversification" phase suggest that its origins lie, at least in part, elsewhere. Having worked with six to seven yearly cohorts of pupils, having associated with the same peers, one begins to repeat the yearly cycle and to find, this time, that it lacks variation. Thus the quest for stimulation, for new ideas, challenges, and engagements. In M. Cooper's (1982) study, for example, engagement in more ambitious, collective projects had to do both with the desire to use one's newly acquired sense of instructional mastery in a more consequential way and with a latent fear of stagnation. What many teachers want at this phase of their career, Cooper claims, is "new stimulation, new ideas . . . deeper commitments, new challenges . . . to become engaged in projects of scope and significance" (p. 81).

Such a fear of stagnation is far more present in other accounts (cf. Newman, 1979; Watts, 1980). In the Huberman (1993a) and Fessler and Christensen (1992) studies, the fear of stagnation was especially strong for teachers with 11 to 19 years of experience, who often cited older peers in their building as examples of what they feared becoming.

"Stock-Taking" and Interrogations at Midcareer

Several of the studies mentioned earlier report a distinct phase, corresponding roughly to 12 to 20 years of experience and 32 to 45 years of age, that informants often describe as problematic. There are some indications that male teachers are more affected than women and full-time teachers more affected than part-time ones. In some instances, this phase follows a "diversification" period that, for various reasons, has proved disappointing or exhausting. In others, there is a move directly from "stabilization" to "interrogations" about one's future. Symptoms can vary from a nagging feeling of routine to a full-fledged crisis over the wisdom of having become a teacher and, once locked in, of trying to break out. One teacher in my study wondered if she was doomed to die in front of a blackboard with a piece of chalk in her hand.

In studies reporting a distinct period of self-questioning, teachers have some of the thoughts that have come to be associated with the "midlife crisis," especially the experience of reviewing one's life and career and contemplating, with a certain sense of urgency, other careers "while it's still possible." Informants in these studies talk explicitly of "assessing what I've done with my life," especially with regard to their original ideals or objectives, and of playing out both the scenario of remaining the rest of their professional lives in teaching and that of taking on the uncertainties—and above all the insecurities—of a career shift.

No study has suggested, however, that the majority of informants traverse such a phase or, for those that do, that these moments constitute a "crisis," in the sense of a radical self-assessment. In my study (Huberman, 1993a), however, there were indications that those teachers who described such a phase in these terms were more likely to relive another such episode some years later, that is, that a period of radical self-questioning did not usually lead to a reconciliation with self five, ten, or fifteen years later. That study also suggested that men who were heavily invested in their careers were more prone to a severe, debilitating phase of self-doubt at midcareer than men with outside interests or than women, many of whom said explicitly that commitments to the family or to other sectors of their life were important sources of equilibrium.

These trends are consonant with the "epidemiological" research literature, in which the idea of a widespread crisis at midlife, especially among men, has been challenged. In recent reviews of empirical studies (Chiriboga, 1988; Hunter & Sundel, 1988), only 2% to 5% of men in the age range 35–55 experience such symptoms as inner turmoil and confusion, dissatisfaction with their jobs or family, a sense of meaninglessness, or a sense of impending physical decline and death. Similarly, studies following both men and women from early adolescence to middle adulthood (Haan, 1981) find no traces of greater turmoil at midlife than at other periods of life.

The evidence is stronger that this phase in the career is associated with periods of "stock-taking" or of "life review" (Butler, 1963), much as Jung (1959) had hypothesized a gradual "turning inward" around 35 to 45 years of age, when a first assessment is made of one's achievements at work, of one's social relationships, of one's emotional self more generally. But this assessment can also be a function of more socially induced pressures associated with what is known as "age-grading" (Atchley, 1975; Riley, 1987)—ideas of what it is appropriate for people to be and to do at various ages. We thus carry around in our heads a set of anticipations of which events in our lives (marriage, having children, promotions, achievements at work) should be occurring and at which time. People who sense themselves to be "out of phase" are thus more likely to be unhappy at moments of "stock-taking." For example, in a seminal study by Lowenthal, Thurner, and Chiriboga (1975), middle-aged men reported that being "off-time" with respect to promotions or salary increases was a major reason for feeling "less satisfied" at this point in their lives.

In the teaching career, age-grading plays out, especially for men, in the progression from classroom teacher to administrator. For example, male teachers in their mid-30s or early 40s in some of the longitudinal studies (Nias, 1985; Prick, 1986; Sikes, 1985) "expected" to be promoted to department head or school headmaster. Those who were not often saw themselves as "failures" in the "normal" progression of their careers.

More prosaically, stock-taking is simply the moment when one contends seriously with the decision to spend the rest of one's career in the same profession or to change before it is too late (cf. Kimmel, 1975; Neugarten, 1968). With 15 to 20 years spent in teaching, the number of alternatives begins to shrink. Having been through 15 yearly school cycles, one easily imagines that the next 15 years are unlikely to bring any major changes; one observes that many older colleagues have lapsed into stagnation or cynicism; one confronts pupils who stay perennially young while one sees oneself aging—this, perhaps, adds to the gradual awareness of the finitude of life. "Stock-taking," then, consists of choosing to make the most of where one is or to leave the profession.

Serenity

Here, again, we have trends in studies of teaching as a career that correspond to more "classic" studies of the human life cycle, especially among men at or after the midpoint of their careers. From this work (e.g., Bray and Howard, 1983; Jung, 1966; Lowenthal et al., 1975) comes the notion of a more relaxed, secure sense of self—a sort of "mellowing" characterized by less drive but also less restlessness, a lesser need to control others or to drive oneself, a greater tolerance for one's limits or weaknesses, a greater acceptance of the "inevitability" of one's life course. The data for women are more equivocal, especially in the case of women with grown children who now have more time and energy to channel into their careers and who, in some studies (e.g.,

Lowenthal et al., 1975; K. Cooper & Gutmann, 1987), perceive themselves as "dominant" and "assertive" at the same point in life when men are presumably letting up and softening their edges.

Moving now to research on the teaching career, no study has most teachers reporting a distinct phase of "serenity" later in their careers, but several have subsets of informants moving at 45 to 55 years of age from an energetic or self-doubting period to a more reflective, self-accepting phase. Generally, the level of career ambition decreases, as does the level of investment, but the perception of effectiveness and serenity appears to compensate for them. One no longer feels one has something important to "prove" to oneself or to others, and one reduces the gap between one's career goals and one's achievements by setting more modest objectives for the coming years.

Across these studies we find, then, three leitmotifs associated with this "phase" of the career. The first has to do with a lessening of one's professional involvement. The second is a perception of increased instructional effectiveness. After 15 to 20 years, teachers will have seen virtually every type of pupil, every alchemy in teacher–pupil interactions, every response to segments of the yearly program; unexpected events will be rare and, for the most part, welcome.

Finally, there is the sense of a greater self-acceptance, as stated, for example, by teachers in Lightfoot's (1985) sample. These are teachers who, echoing one informant, hear themselves, with some amazement, telling pupils "You have to take me as I am" after long years of guilt over their presumed shortcomings.

Conservatism

In Peterson's (1964) study, secondary school teachers of ages 50 to 60 are strikingly negative. A large number bemoan the new cohorts of pupils (less disciplined, less motivated, "decadent"), the negative public attitude toward education, the confused or spineless policies of administrators, the laxity or arrogance of young colleagues. In the same vein, older female teachers in Prick's (1986) sample complain of apathetic or surly pupils and men tend to believe that changes rarely result in an improvement of the school system. In my study (Huberman, 1993a), slightly less than half the sample described themselves as "more prudent," but most had become far more skeptical about attempts at structural reform. On the other hand, there was only one definable subgroup of older teachers corresponding to the profiles in Peterson or Prick. These people had been brought kicking and screaming through earlier periods of change in the local system and continued in their later years to be critical and embittered.

Intuitively, of course, the relationship between age and conservatism is typically taken for granted, buttressed both by a folk literature and by several empirical studies (e.g., Lowenthal et al., 1975; Okun, 1976; Riley & Foner, 1968; Ryff & Baltes, 1976). Modal trends in this research point to gradually increasing levels of rigidity and dogmatism, to increased prudence and resistance to change, to nostalgia for the past, and so forth. On the other hand, these studies do not identify a sequence, nor do they take into account social or contextual factors.

Disengagement

At the most global level, life-cycle research posits what Kuhlen (1964) has called "a curve of expansion and of withdrawal" in the course of the professional career. The initial phases represent an active exploration of the profession and are followed by periods of "mastery," "power," or "advancement," depending on the contours of the profession. There then follows a moment of "stock-taking," gradually giving way to a process of disengagement.

The nature of such a "disengagement" is, however, a subject of some controversy. The principal hypothesis, of a psychological nature, is that of a progressive "internalization" (cf. Neugarten, 1967; Neugarten & Datan, 1974), notably after the mid-40s and among men who have not interrupted a professional career. The indicators in this line of research include increased introspection, greater emotional sensitivity, and more openness to preconscious forces. This evolution is accompanied by what Neugarten (1964) has called a "letting go of external investments" in favor of more immediate and more contemplative sources of satisfaction. Along with others, Neugarten attributes much of this evolution to physiological changes (in hearing, sight, metabolic level) with increasing age.

Others have outlined a similar evolution from a sociological perspective (e.g., Friedman, 1970), emphasizing the social pressures exerted on individuals in their mid- or later 50s to disengage or to make way for others. The landmark study of Cumming and Henry (1961), for example, where the "disengagement" hypothesis was first elaborated, makes a strong case for both intraindividual and social influences.

Finally, some authors (e.g., Maehr & Kleiber, 1981) have introduced the argument that engagement has different meanings at age 25 and at age 55. Later in life, one might invest in activities less connected to material accomplishments, but no less active. One thinks here of Voltaire's anti-hero, Candide, cultivating his garden with as much care and engagement as in his earlier adventures, but at another level of activity, in another, more contemplative, mode of expression.

Does this trend obtain in studies of teachers at the end of their careers? To some extent, it does, simply by virtue of extending trends found earlier in teachers' professional lives. With the so-called phase of "serenity," there begins a gradual process of disengagement, on both the personal and institutional levels. Periods of "conservatism" imply a disagreement with prevailing policies and practices and, thereby, a functional marginality within the school or school system. Other studies (e.g., Becker, 1970; Nias, 1985) identify subsets of teachers who, unable to progress as far as their ambitions, disinvest professionally at midcareer, or who, disappointed by the results of structural change within their school, channel their energies elsewhere.

On the other hand, the existence of a distinct phase of disengagement has not been demonstrated clearly for the teaching profession. Intuitively, there is no reason to believe that teachers behave differently from other professionals undergoing the same physiological evolution and subject to the same social pressures (to "hand the reins over" to younger colleagues, to prepare for one's retirement).

CONCLUSIONS: THE DETERMINANTS OF A SATISFIED CAREER

Let me begin to pull together the several strands of this analysis by representing graphically the succession of modal career sequences outlined earlier (see Figure 9.1). As Figure 9.1 shows, there is a single stream at the point of career entry, running to the "stabilization" phase. Then there are multiple streams throughout the career cycle, converging again into a single path at the end. Depending on the previous trajectory, this final phase can be either serene or acrimonious. The most harmonious sequence runs along the left side of the model [Experimentation/diversification → Serenity → (serene) Disengagement], and the most problematic sequence runs along the right side [Stock-taking/interrogations → Conservatism → (bitter) Disengagement]. But there are paths in which teachers move to and from these harmonious and problematic poles and paths (not shown on the model), in which teachers leapfrog a given stage or revert to a phase experienced earlier in the career (e.g., a stock-taking phase or an experimentation phase). Finally, we should bear in mind that this model is a simplification of trends in the conceptual and empirical literature and that, at best, it accounts for small clusters of individuals in disparate studies. Above all, it is lacking the shapes that order most human lives: the spiral, the gyre, or the helix. In effect, life is much more likely to be a staircase that we descend and ascend at different elevations, finding ourselves in a new territory of stock-taking or stabilization that corresponds to the new trajectory our life has taken.

Staying for a moment with this model, an obvious question comes to mind: What distinguishes those teachers who emerge, after 30 years of experience, in a phase of serene disengagement from those who end their careers

FIGURE 9.1 Modal Sequences of the Teacher Career Cycle: A Schematic Model

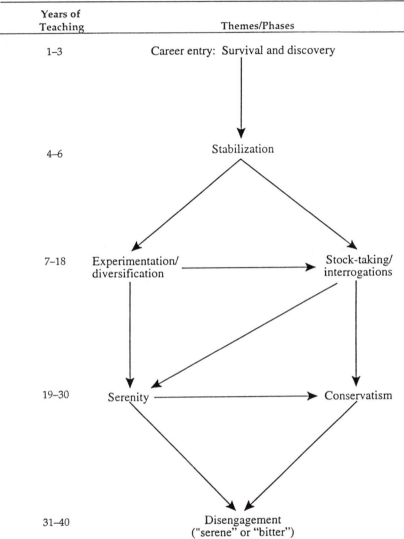

Years of Teaching	Themes/Phases
1–3	Career entry: Survival and discovery
4–6	Stabilization
7–18	Experimentation/ diversification → Stock-taking/ interrogations
19–30	Serenity → Conservatism
31–40	Disengagement ("serene" or "bitter")

in bitter disengagement? In other words, what are the prime determinants of career satisfaction, as identified by teachers who survey their professional lives?

My own study (Huberman, 1993a; cf. Lowther, Gill, Coppard, & Tank, 1982) addressed this issue statistically and was able to predict 89% of the cases of "disenchanted" or "dissatisfied" older teachers and 97% of the cases of "satisfied" teachers. But the study did not predict them early, that is, before teachers were about 12 to 15 years into their career. Still, the few early predictors that emerged are suggestive. Put briefly: Teachers who steered clear of reforms or other multiple-classroom innovations, but who invested consistently in class-room-level experiments—what they called "productive tinkering" with new materials, different pupil grouping, small changes in grading systems—were more likely to be "satisfied" later on in their career than most others, and far more likely to be satisfied than their peers who had been heavily involved in schoolwide or districtwide projects throughout their careers. This latter group felt that the time and effort expended on ambitious attempts to change on-going practices had essentially exhausted and embittered them, given the few concrete results they observed in their classrooms. They accused administra-tors of systematically "caving in" at crucial moments and had harsh words for their colleagues who had used these projects to propel themselves out of the classroom and into administrative jobs (cf. Huberman, 1985). Yet—and this is noteworthy—these same teachers usually described the first experiences of "experimentation" or "renewal" in which they were engaged with colleagues in these building-level changes as the most exciting and formative years of their career.

Three other factors were predictive of professional satisfaction later in the career cycle. Reviewing them will connect this particular study to the broader empirical literature. First, higher levels of perceived satisfaction ob-tained for *teachers who spontaneously sought some form of role shift* when they began to feel stale. In this subset of teachers, every fourth or fifth year brought with it a change in grade level or subject matter or school building or aca-demic stream. Note that these people are not warding off stagnation by leav-ing the classroom but rather by drawing on what diversity there is within the bounds of classroom instruction. And what is significant here is not only that this group of teachers spontaneously sought out such role shifts, but also that so many of their peers were apparently able to avoid them, all the while com-plaining somewhat ritually about professional isolation and stagnation.

The second factor came from elsewhere in the data set, when teachers were asked to describe their "best years." Overwhemingly, teachers mentioned *specific cohorts or classes* with whom they had enjoyed privileged relationships. These were in many ways "magical" years, when classrooms buzzed with pur-poseful activity, when apathetic pupils came alive, and, above all, when teachers felt "stretched" beyond their customary activity formats or materials and met this challenge through revisions of their instructional repertoires.

The third factor was similarly more associated, strictly speaking, with long periods of professional satisfaction than with a career that ended on that note. It had to do, simply, with *the experience of achieving significant results in the classroom*—when sullen or low-performing students engaged well or performed above their previous levels and overall achievement levels were well above the average. In many instances, this corresponded to a major instructional shift on the teachers' part, which brought in its wake some exceptional results (cf. Guskey, 1989), but there were other influences at work as well.

In reviewing this constellation of "predictors" of professional satisfaction in teaching, two impressions stand out. The first is that this list corresponds closely to the mainstream literature on the quality of work life. Ashton and Webb (1986) put it simply and well, noting that "work is likely to be satisfying when we value what we do, when it challenges and extends us, when we do it well, and when we have ample evidence confirming our success" (p. 162). The secondary school teachers in my sample thrived when they were able to tinker productively inside their classrooms or with two or three colleagues in order to obtain the instructional and relational effects they were after.

The second impression is that, on the face of it, such conditions of professional satisfaction are not so difficult to "deliver" at the organizational level. Minimally, sustaining professional growth seems to require manageable working conditions, opportunities—and sometimes demands—to experiment modestly without sanctions if things go awry, periodic shifts in role assignments without a corresponding loss of perquisites, regular access to collegial expertise and external stimulation, and a reasonable chance to achieve significant outcomes in the classroom. These are not utopian conditions. It just may be the case, in fact, that they have not been met more universally because policy and administrative personnel have not deliberately attended to them.

Other Life-Span Models

There is simply not the space here to review other well-developed conceptions of the succession of career stages in teaching. Good examples are Burden (1982), Feiman-Nemser and Floden (1981), Gregorc (1973), and Unruh and Turner (1970). The most fully developed and well-researched example is that of Fessler and his colleagues (see Chapter 8 of this volume). It has the distinctive merit of attending more carefully to institutional parameters than I have.

Professional Development and Career Cycles

Developmental models of the teaching career are basically stereotypical, although they connect to studies of real lives. What do they tell us?

They tell us, for starters, that there are different concerns at different moments in the professional life cycle. A second-year teacher has different preoccupations than one who has been teaching for 30 years. An experienced but shopworn teacher faced with a new, integrated physics curriculum confronts different challenges than a junior colleague trying to inject some meaningful activities into an initial-year French curriculum.

Some analysts have figured, logically enough, that we could devise stage-appropriate staff development opportunities. Burden (1986), Fessler and his colleagues (Fessler & Burke, 1988), and Glickman (1990) have done work in this vein. I am skeptical of career-phase engineering and more inclined toward collaborative work among teachers at different points in their career (see Huberman, 1992).

I am more concerned, in fact, with the forms in which career-appropriate experimentation and mastery can occur. In the Swiss studies (Huberman, 1989, 1993a), pedagogical mastery was increased by specific modes of solitary and communal work. Overall, few were happy with conventional inservice formats ("not aligned with my needs" . . . "specialists who never ran a class of kids" . . . "good exchanges with colleagues, but then it was over and nothing was resolved."). As we know from the empirical literature (Daresh, 1987; Joyce & Showers, 1988; Stevenson, 1987; Wade, 1985), most of these offerings have outlived their eras, both organizationally and pedagogically.

What *had* worked better? The most frequent—but not necessarily the best—procedure was a "lone-wolf scenario"—working alone, with a graduated set of small experiments. The experiments were interspersed with short readings or pieces of advice from a nearby or respected colleague—but seldom from a specialist or teacher educator. Often there were long latency periods—letting things lie for a year or two, then trying a new tack. It is probable that this version of private, self-administered inservice, with whatever tools and expertise lie nearby, is the modal one across most school settings and at most points of the career. Both the architectural and social organization of schooling, make it difficult to work otherwise.

An Exception: The "School Improvement" Scenario

There was one exception. As mentioned above, teachers were almost uniformly enthusiastic when they were in the throes of a major innovation of which they approved: a statewide change to laboratory-centered physics, a combined history and French program, an attempt at heterogeneous grouping across the school, an oral and active approach to teaching German. Why? Because these are simply some of the best conditions for conducting professional development—collaborative work with one's peers; assistance and training from experts; access to new materials and technologies; intensive experimentation, in which all novices are allowed to fail and each success can be celebrated, combined with close collective scrutiny of those experiments, so that the project makes its major errors only once (Huberman & Miles, 1984). The problem, of course, is that such moments come rarely in the professional life span; we can expect, in a 30-year career, four or five such episodes, each lasting three to four years at their peak.

TOWARD A MODEL OF PROFESSIONAL DEVELOPMENT

Let me now move from the "lone-wolf" paradigm described above to a continuous "innovating" model more like the one in the previous paragraph. Issues of the professional life span will come in later.

First, some assumptions. I assume that, structurally, the "lone-wolf" model of trial and error will remain entrenched and that whatever skill-enhancing mechanisms we devise will have to be grafted onto that model, at least partially. In the current organization of schooling, teachers are "professional craftspeople" (see below) who, like artisans, work primarily alone, with a variety of new and scrounged-together materials, in a self-tailored work environment (Huberman, 1993b). Like good artisans, they are active tinkerers, intent on developing an instructional repertoire that responds to—even anticipates— most contingencies in the classroom. In life-cycle terms, this kind of productive tinkering is more pronounced between the 5th and 15th year of experience, but it is always, to some extent, a staple of the profession.

Closed Individual Cycle

Let us now thread our way from the "lone-wolf" to the "innovating" paradigms. Figure 9.2, the closed individual cycle, depicts the way many teachers contend with the instructional challenges they face. Let us take, for example, an official biology textbook that has shown itself to be too difficult for much of the class. The problem is felt, diagnosed, and experimented with (photocopies of "easier" texts, work in mixed-ability groups, an increase in exercises and "debriefing" sessions). If this suffices, the same strategy will be used again. If not, another strategy will be pursued. Literally dozens of instructional matters are resolved—or not—this way in classrooms.

Open Individual Cycle

To gain time, let us assume the same situation—an inadequate biology text. The cycle depicted in Figure 9.3 is similar, except that, at the moment of looking for solutions, the teacher reaches outside the classroom, as it were, and turns to fellow biology teachers, to people at the local teacher educational faculty, or to a wider span of biology materials. This is a primitive, but often successful, form of professional development, given the knowledge acquired, the new resources made available, and the consultations furnished. Still, the success of the enterprise depends almost entirely on the social network of our biology teachers and their willingness to make something of the information and expertise provided. We are still in a "lone-wolf" paradigm.

FIGURE 9.2 "Closed" Individual Cycle

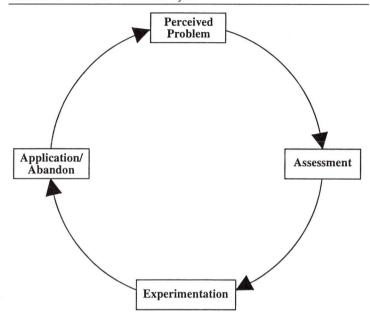

Closed Collective Cycle

The next cycle (see Figure 9.4) brings us closer to a collective enterprise, but one without resources from outside the group. Note that we are not in a school here (although we could be), but among teachers from several schools who share the same discipline, interests, preoccupations, grade level, or type of pupil. An important premise here, at least beyond the elementary school level, is that a biology teacher has more to learn and to give, professionally speaking, in a group of fellow biology teachers than with the one or two peers who also teach biology in that person's own building. In any event, these are "professional craftspeople," and they are traversing a cycle that goes from exchanges to experimentation.

Let us stay with the biology example, although we could easily focus on evaluation, lab work, differences in pupils' ability and motivation, and so forth. In the "experience-sharing" phase, there is an exchange of "case" material ("In my class . . ."). There is also, however, a strong dose of more explanatory or diagnostic discussion: reflection on one's work and discussion of seminal issues about learning and teaching science in different contexts. In other words,

FIGURE 9.3 "Open" Individual Cycle

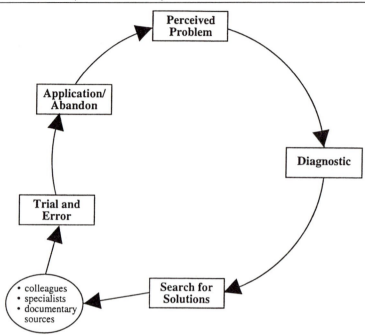

this is one version of the "communities" for teacher research that are increasingly being reported in the literature (e.g., Cochran-Smith & Lytle, 1992). It sensitizes teachers to the facts that (1) their theories have been largely derived from their practices, (2) their experiential base is only one of several possible and equally legitimate ways of construing the same events or the same learning patterns, and (3) the language of exchange is an imperfect and frustrating vehicle until there has been protracted interaction, mutual experience, and gradual development of capacity to imagine perspectives other than one's own from the inside out.

This combination of experience sharing and reflection is a core component of this and the next cycle. As we know, school scheduling provides very little slack time for exchanges that are not purely functional. Most conversation has to do with what Yinger (1987) calls a "language of practical action," as opposed to a forum for representing practice "in larger, more visible patterns" that are accessible to all and that combine meaningful units of thought and action.

Experience sharing leads to the conclusion that new texts and new experiments are called for. Some of the experiments can be done individually; others will call for collaborative work in class. Our biologists work up a series of both and agree to try them out. They come together to discuss these experiments and to make revisions.

The group then decides, let us say, to collect some pupil work samples ("data collection" in Figure 9.4) in order to see how well the new procedures worked. This is a decisive part of the cycle. First, it involves some ongoing monitoring. Next, it renders *public* and *visible* what has gone on in each class. We are no longer in a verbal exchange mode, a "discussion culture," with nothing on the line. These professional exchanges, carried on around real data collected in the class of each member, set up a situation of clarification and comparison, and they only work when the group, in its earlier phases, has come to a level of mutual comfort and complicity.

Practically speaking, the idea here is to set up exchanges around specific products or performances so that the next round of experimentation can be more successful. How did the experiments go? Which constellation of groups worked best? Which misconceptions arose most often? In what form? At the

FIGURE 9.4 "Closed" Collective Cycle

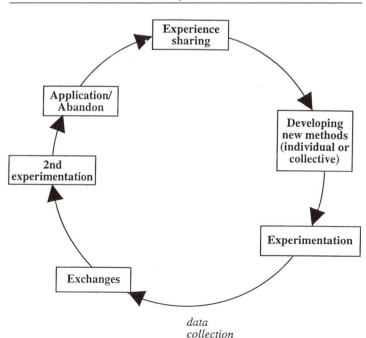

same time, some group cohesiveness has been established. The evidence is fairly clear that such minimal cohesiveness increases performance, and vice versa. As Mullen and Copper (1994) conclude from a set of integrated studies, what distinguishes groups that perform well is not necessarily that their members interact with smooth coordination, or that they like each other that much, or that they are proud of their group, but that "they are committed to successful task performance and regulate their behavior toward that end" (p. 225).

Finally, the remainder of the model shows that a group of this nature can remain together, either to refine the biology module or to work on other issues. We are in the realm of more prolonged "teacher action research" or "collaborative inquiry" (Baird, 1992; Lambert, 1989), both of which closely tied to further experimentation. And we are there, it should be noted, with virtually no recourse to external expertise as would be provided, say, by a science educator or a learning theorist.

Open Collective Cycle

Before going on, let us have a look at Figure 9.5. There are a few core premises to bear in mind:

- In this illustration, the group comes from several schools but shares a subject matter, discipline, grade level, problem, or activity it wants to work on.
- The cycle is managed by the group, not by a consultant or specialist. In some instances a "process facilitator" might be useful. Specialists are called in at various moments, in accordance with the kind of issue with which the group is contending at that moment.
- These are specialists of different kinds, something that is foreign to most inservice work. Also, their intervention can be brief, varying from a couple of weeks two or three months. They are there at specific moments for specific purposes.

Now for the successive stages of the cycle. Let us try a new example, say, hands-on science in the fifth and sixth grades. These teachers have come together because the materials at hand are purely workbook-oriented, and the basic text calls more for memorization than for active problem solving.

Conceptual Inputs. The cycle begins with some conceptual inputs (11 o'clock on the model) from a university psychologist who has worked on social-constructivist perspectives in math and science. She provides a frame for conducting and monitoring experimentation in class in small groups for the kinds of cognitive confrontations and eventual shifts one might observe,

FIGURE 9.5 "Open" Collective Cycle

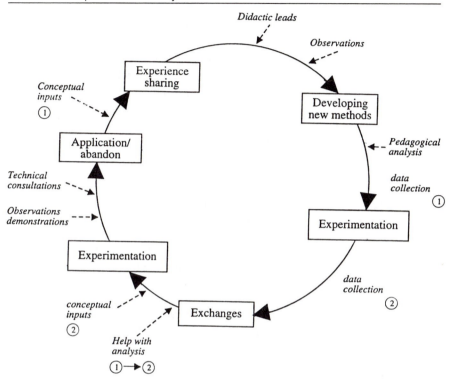

for the relationship between the conduct of small experiments and what actual scientists do, and for the possible links between science and math curricula at the upper elementary level.

Experience Sharing. This next step has two functions. The first is to make acquaintance, via one's own experience with science teaching in the upper elementary grades. This is the reason for the group, and the sharing of experiences has primarily a technical, initiating function (the convivial moments will come in the interstices). At one level, there is the matter of what each person has experienced with the official science curriculum. At another, all members of the group have a professional biography in science teaching that explains why they are dissatisfied and which alternatives would be both appealing and, given one's own pedagogy, acceptable. It is here that the wealth of experience accumulated through the career cycle can be shared—shared, but, as we just saw, not necessarily aligned. The idea is not to come to agreement on a set of pedagogical beliefs, but to get as much understanding of one another as possible in order to continue working together.

The next function has to do with the conceptual inputs the group has just received. What do they signify? How well do they illuminate the cognitions and performances one has observed over the past years? What exactly is a social-constructivist perspective of teaching in real-time, garden-variety classrooms? Presumably, some reading may be done and discussed at this phase of the cycle. It will be in the ongoing shifts from practical experience to more formalized knowledge that we can hope to generate the descriptions, discussions, and debates that constitute for teacher researchers the "joint construction of knowledge through conversation" (Cochran-Smith & Lytle, 1992, p. 309).

Didactic Leads. These, too, are provided in part by outsiders to the group, most likely by science educators from a neighboring university. Their function is to build on the conceptual inputs and sharing of experiences by providing alternative scenarios in class. For example, many hands-on science programs have groups of pupils acting as scientists: making hypotheses, collecting and weighing evidence, drawing conclusions. Common projects have to do with measuring acidity levels in water, building rain collectors, understanding the conditions under which pH levels can be lowered, and so forth. Talking through didactic leads puts flesh and bones on the conceptual inputs and evokes ideas for small experiments one has imagined or done oneself in class.

Observations. These are observations of places in which some of this novel didactic activity is ongoing. These classrooms are identified, typically, by the didactic specialist, and they have the merit of allowing visiting teachers to see how their peers enact new practices under everyday conditions. In terms of learning, of combining conceptual with didactic elements, this is one of the most powerful vehicles for moving from a conventional practice to a novel one. In effect, few modes of learning have shown themselves to be as consequential as observational learning, when the observations are focused and related to one's own experience. Also, again typically, there will be a thousand questions to be asked afterward, and, through the more informal contacts, a possible widening of the network of science teachers in the region.

Development of New Methods. It is here that the group begins to construct an alternative to the science text and workbooks. These are tentative procedures and materials that have been cobbled together, but they represent a start. Some members of the group will want to work on different modules, some on the same.

Pedagogical Analysis. The figure also shows that an external analysis might be useful. By this is meant the entry of a specialist who can take a sympathetic but rigorous look at the procedures and materials that have been put together. Alternatively, one can invite back the person(s) providing the conceptual and didactic leads, asking for a more fine-grained look.

Experimentation. By this point, we could assume that a shared technical culture has developed within the group—at least for those that are still around. What happens now is that each member tries out the materials and sequences that have been elaborated in common. Conceptually, this is an important moment. Group dynamics theory suggests that if a public commitment to change is made—as in this instance—there will be follow-through. Otherwise, the magnitude of effort is likely to be highly variable and, in the mean, trivial. The same lines of research also suggest that groups of this type are more likely to take risks than would the same individuals left alone in their classrooms (Wallach, Kogan, & Bem, 1962). Also, in keeping with social-identity theory, individuals come gradually to comply with the demands and expectations of other group members, owing to the subtle powers that reward or punish individual members. Identifying with the group thus increases accountability to the group (members move to action) and reduces social loafing (Steiner, 1966). Groups with these characteristics are more often what Little (1990) calls subject subcultures: teachers of the same discipline, or at roughly similar grade levels, or who share a similar pedagogical perspective.

Another facet of group dynamics is the facility, in groups drawn from different schools, of giving and asking for help and advice. This turns out to run counter to the norms *within* schools (Glidewell, Tucker, Todt, & Cox, 1983; Huberman, 1993b). There, one does not readily solicit help (in order to preserve one's sense of competence and status equality), nor does one typically offer advice (for fear of appearing arrogant). One can, however, swap experiences in which help is latent or tell a story in return that contains advice ("I once had the same kind of droop just after Easter. So what I tried . . ."). There is evidence that these norms are changing, but not rapidly. Note that in the cycle we are discussing here, help and advice are literally built into the discussions. Also, since what is being tried out is new to all, temporary difficulties, even failures, are socially legitimate. Everyone is stumbling and feels free to talk about it.

Exchanges. The figure also shows another constraint on the group. Each member will collect pre-test data and, after the experimentation, will collect post-test data. The figure also shows that external help can be provided for the analysis of pre-test (1) and post-test (2) data. These data are less there as evaluative instruments than as *an obligation to actually conduct the experimen-*

tation and to debrief with other members in the group in ways that are not purely anecdotal. Ideally, these exchanges will also include work samples, test results, final products, and, in so doing, will make for a more concrete, technical exchange of information. But the core function of the exchanges is the clear evidence of embarking on an adventure together, one in which each member has actually taken some risks, instructionally speaking. In other words, we are close to the school improvement scenario developed in the previous section.

Conceptual Inputs (2) and Experimentation. Following the first experimentation, the analysis of its results in terms of pupils' engagement, productivity, or performance, and ongoing exchanges about the mass of small mysteries, epiphanies, and tragedies, the cycle calls for another visit from a conceptual specialist. It is clear that the discussion at this point will be different from the initial one [conceptual inputs (1)]. There will have been a conceptual articulation of individual frames, didactic and pedagogical leads, the creation and execution of an experiment, and the analysis of its results. For example, one will be talking less about social constructivism in science than about what happened, and especially why, when pupils' expectations were foiled in the first part of the experiment. We would expect, in fact, that the effects of this second conceptual component, built as it is on an experiment that was collectively executed and thoroughly discussed, would be strong ones—would knit theory to instruction. As the figure shows, these inputs lead to a revision of the same experiment or to the design of a new one.

The moments of conceptualization are decisive ones. First, they stave off the rush to action—the eagerness to get the next experiment "right." Next, as the constructivists like to say, they give the time needed for one's confusion. Gradually, members will be able to consider their own views and practices from the perspective of other group members. At the same time, common knowledge is gradually broadened (seeing more ways of acting in one setting) and deepened (conceiving of more aspects of the situation). As Duckworth (1987) puts it, "more situations now make sense; any one situation makes sense in a greater number of ways" (p. 42).

Demonstrations and Consultations. This is a delicate point. We might well imagine that the next experimentation cycle would resemble the first one. I have, however, opted for a more "intrusive" scenario, as shown in Figure 9.5. The figure suggests, in effect, that group members will scan actively for teachers more experienced than they are or for teacher educators familiar with the kind of project they are working on. Why this emphasis on "technical assistance"?

Joyce and Showers (1982, 1988) have shown convincingly, I believe, that we think magically about the mastery of complex instructional procedures—about what learning psychologists call "enactive mastery." It is not simply by trial and error, observation, and verbal exchanges with colleagues that learning of complex skills occurs, in the classroom or elsewhere. In effect, in other areas of expertise—law, medicine, social work, athletics—there are periods of focused observation, demonstration, and at-the-elbow consultation while the novice runs through the successive components of the new practice. In education, by contrast, by falsely extrapolating from the principle that each teacher has a unique instructional and interpersonal style, we may well have come to believe that no rigorous technical support is needed for durable pedagogical change. Because, in so many cases, teachers effectively teach themselves to teach, they may assume that they can teach themselves to teach otherwise. This turns out, in many ways, to be harder. Nor is practice in isolation an adequate solution, not only because it solidifies erroneous activity, but also because it affords so little opportunity for the conceptual clarification that allows teachers to make sense of their cumulative experience.

In fact, most evidence points in the opposite direction: Demonstration by experts, systematic observation of teachers undertaking new practices, and interventions on the spot in the form of "coaching" seem to be required for any major shift in the learning environment created by the teacher—required and, in most instances, appreciated. The same trends appear in the implementation literature (Fullan, 1990). Teachers tend to remain stuck at lower levels of mastery for lack of explicit counsel from external experts or from experienced peers. Note, finally, that in his meta-analysis of inservice training, Wade (1985) concluded that models which incorporate observation, feedback, and practice are more effective than programs that do not use those methods.

In effect, the kind of problem solving built into this cycle *assumes* that the process of learning, experimentation, and change will be moderately complex, novel, ambiguous, contradictory, and conflicting. *These are, in effect, the ideal conditions for significant learning, be it for adults or for children* (see Salomon & Globerson, 1987). Often, too, such a process can trigger self-doubts in more than one sector at once: in one's sense of content mastery, in one's implicit theory of learning, in one's comfort with instructional management. Just as the group literally sets off these unsettling feelings in its members, it also provides a safe haven to experiment with them (Abrams, Wetherell, Cochrane, Hogg, & Turner, 1990).

All this is pertinent to our science teachers. What is unusual, perhaps, in this model is that we have *both* a self-directing group and a set of external interventions. In many respects, it is similar to other rational models that have demonstrated their efficiency, such as that of Stallings (1989): try, evaluate, modify, try again. At the same time, it respects some of the key "collaborative" canons laid out by Lieberman and Miller (1990): (1) a culture of support for teacher inquiry; norms of collegiality, openness, and trust; (2) opportunities and time for disciplined inquiry; (3) teacher learning of content in context; (4) reconstruction of leadership roles; (5) networks, collaborations, and coalitions.

Application/Abandonment. We have come to the end of the cycle shown on Figure 9.5. The group, singly or collectively, will adopt some of the new science approaches they have constructed together. Others will be discarded. More important, perhaps, an enlarged network will have been created: a network of upper elementary science teachers, itself connected to specialists in neighboring universities and resource centers. We have, then, a plausible scenario for the professional development of teachers.

AND THE PROFESSIONAL LIFE CYCLE?

In presenting a model for professional development, we need to be clear about its usefulness over the long haul. What does it bring, in the best instances, to a professional career?

McLaughlin and Yee (1988) have one answer. Their data suggest two components of a "challenging career": *opportunity* and *capacity*. Opportunity has to do with the chance to develop one's basic competence. This implies the availability of stimulation, challenge, and feedback about one's performance, along with support for efforts to acquire new skills. "Opportunity" determines the extent to which an individual can develop heightened degrees of professional competence. Clearly, the open collective cycle laid out earlier (refer to Figure 9.5) is one formula for the achievement of opportunity.

But the cycle is less aligned with "capacity," which the authors define as access to resources and the ability to mobilize them. "Capacity" not only implies the availability of tools to do one's job, but also the capability to influence the direction of one's institution. This is clearly a more building-centered, micro-political dimension of the career.

The main point here is that our model provides opportunity by acting on two fronts. First, if we want to reason in terms of career "phases," this is a forum for everyone. The novice discusses, debates, experiments with more experienced peers, and profits accordingly. "Stabilized" teachers extend their repertoires, both conceptually and practically, and better consolidate the passage from subject-matter mastery to its didactic transposition in class. Teachers in the "diversification" phase will be stretching themselves collaboratively. "Stock-takers" may find it profitable to revive some overused pedagogical routines. In other words, a heterogeneous group reflecting, conversing, debating, and experimenting together is a powerful device for intimacy, mutuality, mastery, and, in the best cases, a resocialization or rebonding to their professional guild.

It needs to be said, finally, that this model does not preclude interactive designs at the level of the school building. In some respects, in fact, this model could be converted to an action research project within an establishment. The differences are threefold. First, we have centered on teachers of similar grade levels or subject matters. In small schools, I may be the only science or math teacher around, and I can go only as far as my best student pushes me. In larger schools, my department may not be—in fact, seldom is—a seedbed of collective reflection, exchange, and experimentation.

Second, this analysis has been largely pedagogical, not structural. I have taken to heart Elmore's (1992) trenchant argument that restructuring alone will not improve teaching practice or student learning. Finally, I have built a mix of conceptual components, then set down some actual obligations to experiment and to follow up somewhat rigorously on the results of those experiments. Both may be harder to do on a schoolwide basis, although the tide is moving that way. Had we exemplars, cross-school experimenting groups, and within-school restructuring groups, we might advance the agenda of professional development and, thereby, enhance the environments of instruction and learning. Finally, we might well resurrect some of the vitality and commitment with which our teachers began their careers and which, over time, have often given way to subtle—sometimes even cynical—forms of disengagement.

REFERENCES

Abrams, D., Wetherell, M., Cochrane, S., Hogg, M., & Turner, J. (1990). Knowing what to think by knowing who you are: Self-categorization and the nature of norm formation, conformity and group polarization. *British Journal of Social Psychology, 29*, 97–119.

Adams, R. (1982). Teacher development: A look at changes in teachers' perceptions across time. *Journal of Teacher Education, 33*(4), 40–43.

Ashton, P., & Webb, R. (1986). *Making a difference: Teachers' sense of efficacy and student achievement.* New York: Longman.

Atchley, R. (1975). The life course, age grading, and age-linked demands for decision-making. In N. Datan & L. Ginsburg (Eds.), *Life-span developmental psychology: Normative life crises* (pp. 261–278). New York: Academic Press.

Baird, J. (1992). Collaborative reflection, systematic inquiry, better teaching. In R. Russell & H. Munby (Eds.), *Teachers and teaching: From classroom to reflection* (pp. 33–48). London: Falmer.

Ball, S., & Goodson, I. (Eds.). (1985). *Teachers' lives and careers.* Lewes, UK: Falmer.

Becker, H. (1964). Personal change in adult life. *Sociometry, 27*(1), 40–53.

Becker, H. (1970). The career of the Chicago schoolmaster. In H. Becker (Ed.), *Sociological work: Method and substance* (pp. 34–69). Chicago: Aldine.

Bray, D., & Howard, A. (1983). The AT&T longitudinal study of managers. In K. Schaie (Ed.), *Longitudinal studies of adult psychological development* (pp. 286–312). New York: Guilford.

Burden, P. (1981). Teachers' perceptions of their personal and professional development. Cited in S. Feiman-Nemser, Learning to teach, in L. Shulman & F. Sykes (Eds.), *Handbook of teaching and policy* (pp. 150–170). New York: Longman.

Burden, P. (1982, February). *Developmental supervision: Reducing teacher stress at different career stages.* Paper presented at Association of Teacher Educators, Phoenix.

Burden, P. (1986). Teacher development: Implications for teacher education. In J. Raths & L. Katz (Eds.), *Advances in teacher education* (Vol. 2; pp. 185–219). Norwood, NJ: Ablex.

Butler, R. (1963). The life review: An interpretation of reminiscence in the aged. *Psychiatry, 26*(1), 65–76.

Butt, R., Raymond, D., McCue, G., & Yamagishi, L. (1986). *Individual and collective interpretations of teachers' biographies.* Lethbridge, Canada: University of Lethbridge.

Chiriboga, D. (1988). Mental health at the midpoint. In S. Hunter & M. Sundel (Eds.), *Midlife myths* (pp. 116–144). Newbury Park, CA: Sage.

Cochran-Smith, M., & Lytle, S. (1992, May). Communities for teacher research: Fringe or forefront? *American Journal of Education*, pp. 298–323.

Cohler, B. (1982). Personal narrative and life course. In P. Baltes & O. Brim (Eds.), *Life-span development and behavior* (Vol. 4; pp. 206–241). New York: Academic Press.

Coloma, J. (1988, September). *Stages of school teachers' professional development.* Paper presented at Association of European Teacher Educators Meetings, Barcelona.

Connelly, M., & Clandinin, J. (1988). *Teachers as curriculum planners: Narratives of experience.* New York: Teachers College Press.

Cooper, K., & Gutmann, D. (1987). Gender identity and ego mastery style in middle-aged pre- and post "empty nest" women. *Gerontologist, 27*(4), 347–352.

Cooper, M. (1982, April). *The study of professionalism in teaching.* Paper presented at American Educational Research Association, New York.

Cumming, E., & Henry, W. (1961). *Growing old.* New York: Basic Books.

Daresh, J. (1987). Research trends in staff development and in-service education. *Journal of Education for Teaching, 13*(1), 11–19.

Duckworth, E. (1987). *The having of wonderful ideas, and other essays on teaching and learning.* New York: Teachers College Press.

Elder, G. H., Jr. (1977). Family history and the life course. *Journal of Family History, 2*, 279–304.

Elmore, R. (1992, April). Why restructuring alone won't improve teaching. *Educational Leadership*, pp. 44–49.

Erikson, E. (1950). *Childhood and society.* New York: Norton.

Featherman, D., Lerner, R., & Perlmutter, M. (Eds.). (1994). *Life-span development and behavior* (Vol. 12). Hillsdale, NJ: Erlbaum.

Feiman-Nemser, S. (1985). Learning to teach. In L. Shulman & G. Sykes (Eds.), *Handbook of teaching and policy* (pp. 150–170). New York: Longman.

Feiman-Nemser, S., & Floden, R. (1981). *A consumer's guide to teacher development.* East Lansing, MK: Institute for Research on Teaching, Michigan State University.

Fessler, R., & Burke, P. (1988). Teacher assessment and staff development. *Journal of Staff Development, 9*(1), 14–18.

Fessler, R., & Christensen, J. (1992). *The teacher career cycle: Understanding and guiding the professional development of teachers.* Boston: Allyn & Bacon.

Friedman, E. (1970). Changing value orientations in adult life. In R. Burns (Ed.), *Sociological backgrounds of adult education.* Syracuse, NY: Center for the Study of Liberal Education for Adults.

Fullan, M. (1990). *The new meaning of educational change.* New York: Teachers College Press.

Fuller, F. (1969). Concerns of teachers: A developmental perspective. *American Educational Research Journal, 6,* 207–226.

Glickman, C. (1990). *Supervision of instruction: A developmental approach.* Boston: Allyn & Bacon.

Glidewell, J., Tucker, S., Todt, M., & Cox, S. (1983). Professional support systems: The teaching profession. In A. Nadler, J. Fisher, & B. Depaulo (Eds.), *New directions in helping* (Vol 3; pp. 189–212). New York: Academic Press.

Gregorc, A. (1973). Developing plans for professional growth. *NASSP Bulletin, 57,* 1–8.

Guskey, T. (1989). Attitude and perceptual change in teachers. *International Journal of Educational Research, 13*(2), 439–454.

Haan, N. (1981). Common dimensions of personality development: Early adolescence to middle life. In D. Eichorn, J. Clausen, N. Haan, M. Houzik, & P. Mussen (Eds.), *Present and past in middle life* (pp. 117–151). New York: Academic Press.

Hamon, H., & Rotman, P. (1984). *Tant qu'il y aura des profs.* Paris: Editions du Seuil.

Handel, A. (1987). Personal theories about the life-span development of one's self in autobiographical self-presentations of adults. *Human Development, 30*(1), 83–98.

Hirsch, G., & Ganguillet, G. (1988). *Einstellungen, Engagement und Belastung des Lehrers: Ein lebensgeschichtlicher Ansatz.* Zürich.

Huberman, M. (1985). Educational change and career pursuits. *Interchange, 16*(3), 54–73.

Huberman, M. (1989). The professional life cycle of teachers. *Teachers College Record, 91*(1), 31–58.

Huberman, M. (1992). Teacher development and instructional mastery. In A. Hargreaves & M. Fullan (Eds.), *Rethinking teacher development* (pp. 122–142). Toronto: OISE Press.

Huberman, M. (1993a). *The lives of teachers* (J. Neufeld, Trans.). New York: Teachers College Press.

Huberman, M. (1993b). The model of the independent artisan in teachers' professional relations. In J. Little & M. McLaughlin (Eds.), *Teachers' work: Individuals, colleagues and contexts* (pp. 11–50). New York: Teachers College Press.

Huberman, M., & Miles, M. (1984). *Innovation up close: How school improvement works.* New York: Plenum.

Hunter, S., & Sundel, M. (1988). An examination of key issues concerning midlife. In S. Hunter & M. Sundel (Eds.), *Midlife myths* (pp. 8–28). Newbury Park, CA: Sage.

Ingvarson, L., & Greenway, P. (1984). Portrayals of teacher development. *Australian Journal of Education, 28*(1), 45–65.

Joyce, B., & Showers, B. (1982, October). The coaching of teaching. *Educational Leadership*, pp. 4–10.

Joyce, B., & Showers, B. (1988). *Student achievement through staff development.* New York: Longman.

Jung, C. (1959). The structure and dynamics of the psyche. In *Collected works* (Vol. 8; pp. 749–795). Princeton, NJ: Princeton University Press.

Jung, C. (1966). *Two essays on analytical psychology.* Princeton, NJ: Princeton University Press.

Kelchtermans, G., & Vandenberghe, R. (1993, April). *A teacher is a teacher is a teacher is a . . . Teachers' professional development from a biographical perspective.* Paper presented at American Educational Research Association, Atlanta.

Kimmel, D. (1975). *Adulthood and aging.* New York: Wiley.

Kuhlen, R. (1964). Developmental changes in motivation during the adult years. In J. Birren (Ed.), *Relationships of development and aging* (pp. 209–246). Springfield, IL: Thomas.

Lambert, L. (1989). The end of an era of staff development. *Educational Leadership, 18*, 78–83.

Levinson, D. (1978). *The seasons of a man's life.* New York: Knopf.

Lieberman, A., & Miller, L. (1990). Teaching development in professional practice schools. *Teacher College Record, 92*(1), 105–122.

Lightfoot, S. (1985). The lives of teachers. In L. Shulman & G. Sykes (Eds.), *Handbook of teaching and policy* (pp. 241–260). New York: Longman.

Little, J. (1990). The persistence of privacy: Autonomy and initiative in teachers' professional relations. *Teachers College Record, 91*(4), 509–536.

Lowenthal, M., Thurner, M., & Chiriboga, D. (1975). *Four stages of life.* San Francisco: Jossey-Bass.

Lowther, M., Gill, C., Coppard, D., & Tank, P. (1982, April). *Job satisfaction among teachers: A multisurvey, multivariate study.* Paper presented at American Educational Research Association.

MacDonald, B., & Walker, R. (1974). *SAFARI.* Colchester, UK: Centre for Applied Research in East Anglia.

Maehr, M., & Kleiber, D. (1981). The graying of achievement motivation. *American Psychologist, 37*(7), 787–793.

McLaughlin, M., & Yee, S. (1988). School as a place to have a career. In A. Lieberman (Ed.), *Building a professional culture in schools* (pp. 23–44). New York: Teachers College Press.

Mullen, B., & Copper, C. (1994). The relation between group cohesiveness and performance: An integration. *Psychological Bulletin, 115*(2), 210–227.

Neugarten, B. (1964). *Personality in middle and later life.* New York: Atherton.

Neugarten, B. (Ed). (1967). *Middle age and aging.* Chicago: University of Chicago Press.

Neugarten, B. (1968). The awareness of middle age. In B. Neugarten (Ed.), *Middle age and aging* (pp. 43–98). Chicago: University of Chicago Press.

Neugarten, B., & Datan, N. (1973). Sociological perspectives on the life cycle. In P. Baltes & K. Schaie (Eds.), *Life-span developmental psychology: Personality and socialization* (pp. 53–69). New York: Academic Press.

Neugarten, B., & Datan, N. (1974). The middle years. In S. Arieti (Ed.), *American handbook of psychiatry* (Vol. 1; pp. 492–608). New York: Basic Books.

Newman, K. (1979, April). *Middle-aged, experienced teachers' perceptions of their career development.* Paper presented at the American Educational Research Association, San Francisco.

Nias, J. (1985). Reference groups in primary teaching. In S. Ball & I. Goodson (Eds.), *Teachers' lives and careers* (pp. 105–119). Lewes, UK: Falmer.

Okun, M. (1976). Adult age and cautiousness in decision: A review of the literature. *Human Development, 19*(3), 220–233.

Peterson, W. (1964). Age, teacher's role and the institutional setting. In B. Biddle & W. Elena (Eds.), *Contemporary research on teacher effectiveness* (pp. 264–315). New York: Holt, Rinehart.

Phillips, S. (1982). Career exploration in adulthood. *Journal of Vocational Behavior, 20,* 129–140.

Prick, L. (1986). *Career development and satisfaction among secondary school teachers.* Amsterdam: Vrije Universiteit.

Riley, M. W. (1987). On the significance of age in sociology. *American Sociological Review, 52,* 1–14.

Riley, M., & Foner, A. (1968). *Aging and society* (Vol. 1). New York: Russell Sage Foundation.

Ryff, C., & Baltes, P. (1976). Value transition and adult development of women. *Developmental Psychology, 12,* 567–568.

Salomon, G., & Globerson, T. (1987). Skill may not be enough: The role of mindfulness in learning and transfer. *International Journal of Educational Research, 11,* 623–638.

Schaie, K., & Schooler, C. (Eds.). (1989). *Social structure and aging: Psychological processes.* Hillsdale, NJ: Erlbaum.

Showers, B. (1984). *Peer coaching and its effect on transfer of training.* Eugene, OR: Center for Educational Policy and Engagement.

Sikes, P. (1985). The life cycle of the teacher. In S. Ball & I. Goodson (Eds.), *Teachers' lives and careers* (pp. 27–60). Lewes, UK: Falmer.

Sikes, P., Measor, L., & Woods, P. (1985). *Teacher careers: Crises and continuities.* Lewes, UK: Falmer

Stallings, J. (1989, April). *School achievement effects and staff development. What are some critical factors?* Paper presented at American Educational Research Association, San Francisco.

Steiner, I. (1966). Models for inferring relationships between group size and potential group productivity. *Behavioral Science, 11,* 273–283.

Stevenson, R. (1987). Staff development in effective secondary schools: A synthesis of research. *Teaching and Teacher Education, 3*(2), 233–248.

Super, D. (1985). Coming of age in Middletown. *American Psychologist, 40*(4), 405–414.

Super, D. (1992). Developmental career assessment and counseling: The C-DAC model. *Journal of Counseling and Development, 71*(1), 74–80.

Unruh, A., & Turner, H. (1970). *Supervision for change and innovation.* Boston: Houghton Mifflin.

Wade, R. (1985). What makes a difference in in-service teacher education? A meta-analysis of research. *Educational Leadership, 42*, 48–54.

Wallach, M., Kogan, N., & Bem, D. (1962). Group influence on individual risk-taking. *Journal of Abnormal and Social Psychology, 65*, 75–86.

Warren, D. (1989). Messages from the inside: Teachers as clues in history and policy. *International Journal of Educational Research, 13*(2), 379–390.

Watts, H. (1980). *Starting out, moving on, running ahead.* San Francisco: Teachers Centers Exchange.

White, R. (1952). *Lives in progress.* New York: Dryden.

Woodruff, D., & Birren, J. (1972). Age changes and cohort differences in personality. *Developmental Psychology, 6*, 252–259.

Yinger, R. (1987). Learning the language of practice. *Curriculum Inquiry, 17*(3), 293–318.

PART IV

The Present and Future of Professionalism

Professional development in education is closely tied to notions of professionalism. The current paradigms of professionalism in education, however, are challenged by the authors in this part. They argue for a new vision of professionalism for educators and then propose models of professional development that coincide with that vision.

In Chapter 10, Michael Eraut of the University of Sussex in England contends that the professional development of teachers cannot be separated from the development of schools as professional institutions that create, monitor, and review their own educational programs and policies. But while the professionalization of schools is necessary, Eraut also argues that such development is dependent upon appropriate modes of accountability. Specifically, schools must give special attention to the impact of their programs and policies on the progress and performance of individual students.

The central role of teachers in the change process is the focus of Chapter 11, by Michael G. Fullan of the University of Toronto. Fullan portrays teachers as not only crucial to all successful improvement efforts, but also as key initiators in these efforts. According to Fullan, the rapid pace of change in education today imposes upon teachers moral and cultural imperatives that compel them to be active change agents. He then goes on to examine how current practices in professional development contribute to, inhibit, or are neutral to teachers' assuming the role of change agent.

10

Developing Professional Knowledge Within a Client-Centered Orientation

MICHAEL ERAUT

TOWARD A MODEL OF TEACHER PROFESSIONALISM

The debate about what precisely constitutes a profession has become sterile, unable to cope either with the changing nature of professional work or the diversity of occupational claims. Johnson (1984) has usefully redefined the framework of inquiry by shifting attention away from the search for a single set of characteristics that distinguish professions from other occupations toward the consideration of professionalism as an occupational ideology. Professionalization can then be viewed as a strategy for gaining status and privileges in accord with that ideology.

Three central features of the ideology of professionalism are a specialist knowledge base, autonomy, and service. The first two are clearly connected by one of the principal arguments expounded by the professions: Their knowledge base is so specialized that only fellow members of the same profession are able to judge the quality of their work. Thus a major feature of professionalization strategies in postwar Britain has been to gain graduate status through some form of alliance with higher education. While the professions gained status and a competitive advantage in recruitment, they lost control of a major part of their training. Higher education norms and interests thus ensured that most of the content of the new courses was dominated by abstract, propositional knowledge. This may have suited the science-based professions, but it seriously distorted the training orientation of the helping professions, which emphasize interpersonal skills. Teaching, however, remained in a somewhat anomalous position because of its dual knowledge base. One knowledge base, that of the subject(s) taught, is largely defined by the universities; the other is based on pedagogy and other education-related processes. The latter is the defining characteristic of teaching as a profession, but traditionally it has been either accorded lower status or academicised beyond recognition. Thus there is endless conflict between the kind of abstract, discipline-based knowledge given most status by higher education and the kind of practical knowledge needed in schools and classrooms. The proper resolution of this conflict will be a major theme in the second part of this chapter.

The argument that professions should be self-regulating and individual professionals autonomous is more complex and increasingly under attack. While it may be true that the most specialized forms of expertise are not fully understood by laypeople, the expert-witness technique is perfectly usable. More dubious still is the professionals' claim that they alone can assess the real needs of their clients. In practice, the proportion of professionals who are self-employed is quite small. Much larger numbers are employed in the public sector, industry, and commerce. Control by consumers is also a significant element in the work of many professionals. The aspiration to acquire the power and status of an elite lawyer or surgeon is but a dream. Hence the pursuit of "autonomy" is primarily a strategy to secure the maximum degree of freedom in one's daily practice and a significant role in determining policy.

Teaching incorporates aspects of all these modes of control. The relationship with pupils comes closest to the ideal of expert professionals determining the needs of their clients. But pupils also exercise a degree of consumer control, as also do their parents. The school district provides employer control, although its officers are usually ex-teachers supported by specialist staff. However, while policy used to be mainly determined within the professional education service, if not within the school itself, the increasing politicization of education has opened up policy issues for public debate. This multiplicity of stakeholders creates major problems for teachers. Are they meant to be serving the pupils, the parents, the local community, the school district, or the whole nation?

Teachers' Concepts of Professionalism

Teachers themselves give the term *professional* different meanings in different contexts, referring as appropriate to professional conduct, professional status, professional quality, professional judgment, and professional responsibilities. The last three are particularly relevant to my purpose.

Teaching quality is especially problematic. Logically, it should relate to the standards by which teachers judge one another's work, so that it becomes both an accolade for good or outstanding performance and an aspiration that stimulates the professional conscience. But in practice, teaching has achieved the unusual status of a private performing art for which there is no commu-

nity of critical discourse able to develop agreed-upon criteria of quality. Theorists may write about such matters and administrators may devise checklists;
but their interpretation is variable. Neither is grounded in public criticism of
performance in the manner of an actor, dancer, or musician. Master classes
in teaching are extremely rare. Moreover, improving the quality of performance
is not seen as part of an ongoing process of professional development.

Professional judgment is also privatized, primarily concerned with decisions about what to do in one's own classroom. The very concept of judgment implies alternative courses of action. So the teacher must have a repertoire of teaching approaches and activities from which to make an appropriate
selection. Similarly, the choice from this repertoire can only be appropriate if
there is a good understanding of the students' needs and an adequate conceptualization of the decision-making process—for example, of matching
learning activities to students' capabilities. Since in most classes there is significant variation among students, this implies that the teacher must be able
to organize different activities simultaneously. Research suggests that a substantial minority of teachers cannot do all these things; and even those teachers
who have this competence do not always make use of it. Time for professional
thinking is limited when routine duties are very demanding. Nevertheless, the
concepts of repertoire, appropriate provision, and differentiation according
to student needs are fundamental to professional practice; and I believe it is
possible to expect the majority of current teachers and all our future teachers
to reach this level of competence.

Another problem affecting professional judgment is the quality of professional discourse. The language introduced in training establishments has
an idealized quality that hinders rather than supports honest discussion about
practice. Nor has it been the tradition in most schools to cultivate such language. The difficulty of judging one's success as a teacher, combined with an
emphasis on what appear to be unattainable ideals, has made teachers vulnerable and lacking in confidence. Hence we have the almost universal adoption
of educational rhetoric as a protective shield against outside criticism. While
the rhetoric does include some important educational principles, it often di-
verts attention from the problems of putting them into practice. It probably
boosts teachers' self-esteem, but it inhibits self-evaluation. Some gap between
aspiration and reality is necessary for progress, as long as the situation is understood. Handling this duality and using it constructively is a central problem
in most professional development. This problem of educational discourse also
makes it difficult for teachers to understand and review their own knowledge
base.

Teachers prefer to use the term *responsibility* rather than *accountability*,
because the adoption of accountability as a slogan by politicians and the mass
media has made it something to be defended against. Yet teachers, when you

talk to them individually, feel accountable in a number of ways; and it is possible to build on their natural feelings of accountability in a manner that safeguards the interests of teachers and clients alike. To summarize briefly, teachers feel (1) morally accountable to students for the effects of their actions, and to a lesser extent to parents; (2) professionally accountable for the quality of their work both to themselves (to their professional conscience, as it were), to their colleagues, and to their profession; and (3) contractually accountable to their principal and their school district (Eraut, 1993d). Under good management these different forms of accountability should rarely conflict. Nevertheless, I will argue later that it is the moral and professional accountability of teachers that should provide the main motivation for their continuing professional development.

The Professional Practitioner

The previous sections have shown that the concept of teacher professionalism is far from simple. But rather than argue about whether teaching fits or ought to fit criteria derived from other professions, I prefer to construct a model of professionalism that is particularly appropriate for the occupation of teaching. Both teachers and the public have become increasingly depressed about the state of education; and what we now need is a positive model for the future role of teachers that includes their relationship with the public. Joint agreement on a model of teacher professionalism would then provide a rationale for teachers' professional development and proper recognition of its importance.

My model has three components: the concept of a professional practitioner, the concept of a professional school, and a framework for determining client needs. My thinking about each component has been informed by research, which I will summarize very briefly. What is new is the bringing together of these hitherto separate areas of inquiry in order to create a model for teacher professionalism.

My concept of a professional practitioner derives from both a view of professional accountability and an analysis of the teacher's knowledge base. At least four kinds of process knowledge play a critical part in the work of a classroom teacher (Eraut, 1993c):

1. *Processes for acquiring information, especially information about students.* These range from deliberate searches to the almost intuitive "reading of an emergent situation."
2. *Routinized action and skilled behavior.* Much classroom teaching falls into this category, intuitive yet following discernible patterns and still under some overall cognitive control.

3. *Deliberative processes such as planning, decision-making, and problem-solving.* These involve analyzing the context, devising options, mulling them over, and eventually choosing a course of action.
4. *Meta-processes such as assessing, evaluating, and controlling.* These processes concern, first, how teachers assess the impact of their actions and evaluate their personal practice; then, second, how they make use of this information to modify or rethink their decisions and work patterns.

The relative significance accorded to these processes determines one's concept of teaching. For example, *teaching as a craft* is principally occupied with process 2, with some attention to process 1 in its intuitive mode. There is considerable evidence to show that routinized action is central to coping in the classroom; but without a significant element of process 4 routines gradually decay and cease to serve their purpose, while at the same time becoming extremely difficult to change. So should we aim to develop *teachers as social scientists* by emphasizing processes 3 and 4? This is extremely unrealistic. Not only does it neglect the need for process 2 knowledge, but it fails to recognize that teachers work in crowded environments where decisions have to be made very rapidly on the basis of insufficient information. The scope for prior deliberation is limited. Moreover, the research of the last 30 years has made it abundantly clear that social science knowledge is not capable, or likely to be capable, of providing blueprints for actions. Most of a teacher's practical knowledge is gained from experience, and it is in the interpretation of that experience that theory plays its most important role (see my later discussion of the role of propositional knowledge in professional thought and action).

Research into teachers' thinking, combined with a more realistic assessment of the role of social science, has led to the development during the last decade of the concept of the *teacher as a reflective practitioner.* This is based on the following set of assumptions:

- A teacher needs to have a repertoire of methods for teaching and promoting learning.
- Both selection from this repertoire and adaptation of methods within that repertoire are necessary to best provide for particular pupils in particular circumstances.
- Both the repertoire and this decision-making process within it are learned through experience.
- Teachers continue to learn by reflecting on their experience and assessing the effects of their behavior and their decisions.
- Both intuitive information gathering and routinized action can be brought under critical control through this reflective process and modified accordingly.

- Planning and pre-instructional decision making is largely deliberative in nature. There is too little certainty for it to be a wholly logical process.
- These processes are improved when small groups of teachers observe and discuss one another's work (Eraut, 1994b).

The most significant features of this concept for our purpose are (1) its dialectic view of the relationship between theory and practice, which challenges the idea of prescription by external experts; (2) its incorporation of a theory of how teachers can change their practice; and (3) its emphasis on process 4 as a distinctive professional element.

I shall argue later that processes 3 and 4 and to a lesser extent process 1 involve drawing upon the teacher's knowledge base and that they need to be conducted within a client-centered orientation. Thus they involve professional thinking of the deepest and most demanding kind. Elsewhere (Eraut, 1993d) I have argued that what makes a reflective practitioner also a professional practitioner is a framework of professional accountability that epitomizes the service ideal. Professional development forms an integral part of this framework, whose implications for professional conduct can be summarized as follows. Being a professional practitioner implies:

1. A moral commitment to serve the interests of students by reflecting on their well-being and their progress and deciding how best it can be fostered or promoted
2. A professional obligation to review periodically the nature and effectiveness of one's practice in order to improve the quality of one's management, pedagogy, and decision making
3. A professional obligation to continue to develop one's practical knowledge both by personal reflection and through interaction with others

The Professional School

One major problem with the concept of professionalism is that it has been applied only to individuals. Most individual professionals work in organizations, and the quality of service depends on those organizations as well as on the individuals. In education, the significance of the organizational dimension is huge. Students are recruited to schools, not to classes; and they normally relate to several different teachers. Schools allocate students to teachers, keep records, organize examinations, provide facilities, communicate with parents, make and implement policy, supervise the work of teachers, and so forth. The "client contract" is formally with the school district but informally, and for most practical purposes, with the individual school. This makes it impossible to construct a credible model of teacher professionalism that does not give high priority to the concept of a professional school.

What, then, are the distinguishing features of a professional school? That it serves the interests of its clients; that it strives to be both effective and efficient; that it demonstrates quality in its processes; that it recruits, nourishes, and develops good staff; that it develops its policy and practice; and that it reviews, evaluates, and controls its affairs on the basis of valid information about its quality, impact, and effect. These features of quality schools are discussed in the research literature on school effectiveness, school improvement, and school management.

One conclusion emerging from this research is that a professional school needs more than good classroom teachers and trained managers. All staff need to participate in school-level processes and develop wider professional roles. Thus the professional practitioner has to take on the further professional obligations of contributing to the professional quality of the school in general; and the school has to respect, use, and develop the professionalism of its teachers by involving them in its professional work.

There is a danger, however, in developing a model of school management in which staff relations and professional development become ends in themselves rather than means for serving the interests of clients. At the student level, there is a need for regular reviews of individual progress in addition to the usual processes of monitoring and trouble-shooting. The purpose of such reviews should not be to revise or reaffirm the school's official definition of the student, but rather to make a joint assessment of the student's needs and to decide what feasible actions by teachers, by the student, and possibly also by parents would do most to promote that student's progress. While there might be preliminary discussions, the final conference should include one or two teachers, the student, and one or two parents.

The consequences for staff development would be threefold. First, the conduct of such reviews would itself require some training. Not only does it require teachers to be skilled in assembling appropriate evidence for discussion, but they will also need negotiating skills and possibly even counseling skills to encourage more reluctant parents and students to articulate their views. Second, the challenges posed in this vivid way by discussions of students' needs will be a continuing impetus to professional development. Third, the review process will encourage the development over time of students' responsibility for their own learning, with the implication that teachers' pedagogy will have to allow sufficient scope for that responsibility to be exercised. Another consequence might be more explicit discussions with students about how and why they learn.

At the school level, learning to undertake reviews of policy and practice that take proper account of the views of students and parents must become an integral part of the process of institutional development. While there is guidance to be obtained from the literature on evaluation, this tends to assume a more expensive and time-consuming operation than schools can afford—so much adaptation is needed, as well as developing the appropriate skills and attitudes. Teachers may need convincing that reviews of students, policies, and accepted practices are both fulfilling their moral obligations to pupils and a central feature of any tenable model of professionalism. This professional approach to improving quality underpins long-term professional development.

PROFESSIONAL KNOWLEDGE AND ITS ACQUISITION

The Domain of Teachers' Knowledge

I start this section with a brief review of the domain of teachers' knowledge. Although I will address only some parts of this domain in detail, I wish to set them in context and briefly draw attention to areas that have hitherto been little explored. The domain can be mapped in two dimensions (Eraut, 1992). The first dimension simply distinguishes among three areas of knowledge:

- *Subject-matter knowledge* is found in school syllabuses and formally taught to pupils.
- *Education knowledge*, both theoretical and practical, impinges upon the teaching process in particular and educational provision in general.
- *Societal knowledge* incorporates both that experiential and commonsense knowledge acquired by living in a society and that more organized and focused knowledge of society deemed important for good citizenship.

Clearly there are overlaps between these three categories, and they are all capable of being subdivided in a number of ways.

The second dimension indicates the range of contexts in which this knowledge is likely to be used:

- *Classroom knowledge* is built into the actual process of teaching and incorporates much of what is sometimes described as "practical know-how." Much of it is learned on the job, and it is difficult to codify and describe.
- *Classroom-related knowledge*, on the other hand, which includes much educational theory, is more easily described than applied. Such knowledge has to be interpreted, transformed, and integrated with classroom knowledge

before it can be said to be genuinely in use. The potential range of such knowledge is very large, and there is considerable professional dispute about which aspects are most important.

- *Management knowledge* is important for senior teachers, principals, supervisors, inspectors, and administrators. Like knowledge of teaching, it can be subdivided into job-embedded and job-related categories (cf. Howey & Joyce, 1978).
- *Other professional knowledge* covers such areas as curriculum development, pupil counseling, and communication with parents, all of which contribute to the life of the school and indeed to the profession in general. It manifests itself through nonteaching roles within the schools and through participation in innovative activities, committees, working parties, development of learning resources, and so forth. Sometimes the acquisition of such knowledge is viewed largely in terms of career development, either because it forms part of some formal qualification or because it is hoped that it will improve the chance of being promoted.

Returning to the first dimension, the area of *societal knowledge* is probably that which is most neglected. Although teachers are members of the society in which they work, they tend to be more familiar with some aspects and subcultures than with others. Their relative isolation from some groups and activities can limit their vision, their understanding, and their capacity to prepare young people for the future. There is even the recognized phenomenon of teachers "who have never left school." Evidence of this emerges from research studies whose primary foci are elsewhere; the issue is often discussed, but no direct research has ensued. We now have programs of In Service Education and Training (INSET) to give teachers the opportunity of gaining experience working in industry, but not for them to experience other occupations or live in other cultural settings. Perhaps this is a sign of the times. Even these programs, however, have been only minimally evaluated.

INSET aimed at improving *subject-matter knowledge* is more common, though much provision is directed not specifically at teachers but at adults in general. Nevertheless, the need to enhance teachers' knowledge of subject matter is generally recognized, even if the complex nature of the task is concealed by the use of terms like *updating*. In science, for example, there is considerable divergence between book knowledge (as tested by typical examination questions) and a working knowledge that allows people to explore and understand real-world phenomena as they encounter them. When science education is successful, both forms of knowledge are acquired, but not necessarily in the same way. Formal teaching develops only book knowledge, while working knowledge is developed through an informal process of socialization into the discipline through practical work and discussions. This requires a working scientific context of a kind that is only developed by imaginative teachers with adequate facilities; and these teachers can benefit from so-called updating courses if given the scope and encouragement to develop their ideas. But teachers with a low knowledge base and little working knowledge of the subject will find it difficult to digest and use new subject matter presented in a traditional way.

A further problem arises from the assumption that subject-matter knowledge is all that is required. While it is obvious that a "higher education–type" lecture is unsuitable for children, the degree of reprocessing involved is grossly underestimated. Learning a subject in higher education does not prepare teachers for structuring, sequencing, or pacing their lessons; for communicating ideas to pupils who may be either less or more intelligent than themselves; for recognizing potential in pupils' questions; or for understanding the nature of pupil misconceptions. To become proficient in these aspects of subject teaching, teachers have to reorganize and rework their knowledge into forms appropriate for classroom use. Their subject-matter knowledge remains job-related rather than job-embedded unless and until this further learning has occurred.

The Dominant Role of Process in Most Professional Work

My earlier analysis of the professional practitioner role referred to four kinds of process that play a critical part in the work of a classroom teacher:

1. Processes for acquiring information
2. Routinized action and skilled behavior
3. Deliberative processes
4. Meta-processes such as evaluating and controlling

These same four categories can be used to describe professional work at the school as well as the classroom level. The quality of professional work depends largely on how these processes are conducted; and this involves both knowledge of the processes themselves and the appropriate use of knowledge from across the domain depicted above (Eraut, 1993b). Closer examination of these processes casts light not only on the nature of a teacher's knowledge base but also on the ways in which it has been and can continue to be developed. Throughout this analysis it is argued that the nature of the knowledge base and the learning process are profoundly influenced by the conditions of the teacher's workplace.

Processes for Acquiring Information. These processes range from study skills concerned with extracting information from documentary sources, through recognized research methods such as interviews and questionnaires, to the experiential acquisition of information through simply being in a particular place at a particular time. They are shared with other professions, although teachers are more likely than most to opt for time-saving intermediate strategies—a short article rather than a book, a short discussion rather than a prepared interview. In addition, there are processes for assessing learning that are unique to the teaching profession—the setting and marking of assignments, tests, and exams. It should be noted, however, that these serve many purposes other than informing the teacher, for example, the motivation and control of pupils.

In general, the manner in which information is acquired and used will depend both on existing cognitive frameworks and on the mode of interpretation. People's search patterns are influenced by what they expect to find; so is what they notice and how they perceive it. Such influences may not be acknowledged or understood, especially when the information is acquired experientially. Another characteristic of such information is that it may not be interpreted at all; if it is not reflected upon, it will remain as a series of personal impressions. In practice there is usually some instant interpretation, involving the recognition of people, but little more of significance may be noted. In classroom situations, there is usually some monitoring of events leading to a decision to continue or intervene. This requires a rapid reading of the situation in which all kinds of prior assumptions are taken for granted. A live encounter passes in a flash, so that what is remembered will depend on the ability of the perceiver to notice and select the right information rapidly at the time of the encounter. Reflection has to take place after the event. It is only out of the classroom that deliberative interpretation can occur, with time for thought and possibly also discussion.

In educational contexts, where there are many actors but some continuity over time, both teachers and managers tend to acquire a great deal of piecemeal information experientially and use it to build up a picture of a person or a situation. For example, let us consider how a teacher acquires information about individual pupils in a class. Although teachers receive some information from records and comments from other teachers, their knowledge of individual pupils is based mainly on direct encounters in the classroom. These encounters are predominantly with the class as a group, but nevertheless a series of incidents involving individuals in whole-class, small-group, or one-to-one settings are likely to be stored in memory, rather like a series of film clips. Insofar as a teacher has made notes, these are likely to serve as memory aids rather than independent sources of information. How is the information then used? Under conditions of rapid interpretation, teachers will respond to situations on the basis of their current images of the pupils, although these images may have themselves been formed by rapid assimilation of evidence with little time for reflection. Under conditions of deliberative interpretation, the most accessible evidence is likely to be carefully considered; but even that may be a sample of remembered encounters selected for their ready accessibility rather than their representativeness.

Psychological research on the information-gathering aspect of human decision making has shown that a number of errors regularly occur, from which professionals are certainly not exempt (Nisbett & Ross, 1980). When retrieval from memory is a critical factor, incidents involving a person are more likely to be recalled if they are more recent and/or more salient: Quiet, unobtrusive people may not be remembered at all. Also, sufficient allowance may not be made when a highly atypical sample of incidents provides the basis of the memory record. For example, a teacher is more likely to notice abnormal behavior in pupils in the form of naughtiness or interesting questions; and a principal usually sees teachers out of their classrooms.

Misunderstanding is also likely to ensue from the strong tendency endemic in all of us to interpret events in accordance with our prior expectations. Thus earlier incidents may affect how later incidents are perceived. Worse still, informal, second-hand reports or rumors may affect how the first direct encounters with a person are interpreted. People tend to see what they expect to see.

Such experiential learning occurs both during the normal process of maturation from child to adult, when many schemata for understanding people and situations are constructed (the basis for Kelly's, 1955, personal construct theory), and during professional practice itself, when further development and modification of frameworks are likely to occur. Even in the professional context, this learning may be at best semiconscious, resulting from experience and socialization rather than any deliberate learning strategy. Such schemata can easily become biased or ineffective because they are subjected to so little conscious reflection. The problem for professionals, however, is not to exclude such experiential learning—they would be lost without it—but to bring it under more critical control. This requires considerable self-awareness and a strong disposition to monitor one's action and cross-check by collecting additional evidence in a more systematic manner with greater precautions against bias.

The crux of this argument is that there needs to be some time set aside for deliberative interpretation and the more controlled collection of evidence. Not only does this provide an ongoing cross-check on one's assumptions and help to avoid serious misunderstandings, but it also creates an opportunity for introducing alternative perspectives and conceptual frameworks. These may be drawn from students, from other teachers, or even from the education literature. Without this vital ingredient, the role of professional practitioner is unachievable and the concept of a professional school is reduced to rhetoric.

Neither needs assessment nor a client-centered orientation can be sustained without a commitment to the regular collection of fresh evidence about students' experience, progress, and well-being.

Routinized Action and Skilled Behavior. Much of what a teacher does in a classroom is aptly described as skilled behavior, for it involves complex sequences of action that have become so routinized through practice and experience that they are performed semi-automatically. This skilled behavior is largely acquired through practice with feedback, mainly feedback from the effect of one's action on classes and individuals. Teachers' early experiences are characterized by the gradual routinization of their teaching, and this is necessary for them to be able to cope with what would otherwise be a highly stressful situation with a continuing "information overload." This routinization is accompanied by a diminution of self-consciousness and a focusing of perceptual awareness on particular phenomena. Hence knowledge of how to teach becomes tacit knowledge, something that is not easily explained to others or even to oneself.

Pearson (1984) makes a distinction between habitual skill knowledge, such as knowing how to tie one's shoes, and intelligent skill knowledge, such as knowing how to teach. In my view this is an oversimplification. There is a continuum of routinization to be considered. Riding a bicycle, for example, involves ongoing monitoring of the environment. Giving a lecture involves rather more thinking on one's feet. Managing a class of children involves a myriad of rapid decisions made on the spur of the moment in response to rapid readings of the situation and the overall purpose of the action. I call the latter semi-automatic because all the decision making is very rapid; there is no time for deliberation during the action itself. Curriculum development, also categorized as intelligent skill knowledge by Pearson, is what I describe below as a deliberative process because it is neither bound by the same time constraints nor as routinized as skilled behavior.

The need for skilled behavior creates a dilemma that characterizes large areas of professional work. The development of routines is a natural process, essential for coping with the job and responsible for increased efficiency, but the combination of tacit knowledge and intuitive decision making makes them difficult to monitor and to keep under critical control. As a result, routines tend to become progressively dysfunctional over time: Not only do they fail to adjust to new circumstances, but shortcuts gradually intrude, some of which only help professionals to cope with pressure at the expense of helping their clients. Apart from these minor modifications, routinized actions are particularly difficult to change, a problem to which we will return in a later section.

If we consider professional work out of the classroom, we can see that it consists of periods of skilled behavior interspersed with periods of deliberation and that most of the skilled behavior takes the form of interpersonal encounters. An interview, for example, can be characterized by a period of deliberative planning, then skilled behavior during the interview itself, followed by a period of deliberative interpretation. Under pressure of time, the deliberative phases get curtailed, with consequent loss of quality.

Deliberative Processes. Deliberative processes such as planning, problem solving, analyzing, evaluating and decision making, lie at the heart of professional work. These processes cannot be accomplished by using procedural knowledge alone or by following a manual. They require unique combinations of propositional knowledge, situational knowledge, and professional judgment. In most situations, there will not be a single correct answer, nor a guaranteed road to success; and even when there is a unique solution, it will have to be recognized as such by discriminations that cannot be programmed in advance. More typically there will be

Some uncertainty about outcomes
Guidance from theory that is only partially helpful
Relevant but often insufficient contextual knowledge
Pressure on the time available for deliberation
A strong tendency to follow accustomed patterns of thinking
An opportunity, perhaps a requirement, to consult or involve other people

These processes require two main types of information: knowledge of the context/situation/problem, and conceptions of practical courses of action/decision options. In each case, there is a need for both information and analysis. What does this mean in practice? I have already discussed the wide range of means by which such information can be acquired, and alluded to the phenomenon of rapid interpretation during the process of collection. Here, I consider the more cognitively demanding activities of deliberative interpretation and analysis, for which professionals need to be able to draw upon a wide repertoire of potentially relevant theories and ideas. Also important for understanding the situation is knowledge of the theories, perceptions, and priorities of clients, co-professionals, and other interested parties. While some may be explicitly stated, others may be hidden, implicit, and difficult to detect. Thus one of the most challenging and creative aspects of the information-gathering process is the elucidation of different people's definitions of the situation.

The other information-gathering task is equally demanding—the formulation of a range of decision options or alternative courses of action. This depends both on knowledge of existing practice and on the ability to invent or search for alternatives. One problem for the professional is the difficulty of evaluating new ideas on the basis of limited information. All too often reports refer to work in contexts different from one's own and are written by advocates and enthusiasts. Thus the skills of acquiring and evaluating information about new ideas and new forms of practice are probably more important than the retention in memory of an increasingly obsolescent block of propositional knowledge.

If we confine our attention for the moment to processes such as problem solving and decision making, much of the literature tends to suggest a rational linear model, in which a prior information-gathering stage is succeeded by deductive logical argument until a solution/decision is reached. In practice, this rarely occurs. Research on medical problem solving, for example, shows that hypotheses are generated early in the diagnostic process and from limited available data (Elstein, Shulman, & Sprafka, 1978). Further information is then collected to confirm or refute these hypotheses. Although described as intuitive, the process is essentially cognitive, but it allows pattern recognition and other experiential insight to contribute at the first stage. In less scientific areas, the need for continuing interaction between information input and possible courses of action is even greater. The information cannot be easily summarized and can usually be interpreted in a number of ways. There is also a need for invention and insight when considering possible actions, so new ideas have to be generated, developed, and worked out. The process is best considered as deliberative rather than deductive, with an interactive consideration of interpretations of the situation together with possible actions continuing until a professional judgment is reached about the optimal course of action.

Hitherto I have been considering deliberation primarily as an individual activity. This is usually valid when it pertains to individual teachers deliberating about their classroom decisions, for even when other teachers contribute comments or observations, the reference is a single classroom and the decision maker a single teacher. But when we move to consider policy making, curriculum development, or school review, much of the deliberation will take place in groups of teachers, all of whom have a similar stake in the outcome. The arena is public rather than semiprivate, and discussions are permeated with multiple agendas and school micro-politics. For effective group deliberation not only leaders but participants need social and political skills as well as knowledge of the area under discussion. Mutual knowledge, experience of working together, and an ability to conceptualize the nature of the deliberative process itself are also important. Many people find it difficult to handle the combination of creative and analytic thinking required in problem solving. Some find it difficult to focus sufficiently or are too impatient to think things through. Others feel uncomfortable with any departure from routine patterns of thinking. The need for adopting several contrasting perspectives is also increasingly recognized, and this is one of the arguments for teamwork.

Meta-Processes. The fourth type of process knowledge comprises those processes used to evaluate and control one's own actions, commonly referred to as meta-processes. The word *control* in this context has a cybernetic meaning. It refers at one level to monitoring and adjusting what one is doing and thinking, without any significant reorientation; while at a deeper level it may involve the reorientation of one's approach through redefining priorities following evaluation or the critical modification of cognitive frameworks and assumptions. Its central features are self-knowledge and self-management, so it includes the organization of oneself and one's time, the selection of activities, the management of one's learning and thinking, and the general maintenance of a meta-evaluative framework for judging the import and significance of one's actions. Evaluation as a formal activity is a deliberative process, but a personal assessment of one's contribution to that process belongs here. So also would be thinking about whether such an evaluation was appropriate, was being well conducted, or was achieving its purpose.

The value of this control process was highlighted by Argyris and Schön (1976), who demonstrated that for many professionals there is a significant gap between their espoused theories (their justifications for what they do and their explicit reasons for it) and their theories in use, those often implicit theories that actually determine their behavior. This gap between account and action is a natural consequence of people's perceptual frameworks being determined by what they want or expect to see, and by people reporting back to them what they think they want to hear. The solution Argyris and Schön recommend is to give priority not so much to objectives—for then one reads situations purely in terms of one's own preplanned ideas of how they ought to develop—as to getting good-quality feedback. Unless one is prepared to receive, indeed actively seek, feedback—which may be adverse or distressing—one will continue to misread situations and to deceive oneself that one's own actions are the best in the circumstances.

Learning from Experience

In the first part of this chapter I explained my view that ongoing learning by individual teachers and by schools is central to their professionalism. In the second part I have described how different professional processes both draw on prior knowledge and provide the experience from which new knowledge can grow. This involves a range of learning modes: At one extreme learning is wholly intuitive and the resultant knowledge is tacit; at the other it is purely cognitive, explicitly based on theory and accounts of past experience with no new experiential input. In between we find a shifting balance between experience and thinking, depending on the time devoted to reflection and deliberation and the quality of that process. Rapid interpretation is near the intuitive end of the spectrum; planning is near the cognitive end.

Experience is initially apprehended at the level of personal impressions, which contribute little to one's thinking until there has been a further period of reflection. Most models of experiential learning assume that this further reflection will happen, but that will depend on the disposition of the learner— hence our ability to discuss the extent to which somebody has learned from experience. One reason for learning to remain initially at the level of impressions may be that there is no specific learning intent; another is that the flow of experience and need for simultaneous action are so rapid that little further attention can be devoted to reflection until some later occasion.

Experiential learning is fallible at two levels. At the level of attention, what is noticed depends on saliency, recency, and prior expectations; and at the level of interpretation, preexisting constructs, perspectives, and frames of reference are likely to strongly affect the outcome. Without significant self-monitoring these processes will be out of critical control, based only on taken-for-granted and largely implicit cognitive and perceptual frameworks. The following suggestions for developing expertise in acquiring and interpreting information follow from the analysis presented earlier:

1. Be aware of one's own constructs, assumptions, and tendencies toward misinterpretation.
2. Use additional sources of evidence to counteract any possible bias in one's information base.
3. Find out about the perspectives of the other people involved.
4. Expand the range of one's interpretative concepts, schemata, and theories.
5. Make time for deliberation and review. (Eraut, 1993a)

The development of skilled behavior also depends on learning from experience, though this is constrained by the natural limits on self-awareness, not knowing how to go about it, inappropriate support, and consequent lack of motivation. Possible approaches to self-development in the area of skilled behavior and routinized action include:

1. Getting feedback from an independent observer
2. Making recordings and studying them, preferably with some friendly support
3. Monitoring oneself and collecting evidence from others to develop awareness of the effects of one's actions
4. Observing other people in action
5. Using the information gained from 1–4 to improve the quality of one's current routines

6. Expanding one's repertoire of routines to meet the needs identified above
7. Using the information gained (and possibly consultancy support) to optimize the conditions for effective performance (e.g., timing, grouping, ambience, resources, flexible planning of introductions/phasing/transitions/conclusions). (Eraut, 1993a)

It is difficult to see professional development making a significant impact on classroom action until these approaches to quality improvement have been accepted as the norm. Although many educators will dismiss them as impractical (Doyle & Ponder, 1977), they have been tried with some success by a significant minority of teachers and schools. The real issue is the cultural disposition of the majority.

The Process of Theorizing

At this stage, it is useful to introduce the term *theorize* to cover those aspects of professional thinking in which there is some attempt to relate specific intentions, actions, or experiences either to other examples or to more general ideas. Thus it includes both the construction of a private theory and the use of a public theory, not that these processes are necessarily so very different. Using a public theory involves giving it a contextually specific meaning, so there is always an element of reinterpretation or reconstruction, and private theories often include elements of public theories that get "picked up" without being recognized.

Theorizing is central to teachers' thinking during reflection and deliberation, and therefore it plays a part in all the professional processes I have examined. As noted above, good theorizing partly depends upon having a repertoire of theory—concepts, frameworks, ideas, and principles—readily available for use. Some will be derived from publicly available theory and some from reflection and discussion of personal practice. However, for reasons discussed below, concepts and principles are unlikely to be available in this repertoire unless they have been previously used in some personally meaningful way. The use of an idea depends not only on its being "in mind" but also on its being perceived as relevant because examples are known of its use in similar situations. Without such examples and without the ability or disposition to draw fresh concepts into their theorizing, teachers are likely to disregard it (Eraut, 1994a).

Thus theory has to be introduced and discussed in constant dialogue with practical experience. Otherwise it will simply be consigned to some remote attic of the mind before it has had a chance to flourish in use. Student teachers have insufficient practical experience to assimilate much educational theory. So considerable development of teachers' conceptual repertoire has to be postponed until after certification, when it can be used to reinterpret and share experience and to provide a platform for further professional development.

A second problem arises because the selection of an interpretation is influenced by conceptual frameworks, which may derive primarily from prior experience and not be at all explicit. These frameworks may change through accommodation to new experiences, but the process is slow, gradual, and uncertain.

The acquisition of a new idea or theory, to the extent that enables one to comprehend it or use it in conversation, is but a small part of the learning process. I compare it with that part of an iceberg that remains above the surface. But to make use of that idea in professional thinking and to build it into one's conceptual framework takes a great deal more cognitive effort. That is the larger part of the learning process that remains below the surface. Traditionally all the resources of education have been put into the visible part above the surface, leaving learners in dark isolation when they attempt to put their knowledge to use. Ill prepared for such cognitive difficulty, they succumb to feelings of inadequacy and/or reject theory as irrelevant to their needs.

MANAGING PROFESSIONAL DEVELOPMENT

Purposes of Professional Development

This section brings together the various purposes for professional development that were advocated and justified in previous sections. First, I presented a view of the professional classroom teacher that was characterized by:

- Continuing development and adaptation of his or her repertoire
- Ongoing learning from experience, reflection, and theorizing about how best to meet the needs of students, individually and collectively
- Ongoing learning through mutual observation and discussion with colleagues

Professionalism, however, extends beyond classroom practice, and I argued that all teachers should develop professional roles. Hence there are two additional purposes for professional development:

- Continuing development of the capacity to contribute to the professional life of the school (e.g., through policy making, internal reviews, management roles)
- Continuing development of the capacity to interact with clients and stakeholders, both as a class teacher or form tutor and on behalf of the school as a whole

These five purposes might seem rather insular, though they should not be limited to the world of the school and its immediate environment. However, I also argued the need for external sources of knowledge. In addition to the process knowledge embedded in the purposes listed above, four other knowledge acquisition processes can be discerned:

• Continuing proficiency in relevant, up-to-date subject matter and continuing development of ways to make it accessible to students
• Ongoing collection of evidence about policies and practices in other schools
• Ongoing access to new educational thinking relevant to improving the quality of the school
• Continuing acquisition of relevant knowledge about one's changing society, both to support good communication with students and other stakeholders and as a basis for reviewing curriculum priorities

Finally, there is what many politicians and higher-level administrators regard as the primary purpose of professional development:

• The need to gather intelligence about and later implement the decisions of external policy makers who have jurisdiction over the school

These could be at the level of the school district, a state department of education, or a national ministry of education.

We thus have ten different reasons for engaging in professional development. Many professional development activities are designed to satisfy more than one of these purposes; there can also be much conflict between them. The more obvious conflicts derive from differences of approach and ideology. But there are also conflicts of power between different levels of jurisdiction: the teacher, the school, and the district, state, or nation. Least obvious but equally pervasive are conflicts over the prioritization of personal time. Keeping professional development relevant to these ten purposes and resolving conflicts of priority among them must always be a major concern for those charged with promoting and managing professional development.

The Role of the School

Research into inservice education has focused around three types of model: personal-learning models linked to the concept of a *reflective practitioner*, institutional-development models centered around the notion of *school improvement*, and curriculum-implementation models associated with *centrally planned change*. Although the first and last of these types ascribe the initiative to the individual and to the state or district, all three depend for their success on the quality of school management of the professional development process.

My analysis of the professional learning process suggests that the professional development of reflective practitioners requires:

Time set aside for deliberation and review
Self-awareness developed through collecting evidence from others on the
    effects of one's actions
Opportunities for observation of alternative practice
Access to feedback and support when significant change is being attempted

None of these can happen without the practical and psychological support of school management.

Another conclusion to be drawn is that almost any type of professional work can provide an opportunity for professional development if there is appropriate time and stimulus for reflection. Hence it is important to include within the scope of professional development planning any activity that has been assigned a professional development purpose, even if that is not its main purpose. However, the ascription of a professional development purpose should be neither trivial nor *post hoc.* It should normally involve (1) prior recognition of a professional development need; (2) agreement that engaging in the activity will provide a learning opportunity that contributes to that need; and (3) planning for an experiential learning cycle of setting targets, providing support, self-evaluation, and feedback from others.

Thus personal opportunities for professional development can be jointly created by a teacher and a support person, either by selecting some of the teacher's normal professional tasks for special attention or by choosing some special learning activity to assist in the achievement of agreed-upon learning goals. Examples of the former might be conducting an unusually thorough review of the progress of a particular student causing concern or giving special attention to preparing the teaching of a new topic. Targets would include both professional-quality reports on the task (important for confidence and sustaining a sense of professionalism) and learning goals (with potential for transfer to other cases and situations). Examples of the latter might include studying practice in another classroom (or even another school), shadowing another member of the staff prior to taking on some new responsibility, or chairing a school committee. In all such cases, there will be a clear learning focus agreed upon at the beginning; advice and support will be provided as appropriate (not only by the designated support person, who may negotiate for additional help); and self-evaluation of what has been achieved and what has been learned will be followed by constructive feedback from others. The support person could be a colleague, a senior teacher, or a manager, and I would hope that all post-probationary teachers would take on this role.

Similar kinds of activity may be undertaken by groups of teachers who have identified a common need or who gain special motivation from learning together. Both personal and group activities need to be supported by goal setting, discussion, and feedback; while further support may include demonstration and explanation of some practice, coaching in some process or skill, sharing experience, and providing or recommending relevant reading or videos.

This system of formalized professional development opportunities (PDOs) can also contribute to the development of teachers' wider professional roles in a manner that takes appropriate account of their diverse talents and aspirations. Sometimes such PDOs will be within the school; sometimes they will involve external visits to other schools, members of the community, or courses and conferences, with the express intention of adding to the school's knowledge base as well as that of the individual teacher. The implications for school management are that they need to:

- Incorporate professional development into the way they deploy staff and allocate tasks
- Develop a learning culture focused on the needs of students
- Learn how to take advantage of professional development opportunities and how to support others engaged in the process
- Acquire up-to-date information about external networks and professional development opportunities
- Learn how best to share and use both the current expertise of staff and knowledge acquired externally
- Expand the repertoire of professional development ideas and be aware of good professional development practice in other schools

This list provides but one example of how schools need to develop their in-house expertise, in this case expertise in professional development itself. Similar lists can be constructed for the other processes stressed by the school-improvement approach: needs assessment, policy reviews, development planning, and so forth. The school-improvement literature gives relatively little attention to the development of a school's knowledge base and the expertise needed to manage and contribute to the deliberative processes on whose quality its success is so dependent.

The school-improvement literature, however, does emphasize the need for a professional school that is seeking to improve the quality of its work to restrict the amount of change to what it can properly implement and to consolidate what it has already achieved. Thus it will need a school-development plan to express and phase its priorities for change that will provide enough continuity to develop and implement selected changes effectively yet remain sufficiently flexible to allow adaptation to meet newly identified needs.

While the school-improvement approach emphasizes the internal identification of needs as the starting point for professional development, there are times in most countries when the external identification of needs leads to comprehensive programs of school reform that swamp internal initiatives. Sometimes a succession of single-issue external directives has a similar, but unintended, effect. Griffin (1987) noted that mandated change is rarely accompanied by sufficient additional resources, so the system has to redirect resources to meet the new requirements. "The implementation [of mandated change] pulls away energy, time and other resources, often well beyond the expected level of effort, that might be allocated to a competing staff development program" (p. 22). Hence there are clear limits to the amount of mandated change a school system can handle without rendering impotent attempts to develop school-based staff development programs.

Research on the implementation of externally mandated change has shown, however, that the role of school management is still extremely important (Fullan, 1991). Change in the classroom is a complex and lengthy process, requiring not only orientation and preparation but appropriate support during the implementation process itself. My earlier analysis of the respective roles of direct experience and reflective theorizing helps to explain why such support has to be mainly classroom-focused. Neither clarity of practical understanding nor appreciation of the significance of an innovation fully develop until teachers have gained some experience in trying it out in their own classrooms. Effective change has to include a period of development through use; and research suggests that INSET support should be linked to formative evaluation, mutual sharing of experience, and making of consequent adjustments to plans and activities. Although districts may be able to provide initial training and possibly some ongoing consultancy support, most of the support offered to individual teachers has to come from within the school itself.

Our recent research at Sussex on the effectiveness of inservice education for supporting curriculum change (Steadman, Eraut, Fielding, & Horton, 1995) suggests that schools need two kinds of expertise. First, they need to be able to design INSET events that both reflect local needs and concerns and are properly based on theories of professional learning. Second, they need a deep understanding of the longer-term process of change and the role within it of appropriate professional development activities. This involves thinking in terms of sequences and combinations of INSET activities rather than isolated courses or events. Sequences have to include:

Early intelligence gathering outside the school
Internal planning and preparation

Providing support for attempts to implement change in the classroom

Giving time for individuals and groups to reflect purposefully on their attitudes, beliefs, and practices

Allowing evaluative feedback from one event to shape the next

Combinations of INSET experiences have to contribute to an effective mixture of practical know-how, understanding of curriculum issues, resocialization of norms and attitudes, and the ability to plan, prepare, evaluate, and adjust both individually and cooperatively.

We found that this latter kind of expertise, embodying a capacity to conceptualize both professional development and the process of mandated change, was relatively rare. Significantly, such expertise was associated with previous experience of a school-improvement approach. Implementing mandated change requires a much higher degree of internal initiative and eventual internal ownership than is commonly recognized. Moreover, the necessary leadership and expertise are unlikely to be developed under continuing external direction.

Personal Development Plans for Individual Teachers

From the perspectives of the individual teachers, externally mandated change is transmitted through the school and becomes part of the school's expectations for them. Even when they have been involved in planning its implementation or in developing school-based initiatives, they will still have personal needs and aspirations in addition to those of their school. Such individual needs may arise naturally from personal review of classroom practice, from changing perceptions of the needs of students, or from changes of role and new responsibilities. There is also the desire for personal growth and career development. When these are combined with needs arising from school-wide priorities, the risk of "need overload" is clearly considerable. Elsewhere, I have recommended that three principles be observed when handling this issue:

1. Change should be managed and phased so as not to put impossible demands on a person at any time. Teacher development also needs to be planned over a period of time to keep its demands at a realistic level.
2. Each professional development activity has to be resourced and supported at a level that gives it a reasonable chance of achieving its purpose. Distributing resources over too many separate activities is likely to result in none of them being effective.
3. Negotiation should take place, preferably with each individual teacher, about the proper balance between the school's supporting that teacher's personal needs and the teacher's supporting the needs of the school. A

teacher's professional development plan should normally incorporate elements of both. (Eraut, 1993d)

In my view the proper context for such a negotiation is an annual staff development interview, interspersed with regular professional contact between the pair of colleagues concerned. Each interview will aim to produce a personal development plan that incorporates targets, participation in schoolwide professional development activities, and a small number of professional development opportunities (of the kind discussed in the previous section).

There are also, I believe, good arguments for establishing a rhythm in which the ongoing professional development of teachers is given a special focus every five or six years, when sufficient release time and support can be granted to change or review some major aspect of their practice. Personally planned and supported periods of development and consolidation throughout a teacher's career can help sustain a sense of lifelong learning, flexibility, and efficacy. Such focusing on individual development within a professional school context may be a more effective approach to change than continuous tinkering with innovations that never quite work as intended.

REFERENCES

Argyris, C., & Schön, D. A. (1976). *Theory in practice: Increasing professional effectiveness.* San Francisco: Jossey-Bass.

Doyle, W., & Ponder, G. A. (1977). The practicality ethic in teacher decision-making. *Interchange, 8*(3), 1–11.

Elstein, A. S., Shulman, L. S., & Sprafka, S. A. (1978). *Medical problem solving: An analysis of clinical reasoning.* Cambridge, MA: Harvard University Press.

Eraut, M. (1992). Review of research on in-service education: A UK perspective. In J. Wilson (Ed.), *The effectiveness of in-service education and training of teachers and school leaders* (Report of the Fifth All-European Conference of Directors of Educational Research Institutions Triesenberg, Liechtenstein, 11–14 October 1988, Council of Europe, UNESCO Institute for Education) (pp. 49–68). Amsterdam: Swets and Zeitlinger BV.

Eraut, M. (1993a). The characterisation and development of professional expertise in school management and in teaching. *Educational Management and Administration, 21*(4), 223–232.

Eraut, M. (1993b). Developing the knowledge base: A process perspective on professional training and effectiveness. In R. A. Barnett (Ed.), *Learning to effect* (pp. 98–118). Buckingham, UK: Open University Press.

Eraut, M. (1993c). Mid-career professional education. In I. E. Pirgiotakis & I. N. Kanakis (Eds.), *Worldwide crisis in education* (Proceedings of the Greek Education Society 1989 Conference) (pp. 310–328). Athens: Gregory Editions. (in Greek)

Eraut, M. (1993d). Teacher accountability: Why it is central to teacher professional development. In L. Kremer-Hayon, H. C. Vonk, & R. Fessler (Eds.), *Teacher professional development: A multiple perspective approach* (pp. 23–43). Amsterdam: Swets and Zeitlinger BV.

Eraut, M. (1994a). The acquisition and use of educational theory by beginning teachers. In G. Harvard & P. Hodkinson (Eds.), *Action and reflection in teacher education* (pp. 69–88). Norwood, NJ: Ablex.

Eraut, M. (1994b). Indicators and accountability at the school and classroom level. In Centre for Educational Research and Innovation, *Making education count: Developing and using international indicators* (pp. 289–306). Paris: Organization for Economic Cooperation and Development.

Fullan, M. (1991). *The new meaning of educational change.* New York: Teachers College Press; London: Cassells; Toronto: Ontario Institute for Studies in Education.

Griffin, G. A. (1987). The school in society and social organization of the school: Implications for staff development. In M. F. Wideen & I. Andrew (Eds.), *Staff development for school improvement* (pp. 19–37). London: Falmer.

Howey, K. R., & Joyce, B. (1978). A database for future directions in-service education. *Theory into Practice, 17,* 206–211.

Johnson, T. J. (1984). Professionalism: Occupation or ideology. In S. Goodlad (Ed.), *Education for the professions: Quis custodiet?* (pp. 17–25). Slough, UK: Society for Research in Higher Education and National Foundation for Educational Research–Nelson.

Kelly, G. A. (1955). *The psychology of personal constructs.* New York: Norton.

Nisbett, R. E., & Ross, L. (1980). *Human inference: Strategies and shortcomings of social judgment.* Englewood Cliffs, NJ: Prentice-Hall.

Pearson, A. T. (1984). Competence: A normative analysis. In E. C. Short (Ed.), *Competence: Inquiries into its meaning and acquisition in educational settings* (pp. 31–38). Lanham, MD: University Press of America.

Steadman, S., Eraut, M., Fielding, M., & Horton, A. (1995). *Inset effectiveness* (Occasional Paper 15). Brighton, UK: University of Sussex, Institute of Continuing and Professional Education.

11

The Limits and the Potential of Professional Development

MICHAEL G. FULLAN

Professional development for teachers has a poor track record because it lacks a theoretical base and coherent focus. On the one hand, professional development is treated as a vague panacea—the teacher as continuous, lifelong learner. Stated as such, it has little practical meaning. On the other hand, professional development is defined too narrowly and becomes artificially detached from "real-time" learning. It becomes the workshop, or possibly the ongoing series of professional development sessions. In either case, it fails to have a sustained cumulative impact. At best it serves to support the implementation of specific innovations, but it lacks any integration with the day-to-day life of teachers. Professional development becomes reified as episodic events that occur as an appendage outside of the normal workday.

In this chapter, I provide three interrelated components of what constitutes a more substantial and articulated framework for rethinking professional development so that it becomes fundamentally integrated into the essence of teaching and being a teacher. The three components taken up in the following pages are:

1. Moral purpose and professional development
2. The culture of the school and professional development
3. Linking preservice and inservice teacher education

MORAL PURPOSE AND PROFESSIONAL DEVELOPMENT

Teaching at its core is a moral enterprise. It is about making a difference in the lives of students—all students regardless of class, gender, and ethnicity (Fullan, 1993). Traditionally, the task of teaching was comparatively stable and less complex than it is today. It was about the transmission of knowledge, skills, habits, and culture. It was a "conservative" proposition. Teaching has changed radically over the past 30 years. Not only has teaching become complex, but it is ever-changing. Postmodern society is a dynamically complex and nonlinear one in which change is ubiquitous and relentless. New knowledge, new ways of knowing and learning, and global interdependencies are changing all the time in unknown ways. Individual and societal problems become more intractable.

In their major study of teacher education, Goodlad and his colleagues found themselves being pushed deeper to the moral purposes of education in order to understand the basic rationale for teaching in postmodern society: "We came to see with increasing clarity the degree to which teaching in schools, public or private, carries with it *moral imperatives*—more in public schools, however, because they are not schools of choice in a system requiring compulsory schooling" (Goodlad, 1990a, p. 47, emphasis added; see also Goodlad, Soder, & Sirotnik, 1990). Goodlad (1990b) singles out four moral imperatives:

Facilitating Critical Enculturation
The school is the only institution in our nation specifically charged with enculturating the young into a political democracy. . . . Schools are major players in developing educated persons who acquire an understanding of truth, beauty, and justice against which to judge their own and society's virtues and imperfections. . . . This is a moral responsibility. (pp. 48–49)

Providing Access to Knowledge
The school is the only institution in our society specifically charged with providing to the young a disciplined encounter with all the subject matters of the human conversation: the world as a physical and biological system; evaluative and belief systems; communication systems; the social, political, and economic system that make up the global village; and the human species itself. . . . [Teachers] must be diligent in ensuring that no attitudes, beliefs, or practices bar students from access to the necessary knowledge. (p. 49)

Building an Effective Teachers–Student Connection
The moral responsibility of educators takes on its most obvious significance where the lives of teachers and their students intersect. . . . The epistemology of teaching must encompass a pedagogy that goes far beyond the *mechanics* of teaching. It must combine generalizable principles of teaching, subject-specific instruction, sensitivity to the pervasive human qualities and potentials always involved. (pp. 49–50)

Practicing Good Stewardship
If schools are to become the responsive, renewing institutions that they must, the teachers in them must be purposefully engaged in the renewal process. (p. 25)

At a policy level, growing concerns about educational equity and economic performance mirror the more particular issues just described. The restructuring movement, in intent at least, places a renewed focus on the education of *all* students, "especially those who have been ineffectively served in the past," and attempts to reorganize schools for that purpose (Murphy, 1991, p. 60). Poverty, especially among children and women, racism, drug abuse, and horrendous social and personal problems all make the equity and excellence agenda more serious and poignant day by day (Hodgkinson, 1991).

The moral purpose of the teacher is the building block for change. But it cannot be done alone, or without the skills and actions that would be needed to make a difference. The key to enacting moral purpose is "continuous learning," which is another way of saying that continuous professional development is essential. Basically, professional development at its core is learning how to make a difference through learning how to bring about ongoing improvements.

I see four core capacities for being able to learn on a continuous basis:

1. Personal vision-building
2. Inquiry
3. Mastery
4. Collaboration

I start with personal vision-building because it connects so well with moral purpose contending with the forces of change. Shared vision is important in the long run, but for it to be effective you have to have something to share. Working on vision means examining and reexamining, and making explicit to ourselves, why we came into teaching. Asking "What difference am I trying to make personally?" is a good place to start. For most of us it will not be trying to create something out of nothing. The reasons are there, but possibly buried under other demands, stagnant through years of disuse, or, for the beginning teacher, still underdeveloped. It is time to make them front and center. We should not think of vision as something only for leaders. It is not a far-fetched concept. It arises by pushing ourselves to articulate what is important to us as educators. Block (1987) emphasizes that "creating a vision forces us to take a stand for a preferred future" (p. 102); it signifies our disappointment with what exists now. To articulate our vision of the future "is to come out of the closet with our doubts about the organization and the way it operates" (p. 105). Indeed, it forces us to come out of the closet with doubts about ourselves and what we are doing.

Block, writing more generally about organizations, states: "We all have strong values about doing work that has meaning, being of real service to our customers, treating other people well, and maintaining some integrity in the way we work" (p. 123). Teachers, as I have indicated, are in one of the most natural occupations for working on purpose and vision, because underneath that is what teaching is all about.

The second core capacity—inquiry—implies that moral purpose is not a static matter. Richard Pascale (1990) captures this precisely: "*The* essential activity for keeping our paradigm current is persistent questioning. I will use the term *inquiry.* Inquiry is the engine of vitality and self-renewal" (p. 14). Stacey (1992) puts it this way: "A successful, innovative organization must have groups of people who can perform complex learning spontaneously. Because in open-ended situations no one can know what the group is trying to learn, the learning process must start without a clear statement of what is to be learned or how" (p. 112).

Inquiry is necessary at the outset for forming personal purpose. While the latter comes from within, it must be fueled by information, ideas, dilemmas, and other contentions in our environment. The beginner, by definition, is not experienced enough with the variety and needs of students, or with the operational goals and dilemmas of improvement, to have clear ideas of purpose. Habits of "questioning, experimentation, and variety" are essential (Stacey, 1992, p. 112). Reflective practice, personal journals, action research, working in innovative mentoring and peer settings are some of the strategies currently available (see Fullan & Hargreaves, 1991). Inquiry means internalizing norms, habits, and techniques for *continuous learning.*

Mastery is another crucial ingredient. Mastery and competence are obviously necessary for effectiveness, but they are also *means* (not just outcomes) for achieving deeper understanding. New mindsets arise from new mastery as much as the other way around. Mastery, then, is very much interrelated with vision and inquiry, as is evident in this passage from Senge (1990):

> Personal mastery goes beyond competence and skills, though it is grounded in competence and skills. . . . It means approaching one's life in a creative work, living life from a creative as opposed to a reactive viewpoint. . . .
>
> When personal mastery becomes a discipline—an activity we integrate into our lives—it embodies two underlying movements. The first is continually clarifying what is important to us (purpose and vision). We often spend so much time coping with problems along our path that we forget why we are on that path in the first place. The result is that we only have a dim, or even inaccurate, view of what's really important to us.
>
> The second is continually learning how to see current reality more clearly. . . . The juxtaposition of vision (what we want) and a clear picture of current reality (where we are relative to what we want) generates what we call "creative tension." "Learning" in this context does not mean acquiring more information, but expanding the ability to produce results we truly want in life. It is lifelong generative learning. (p. 142)

It has long been known that skill and know-how are central to successful change, so it is surprising how little attention we pay to it beyond one-shot workshops and disconnected training. Mastery involves strong initial teacher education and continuous staff development throughout the career, but it is more than this when we place it in the perspective of being an agent of comprehensive change. It is a learning habit that permeates everything we do. It is not enough to be exposed to new ideas. We have to know where new ideas fit, and we have to become skilled in them, not just agree with them. Block (1987) says that the goal is to learn "as much as you can about the activity you are engaged in. There's pride and satisfaction in understanding your function better than anyone else and better than you thought possible" (p. 86).

Collaboration is the fourth capacity (which I take up in more detail in the next section). Collaboration is essential for personal learning (Fullan & Hargreaves, 1991). There is a ceiling effect to how much we can learn if we keep to ourselves. The ability to collaborate—on both a small and large scale—is becoming one of the core requisites of postmodern society. Personal strength, as long as it is open minded (i.e., inquiry oriented), goes hand-in-hand with effective collaboration—in fact, without personal strength collaboration will be more form than content. Personal mastery and group mastery feed on each other in learning organizations. People need one another to learn and to accomplish things.

Small-scale collaboration involves the attitudes and abilities needed to form productive mentoring and peer relationships, team building, and the like. On a larger scale, it consists of the ability to work in organizations that form cross-institutional partnerships, such as various alliances among school districts, universities, and communities, and businesses, as well as global relationships with individuals and organizations from other cultures. In short, without collaborative skills and relationships it is not possible to learn and to continue to learn as much as you need in order to be an agent for societal improvement.

In summary, teachers are no longer just in the conservation business; they are in the change business (Fullan, 1993). To be in the change business these days, by definition, means that you are in the business of having to learn autonomously and collaboratively because so much is happening, much of it unpredictable.

All of this is to say that professional development is continuous learning and as such is not an add-on. It is the essence of teaching and learning to teach better. The first basic point, then, is that professional development must be reconceptualized as continuous learning, highly integrated with the moral task of making a difference in the lives of diverse students under conditions of somewhat chaotic complexity.

THE CULTURE OF THE SCHOOL AND PROFESSIONAL DEVELOPMENT

A second and related component is that continuous learning must be *organically* part and parcel of the culture of the school. Professional development is currently limited because it is seen as and experienced as separated events, as though teachers' learning can be segmented from their regular work. Research on collaborative school cultures shows clearly that learning is "built-in" to the day-to-day interactions among staff who are preoccupied with continuous learning.

Nias, Southworth, and Campbell (1992) studied five primary schools in England. The themes they discuss confirm as well as shed additional light on the key factors related to continuous improvement. Four themes stand out in the investigation of Nias and colleagues: (1) the central importance of teachers' learning, individually and in relation to colleagues; (2) how changes in teachers' beliefs and practices toward sharing evolve over time and how independence and interdependence coexist in dynamic tension; that is, conflict is normal; (3) how the working conditions for continuous learning and continuous development of a whole-school curriculum inhibit or facilitate the process; and (4) the inevitability of complexity, unpredictability, and constant shifts both within the school and in the external policy environment.

The first and foundation theme identified by Nias and colleagues is *teachers' learning*:

> Both teachers and heads saw professional learning as the key to the development of the curriculum and as the main way to improve the quality of children's education. Although they responded during the year to internal and external pressures for change, the main impetus for their learning came from the shared belief that existed in all the schools that practice could always be improved and hence that professional development was a never-ending process, a way of life. (p. 72)

> Teachers who wanted to improve their practice were characterized by four attitudes: they accepted that it was possible to improve, were ready to be self critical, and to recognize better practice than their own within the school or elsewhere, and they were willing to learn what had to be learned in order to be able to do what needed or had to be done. (p. 72)

It is important to note that this personal commitment to learn played itself out in a community of learners in which teacher colleagues and the principal continually reinforced the expectations and conditions conducive to learning. As Nias and colleagues observe:

> Seeing colleagues learning was an added encouragement, because individuals realized that they were not alone in their need to learn. Learning was regarded as a means of increasing one's ability, not as a sign of inadequacy; the desire to

improve practice also led to a constant quest for "good ideas", that is ideas that were relevant to classroom practice. (p. 88)

A critical finding was that the climate of support, combined with a commitment to learning together, generated a more, rather than less, questioning approach to improvement, and more rather than less risk-taking: "When such support was available, individuals felt encouraged to take risks, to do something they had perhaps never done before, knowing that whether success or failure followed, they would be able to share the results with their colleagues" (p. 103).

Finally, this commitment to learning was continually reinforced through the actions and expectations of principals or head teachers:

> Habitual learners themselves, these headteachers valued learning, and were willing to contribute to the growth of others, particularly to that of their colleagues. This they did in several ways. They encouraged and actively supported the interests of staff and responded to their concerns by recommending courses, other schools to visit, people to talk to or appropriate reading. They initiated developments themselves and supported the initiatives taken by others. (p. 104)

Similarly, in her case studies of high schools, McLaughlin (1994) found that some schools differed fundamentally in how they defined professional development. McLaughlin's research demonstrates that effective professional development permeates the culture of the school.

> My analysis is based on the view that teachers' professional development of the most meaningful sort takes place not in a workshop or in discrete, bounded convocations but in the context of professional communities—discourse communities, learning communities. Further, I show that teachers can and typically do belong to multiple professional communities, each of which functions somewhat differently as a strategic site for professional growth. Thus the argument is made that enabling professional growth is, at root, about enabling professional community. (p. 31)

Such "professional discourse communities" were structurally and culturally embedded in the regular workflow of teachers as they continually tried to make improvements in student learning.

> As we looked across our sites at teachers who report a high sense of efficacy, who feel successful with today's students, we noticed that while these teachers differ along a number of dimensions—age and experience, subject area, track assignment and even conceptions of pedagogy—all shared this one characteristic: membership in some kind of a strong professional community. Further, almost without exception, these teachers singled out their professional discourse community as the reason that they have been successful in adapting to today's stu-

dents, the source of their professional motivation and support, and the reason that they did not burn out in the face of some exceedingly demanding teaching situations. (p. 33)

McLaughlin concludes:

These department, school, district, and collaborative communities illustrate the extent to which professional development is not a special project activity or only an in-service problem. Issues of and opportunities for professional development occur in assorted form, formats, and forums in the daily lives of teachers. (p. 47)

Rosenholtz's (1989) study of 78 elementary schools is also clear about the differences between nonlearning and learning schools in her depiction of "stuck" and "moving" schools. Rosenholtz found that in the 13 "moving" schools in her study, teachers learned from one another and from the outside. Most teachers of these schools, even the most experienced, believed that teaching was inherently difficult. They believed that teachers never stopped learning to teach. Since most teachers acknowledged that teaching was difficult, almost everyone recognized they sometimes needed help. Giving and receiving help did not therefore imply incompetence. It was part of the common quest for continuous improvement. Having their colleagues show support and communicating more with them about what they did led these teachers to have more confidence, more certainty about what they were trying to achieve and how well they were achieving it.

As Rosenholtz observes, in effective schools, collaboration is linked with norms and with opportunities for continuous improvement and career-long learning: "It is assumed that improvement in teaching is a collective rather than individual enterprise, and that analysis, evaluation, and experimentation in concert with colleagues are conditions under which teachers improve" (p. 73). As a result, teachers are more likely to trust, value, and legitimize sharing expertise, seeking advice, and giving help both inside and outside the school. They are more likely to become better and better teachers on the job: "All of this means that it is far easier to learn to teach, and to learn to teach better, in some schools than in others" (p. 104).

The recognition that the culture of the school is paramount for professional development is critical in light of recent findings about site-based management. The findings are clear: Site-based management has resulted in some changes in governance at the school level—such as participation in site-based councils—but *not* in substantial changes in the teaching–learning and teacher–teacher culture of the school. Put positively, we need to focus on the professional learning culture of the school. Organic professional development is primarily about "reculturing" the school, not about "restructuring" its formal elements (Fullan, 1993).

The Japanese concept of *kaizen* helps to explain how learning and continuous improvement become inseparable. *Kaizen* means unending improvement by focusing on continuous changes to achieve ever higher standards (Imai, 1986). Institutionalized professional learning cultures do just that. When professional development becomes absorbed as part of the core culture of the school, attention to never-ending improvements becomes a natural part of the teachers' *raison d'être*. The school becomes culturally wired for "real-time," everyday professional development.

LINKING PRESERVICE AND INSERVICE TEACHER EDUCATION

The third reason that conventional professional development is seriously flawed relates to the conceptual and programmatic failure to link (and in so doing redesign) preservice and inservice teacher education. Professional development will never amount to much until pre- and inservice strategies are coordinated. Initial teacher preparation programs are notorious for being individualistic and lacking in coherence and connectedness. Faculties of education must revamp their programs to focus directly on developing the beginner's knowledge base for effective teaching *and* the knowledge base for making changes in the conditions that affect teaching. Sarason (1993) puts it this way: "Is it asking too much of preparatory programs to prepare their students for a 'real world' which they must understand *and seek to change* if as persons and professionals they are to grow, not only to survive?" (p. 252, emphasis added). Goodlad (1991) asks a similar question: "Are a large percentage of these educators thoroughly grounded in the knowledge and skills required to bring about meaningful change?" (p. 4).

Thus, if collaborative skills and continuous learning are essential for teachers, they must be fostered from the beginning in teacher preparation programs explicitly designed for that purpose. At the same time, synergy can be achieved through partnerships with schools and districts by working simultaneously on the inservice component (mentor training and the development of collaborative schools) to develop school cultures supportive of preservice, beginning, and tenured teachers.

One example, among several now underway, is our Learning Consortium. The Learning Consortium is a long-term partnership (renewable three-year terms), entering its sixth year as of July 1993, involving four school districts and two higher education institutions in and around metropolitan Toronto, Canada. The districts are large: Durham Board of Education has 55,000 students; Halton, 44,000; North York, 59,000; Scarborough, 75,000. Altogether there are 500 schools and 13,700 teachers in the Consortium boards. The two higher education institutions are also large: the faculty of education, University of Toronto, has some 90 faculty, 1,100 preservice teachers, and 500 inservice teachers; the Ontario Institute for Studies in Education has 140 faculty and more than 2,300 part- and full-time graduate students.

The aim of the Consortium is to improve the quality of education for students in schools and universities by focusing on teacher development, school development, and the restructuring of districts and the faculty of education to support improvement on a continuous basis. The Consortium has three core objectives:

1. To plan and initiate new programs in teacher development and school improvement
2. To generate knowledge through documenting and researching these initiatives
3. To disseminate what we are learning about teacher development and school improvement

While the basic assumptions and objectives were broadly stated, we were committed to launching specific initiatives to realize our aims. We began in 1988 with an emphasis on cooperative learning, a theme that provided a concrete point of department. By the third year, summer and winter institutes on cooperative learning and follow-through support were well established; a new field-based teacher certification program was in place; and dissemination conferences and inservice were carried out with such collaborative approaches as mentoring, induction, peer coaching, and school-improvement planning. The Consortium partners attempted to link these activities by paying attention to such consistent themes as teaching as career-long learning, fostering collaborative cultures, and focusing on instruction.

More recently the Learning Consortium has begun to incorporate innovative teacher preparation programs as part of its commitment to integrating the teacher education continuum. Longstanding concerns about the inadequacy of teacher education (from initial preparation to the end of the career) and the isolationist culture of schools have led to various attempts to improve either component, but rarely in conjunction. Such integration is essential to the further development of more fundamental professional development itself.

Professional development schools (PDSs) represent one new initiative that attempts to link the teacher-as-learner and the development of collaborative work cultures. Stoddart, Winitzky, and O'Keefe (1992) summarize the Holmes Group's (1990) definition of a PDS:

A Professional Development School (PDS) is a school in which university faculty work collaboratively with practitioners over time with the goal of improving teaching and learning through: 1) upgrading the education of pre-service teachers, 2) providing professional development for experienced teachers, and 3) field-based research. Inherent in the PDS models is the notion of school sites evolving as models of excellence and centers of inquiry through collaboration between school and university faculties over time. (p. 2)

In principle, then, the PDS is a model that is on the right track in promising to produce learning educators and learning organizations through school–university partnerships. There are three main observations that can be made at this early stage of its development: The concept is ambitious and vague; little research data are available as yet; and the university side of the partnership is underdeveloped.

First, as to the ambitiousness and vagueness of the concept, the idea is that collaborative groups would develop the particular programs within the broad principles of the model. Thus it is assumed that specificity would come from the development of the model in practice.

Second, little evaluative data are available because the first published reports on PDSs are just beginning to appear. These take on considerable importance given the ambiguity of what the model might look like in practice. Grossman (1994), for example, reports on a case study of a PDS at Lark Creek Middle School as part of the Puget Sound Professional Development Center (PSPDC) in Washington state. The PSPDC program places small groups of student teachers at the school for an extended period of time under the supervision of teams of mentor teachers. This field experience is inquiry-oriented and linked to a core team-taught seminar that attempts to integrate theory and practice. An extensive professional development program for experienced teachers has also been undertaken, one that includes professors of education spending blocks or regular amounts of time at the school (see Grossman, 1994, for more details).

Lark Creek is a good example of the difficulties and potential involved in establishing a PDS. One problem common to both schools and universities is whether PDS is just another project or whether it becomes a new, more integrating way of life. One sees this dilemma at Lark Creek, which was already heavily involved in a high-profile, state-sponsored school renewal program called "A School for the Twenty-First Century," when a decision was taken to also become a PDS. Grossman calls this a "dual agenda":

From its very inception as a PDS, Lark Creek Middle School would be pursuing a dual agenda—to restructure itself in accordance with the goals of Outcome-Based Education, as proposed in the Schools for the 21st Century grant, and to transform itself into a site for the career-long professional development of teachers, with special emphasis on the preparation of preservice teachers. (p. 51)

These two programs, of course, are not in principle mutually exclusive—a point that the school principal stresses. But teachers, partly because they are not used to linking particular programs to larger concepts (and do not have time to do so), and partly because of the "projectitis" decision-making patterns of school systems, usually experience overload and fragmentation. As observed by Grossman (1994): "The teachers' feelings of being overwhelmed by change efforts reflect their sense of fragmentation. [They need] opportunities . . . to undedrstand the larger goals" (p. 70). Despite these programs, most teachers intuitively feel and sometimes experience first-hand the great potential of the new model for preparing new teachers and for revitalizing themselves.

Third, on the university side of the equation the issues are both understated and undeveloped. In addition to seeking changes in the culture of schools toward collaborative learning environments, similar changes *in universities* are required. So far, faculties of education have not looked inward. Even professional development schools, which are purportedly based on equal school–university partnerships, tend to focus only on the school side of the relationship. Grossman (1994) makes the following observation about the Puget Sound Professional Development Center:

> Change has been no easier, and perhaps even more difficult, on the university side. From its inception, the professional development center has been cast as the on-going concern of relatively few faculty, rather than as the responsibility of the college as a whole, despite efforts by the dean and director to change this perception. The PSPDC has been seen as simply another project, rather than as an effort to change the way the college functions. (p. 32)

In short, professional development will remain impotent as long as initial teacher preparation and on-the-job teacher learning are not conceived *and* treated in practice as working in the same direction. When all is said and done, reform in teacher education must begin simultaneously in schools and in faculties of education, both independently (because one cannot wait for the other) and together through multiyear alliances (which serve to put pressure on and support both institutions to change their ways and realize their relationship to each other).

CONCLUSION

Professional development has been miscast. By being treated as a discrete entity outside the regular job, its effectiveness has been severely limited. In addition to being artificially detached, professional development has no coherent theoretical framework that governs it. It thus becomes relegated to ad hoc events or diffuse rhetoric.

I have attempted in this chapter to develop a more compelling basis and rationale for the role and meaning of professional development. By conceiving professional development as integral to accomplishing moral purpose, as central to continuous improvements in professional work cultures, and as embedded in the continuum of initial and career-long teacher education, a new mindset is created. This is not to say that workshops, institutes, and the like should be discontinued. Rather, it puts them in perspective. Professional development is the sum total of formal and informal learning pursued and experienced by the teacher in a compelling learning environment under conditions of complexity and dynamic change.

By reconceptualizing professional development as I have done, its role becomes defined more coherently and comprehensively. Such a fundamental redefinition is required in order to move beyond the current rhetoric in which professional development is largely ineffective because it lacks a compelling and clear framework to guide its action. There are numerous implications that arise from this new mindset about professional development. As an illustration, several guidelines are offered for teachers, principals, and faculties of education. The guidelines for teachers are:

1. Locate, listen to, and articulate your inner voice.
2. Practice reflection in action, on action, and about action.
3. Develop a risk-taking mentality.
4. Trust processes as well as people.
5. Appreciate the total person in working with others.
6. Commit to working with colleagues.
7. Seek variety and avoid Balkanization.
8. Redefine your role to extend beyond the classroom.
9. Balance work and life.
10. Push and support principals and other administrators to develop interactive professionalism.
11. Commit to continuous improvement and perpetual learning.
12. Monitor and strengthen the connection between your development and students' development. (Fullan & Hargreaves, 1991, p. 64)

For principals the guidelines are:

1. Understand the culture.
2. Value your teachers; promote their professional growth.
3. Extend what you value.
4. Express what you value.
5. Promote collaboration, not cooptation.
6. Make menus, not mandates.
7. Use bureaucratic means to facilitate, not to constrain.

8. Connect with the wider environment. (Fullan & Hargreaves, 1991, pp. 84–85)

And for faculties of education, the guidelines are that each faculty should:

1. Commit itself to producing teachers who are agents of educational and societal improvement.
2. Commit itself to continuous improvement through program innovation and evaluation.
3. Value and practice exemplary teaching.
4. Engage in constant inquiry.
5. Model and develop lifelong learning among staff and students.
6. Model and develop collaboration among staff and students.
7. Be respected and engaged as a vital part of the university as a whole.
8. Form partnerships with schools and other agencies.
9. Be visible and valued internationally in a way that contributes locally and globally.
10. Work collaboratively to build regional, national, and international networks. (Fullan, 1993, p. 114)

The task is as fundamental as redefining the roles of the teacher, university faculty, and administrators, and restructuring and reculturing the organizations in which they work. Fortunately, there are elements of this new paradigm currently in practice. There are many institutes and partners working along these lines—schools and school districts, teacher unions, universities, and foundations (see Fullan, 1993). There is a great deal of attention currently paid to professional development. Ironically, being preoccupied with the term *professional development* as a separate phenomenon may inhibit its becoming central to the work of all teachers.

Be that as it may, radical changes are required in how teachers learn and in their opportunities to learn. Focusing on the interrelationship among moral purpose, professional cultures, and the teacher education continuum provides a powerful framework for making professional development central to the work of all teachers.

REFERENCES

Block, P. (1987). *The empowered manager.* San Francisco: Jossey-Bass.
Fullan, M. (1993). *Change forces: Probing the depths of educational reform.* London: Falmer.
Fullan, M., & Hargreaves, A. (1991). *What's worth fighting for in your school?* Toronto:

Ontario Public School Teachers Federation; Buckingham, UK: Open University Press.

Goodlad, J. (1990a). Studying the education of educators: From conception to findings. *Phi Delta Kappan, 71*(9), 698–701.

Goodlad, J. (1990b). *Teachers for our nation's schools.* San Francisco: Jossey-Bass.

Goodlad, J. (1991). Why we need a complete redesign of teacher education. *Educational Leadership, 49*(3), 4–10.

Goodlad, J., Soder, R., & Sirotnik, K. A. (Eds.). (1990). *The moral dimensions of teaching.* San Francisco: Jossey-Bass.

Grossman, P. (1994). In pursuit of a dual agenda: Creating a middle level professional development school. In L. Darling-Hammond (Ed.), *Professional development schools: Schools for developing a profession* (pp. 50–73). New York: Teachers College Press.

Hodgkinson, H. (1991). Reform versus reality. *Phi Delta Kappan, 72*(1), 9–16.

Imai, M. (1986). *Kaizen: The key to Japan's competitive success.* Toronto: McGraw-Hill.

McLaughlin, M. (1994). Strategic sites for teachers' professional development. In P. Grimmett and J. Neufeld (Eds.), *Teacher development and the struggle for authenticity: Professional growth and restructuring in the context of change* (pp. 31–51). New York: Teachers College Press.

Murphy, J. (1991). *Restructuring schools.* New York: Teachers College Press.

Nias, J., Southworth, G., & Campbell, P. (1992). *Whole school curriculum development in the primary school.* Lewes, UK: Falmer.

Pascale, R. (1990). *Managing on the edge.* New York: Touchstone.

Rosenholtz, S. (1989). *Teachers' workplace: The social organization of schools.* New York: Longman.

Sarason, S. (1993). *The case for change: The preparation of education.* San Francisco: Jossey-Bass.

Senge, P. (1990). *The fifth discipline.* New York: Doubleday.

Stacey, R. (1992). *Managing the unknowable.* San Francisco: Jossey-Bass.

Stoddart, T., Winitzky, N., & O'Keefe, P. (1992, April). *Developing the professional staff development school.* Paper presented at the annual meeting of the American Educational Research Association, San Francisco.

CONCLUSION

The Diversities of Professional Development

MICHAEL HUBERMAN AND THOMAS R. GUSKEY

The essays in this volume have rendered well the diversity that exists in the ways professional development is construed, designed, and carried out. They also have shown that there remains some muddiness in the constructs deployed in this field. Furthermore, they have brought to the surface some underlying tensions in the primary orientations of those responsible for the professional development of educators. We close with a review of two of these tensions.

THE TENSION BETWEEN "DEFICIT" AND "GROWTH" MODELS

It was not long ago that specialists in the field of professional development referred to their work as "inservice teacher education." They reasoned simply that the preservice education of teachers was woefully incomplete. Changes in learning and instructional theory, in assessment, in classroom management, and in the curriculum therefore warranted more systematic exposure or outright training if levels of competence among educators were to be maintained.

To some, this scenario reflects a "deficit" model of professional development. It is based on the idea that something is lacking and needs to be corrected. Typically these deficits are determined by others, notably by administrators, program evaluators, or researchers. Teachers are, in turn, seen as the objects, rather than the subjects, of their professional growth.

To update the terms used in this scenario does not alter the perception of "deficit." The critics of "staff development," for example, make the same arguments. They contend that there is an implicit thesis of inadequacy in most programs and that teachers are not in control of the agenda by which they are "developed."

It is difficult to fully discredit the "deficit" model, however. As Borko and Putnam show in Chapter 2, a lack of intrinsic subject-matter mastery on the part of teachers is related to lesser content mastery, which, in turn, is related to lower student performance. Similarly, in Chapter 6 Tillema and Imants offer evidence showing that teachers often are not aware of shortcomings that have direct consequences on the learning environments they create and manage. As a result, they tend not to work on them. And it is explicitly through this kind of work, Eraut claims in Chapter 10, that we can legitimately talk about "professionalism." To be fair, those who refute the "deficit" model contest not the need for professional development but, rather, the disempowered, passive image of teachers the model projects.

The countervailing model is known as a "growth" model. It consists of a variety of professional development activities that accompany "continuous inquiry" into one's own instructional practice. These activities include teacher study groups, curriculum writing groups, teacher-designed research projects, teacher resource center activities, program evaluations conducted internally, and participation in workshops and seminars that are often given by more experienced peers. They are characterized by the secondary role or even the absence of external expertise or external direction and by their heavily interactive nature. They are typically site-based. They are meant to produce the joint construction of craft knowledge by surfacing tacitly held data about classroom life, learning conditions, and the cultures of teaching. In this way, they heighten awareness and facilitate experimentation in didactic and organizational arrangements. They can, and do, take a critical turn, by rendering teachers more sharply reflective about their own instructional and social practices in the classroom. Several chapters here, most notably, Chapters 4 and 10, take up these themes.

INDIVIDUAL VERSUS INSTITUTIONAL MODELS

In several chapters, notably Chapters 4, 7, 8, and 9, professional development is seen as largely an individual enterprise. It meshes with instructional concerns for particular pupils and classes, with particular moments in the professional life cycle, and with individual aspirations toward growth, change, and challenge. But as Mevarech suggests in Chapter 7, under certain conditions it can be a disorienting, even temporarily regressive, experience. This is the phenomenological dimension of professional development.

In some cases, however, individual change is associated with overdue changes in the working conditions in schools. That is, it may have less to do with genuine tension between individual and institutional facets, and more to do with emphasis and equilibrium at different moments. This is what Guskey calls the "optimal mix" in Chapter 5.

At another level, Hargreaves in Chapter 1 evokes individual development in the social and moral spheres, noting the overwhelming focus on the cognitive, managerial, and pedagogical dimensions. He argues that focusing solely on technical competence renders professional development a "narrow, utilitarian exercise that does not question the purposes and parameters of what teachers do." It should also address "the place of moral purpose in teaching, political awareness, acuity, and adeptness among teachers, and teachers' emotional attachments to engagements with their work."

Still, we remain within the traditional perspective of professional development: matching individual teachers with opportunities for growth and proficiency that are self-defined or externally determined, organized or more incidental, carried out with peers or with a mixture of peer and "expert" leadership. With the exception of Hargreaves's call for greater political acuity, the implication throughout is that educators will take these opportunities back into their professional lives and back into the classroom, but not trade on them institutionally.

There is, again, a countervailing orientation. Hargreaves puts it sharply by stating that in time of voluntary or enforced restructuring, "retreating to an enclosed world of the personal and practical" creates political quiescence and professional disempowerment. In other words, professional development is a subinstitutional or fully institutional affair. It can take the form of systematic collaboration among subsets of teachers, as in the "professional growth" model. But, at the same time, it shares a commitment to greater risk-taking across settings, to more continuous attempts to coordinate work across grade levels, and to modification of instructional arrangements that depress student learning and motivation.

At the institutional level, professional development is synonymous with enacting change. These may be warranted changes in tracking, sequencing, and divisions of labor among teachers and other professionals who minister to students. They require finding some logic and harmony between the multiple and contradictory demands of day-to-day work in the classroom. The list is endless. As Fullan points out in Chapter 11, change does not involve one implementation, but rather the management of several at once. Similarly, Fullan views the role of the teacher as that of change agent: construing, designing, implementing, and monitoring desirable changes that affect working conditions throughout the school. In Chapter 5 Guskey provides a series of guidelines to this effect, derived from the empirical research literature on educational change.

Several authors point out that conflict and disagreement are part of the change process and, as such, are mostly formative. They sharpen individual and collective reflection; they surface critiques of current practices that were long kept unconscious or subterranean; and, when well managed, they change minds. They are also signs that nontrivial changes at least are on the table. When internal tensions persist during implementation, they may, as Mevarech shows in Chapter 7, lead to temporary disorientation. But they are also indications that the school is actually coming to terms with consequential change. At a later phase of the pilgrimage, when meaningful changes are enacted, they may well turn into the glue that binds a collective mission and vision.

But conflict and disagreement are also characteristics that can be turned outward, notably toward authorities who have explicit control over key school practices such as tracking, testing, staff assignments, class size, promotion criteria, and curriculum frameworks. Some of these changes are negotiable and, in fact, are often initiated from outside the school. In other cases, however, to change these procedures is to engage politically, as both Hargreaves (Chapter 1) and Smyth (Chapter 3) point out.

Professional development therefore includes political sensitization and, for some analysts, "emancipation" from the rules and constraints that dominate one's work but seldom come to full personal or collective awareness. More globally, to understand the proper context of internal change, Hargreaves and Smyth claim it is important to look at the macro-issues. We must see how dysfunctions and inequities in the school connect to socially generated constraints, the distribution of political influence and power, social class distinctions, and, for Smyth, the changing nature of the labor process in advanced capitalist societies.

This is an enormous range of issues, from the micro-analysis of changing cognitive strategies in the classroom (Chapter 6) to the macro-analysis of critical social theory (Chapter 3). While all these perspectives cast useful light, they also show how the construct of professional development has become protean and multivocal. Furthermore, they show how we are embedded both in ideologies and in models for reorganizing core facets of the profession. These ideologies and models are not always conciliatory, but they have provided for readers, as promised, a set of alternative paradigms and practices to consider and, eventually, to choose among for their own professional purposes.

About the Contributors

Hilda Borko is Professor of Educational Psychology and Curriculum and Instruction, and Chair of the program area in Educational Psychology in the School of Education, University of Colorado at Boulder. Dr. Borko's primary research interests are in the areas of teacher cognition, expert/novice differences in teaching, and the process of learning to teach. Her publications include *Designing Classroom Research: Themes, Issues and Struggles* (1993, with Margaret Eisenhart) as well as chapters in edited volumes and articles in journals such as *American Educational Research Journal, Journal for Research in Mathematics Education, Journal of Educational Psychology, Teaching and Teacher Education.*

Michael Eraut is Professor of Education at the University of Sussex. He currently works in professional education, including professions other than teaching, and the management of change in public sector organizations. Previous publications have been in curriculum development, evaluation, and educational technology. His most recent book, *Developing Professional Knowledge and Competence*, provides a strong theoretical base for rethinking approaches to professional education through its analysis of how and what people learn from experience and what is involved in putting theory into use.

Ralph Fessler is Professor and Director of the Education Division at Johns Hopkins University. He received his B.S., M.S., and Ph.D. degrees from the University of Wisconsin-Madison. Prior to coming to Johns Hopkins in 1983, he was a faculty member and held various administrative positions in the University of Wisconsin system. His professional interests include developing programs and conducting research that address the continuing growth and development needs of teachers. Recent activities have included planning and implementing school-university professional development school partnerships that promote career-long approaches to teacher growth and development.

Michael G. Fullan is the Dean of Education, University of Toronto. He is a writer, consultant, and trainer in the area of the management of change. His recent books include *Change Forces* (Falmer Press), *The New Meaning of Educational Change, What's Worth Fighting for in the Principalship*, and with Andy Hargreaves, *What's Worth Fighting for in Your School.*

Thomas R. Guskey is Professor of Educational Policy Studies and Evaluation at the University of Kentucky. Prior to joining the faculty at Kentucky he served as Director of the Center for the Improvement of Teaching and Learning, a national research center located in Chicago, and as a school administrator in the Chicago Public Schools. A graduate of the University of Chicago, Dr. Guskey has been a visiting professor at numerous colleges and universities, and has served as consultant to educators in over forty-five states and several foreign countries. His primary research interests are instructional quality, educational change, and assessment and evaluation. His most recent books include *High Stakes Performance Assessment* (Corwin, 1994) and *School Improvement Programs: A Handbook for Educational Leaders* (Scholastic, 1995) with J. Block and S. Everson.

Andy Hargreaves is Professor in Educational Administration at the Ontario Institute for Studies in Education in Toronto, Canada and currently also International Research Professor at the Roehampton Institute in London, England. He has previously been a primary school teacher and has been a university lecturer at the Open University and the University of Oxford and Warwick in England. His Ph.D. is in Sociology, from Leeds University, England. Andy has written or edited many books in education, the most recent of which are *Changing Teachers, Changing Times: Teachers Work and Culture in the Postmodern Age* (London: Cassells; New York: Teachers College Press, 1994), *Understanding Teacher Development* (edited with Michael Fullan; London: Cassells; New York: Teachers College Press, 1992), and *Teachers' Professional Lives* (edited with Ivor Goodson; New York: Falmer Press, forthcoming).

Michael Huberman has been Visiting Professor at Harvard Graduate School of Education and Senior Research Associate at the Network, Inc. since 1991. He was previously Professor of Education for 20 years at the University of Geneva, Switzerland. His main interests are adult cognition and development, qualitative research methodologies, and "life-cycle" research. His most recent books are *Qualitative Data Analysis* (2nd ed.; Sage, 1994), with Matt Miles, and *The Lives of Teachers* (Teachers College Press, 1994).

Jeroen Imants is Assistant Professor at the Center for Research in Education and Instruction at the University of Leiden, The Netherlands. His main fields of interest are school organization and educational leadership.

Zemira R. Mevarech is an Associate Professor in the School of Education and the Institute for the Advancement of Social Integration in Schools at Bar-Ilan University in Israel. A graduate of the University of Chicago, Dr. Mevarech was a visiting professor and visiting researcher in various universities and research institutes. Prior to joining the faculty at Bar-Ilan, she was a mathematics teacher and served as a high school administrator. She also worked in a teacher training college and was a research coordinator in the Research and Development Office of the Chicago Board of Education. Her primary research interests are: computer learning environments, mathematics education, cooperative learning methods, and the development of instructional methods for enhancing higher-order thinking processes.

Ralph T. Putnam is Associate Professor in the Department of Counseling, Educational Psychology and Special Education at Michigan State University. Dr. Putnam's teaching and research focuses on cognitively oriented studies of classroom teaching and learning. His recent research has examined the teaching and learning of mathematics in elementary school classrooms, especially the knowledge and beliefs of teachers as they strive to teach mathematics for understanding and the different ways that students learn about mathematics from various kinds of instruction.

Mark A. Smylie is Associate Professor of Education at the University of Illinois at Chicago. He received his Ph.D. degree from Vanderbilt University and his B.A. and M.Ed. degrees from Duke University. Smylie's research interests concern school organization, leadership, and change; the design and redesign of teachers' work; teachers' professional learning and development; and coordinated children's services. His recent publications include "Redesigning Teachers' Work: Connections to the Classroom" in *Review of Research in Education,* "Teacher Leadership: Tensions and Ambiguities in Organizational Perspective" in *Educational Administration Quarterly,* and "Teacher Participation in Decision Making: Assessing Willingness to Participate" in *Educational Evaluation and Policy Analysis.* Smylie, a former high school teacher, was a 1992 National Academy of Education Spencer Fellow.

John Smyth is Foundation Professor of Teacher Education and Associate Dean for Research at the Flinders University of South Australia and Director of the Flinders Institute for the Study of Teaching. Previously he was an associate professor at Deakin University. Originally a high school teacher, he has held academic positions at the University of New England, the Papua New Guinea University of Technology, and the Centre for Research on Teaching at the University of Alberta. His research, scholarly and academic interests are in the area of teachers' work, teacher appraisal, and the professional development of teachers. He was awarded the Palmer O Jonston Memorial Award for the most outstanding contribution to an American Educational Research Association Journal for 1992. He is the author or editor of six books, including *Teachers as Collaborative Learners* (Open University Press, 1991), *A Socially Critical View of the Self-Managing School* (Falmer Press, 1993), *Academic Work* (Open University Press, 1995) and has published over 200 articles in scholarly journals.

Harm H. Tillema is Associate Professor and Senior-Researcher at the Center for Research in Education and Instruction at the University of Leiden, The Netherlands. His main fields of interest are the professional development of teachers and training research.

Index